D1617052

The Rest of the Dream

R^{THE}est OF THE Dream

The Black Odyssey of LYMAN JOHNSON

WADE HALL

THE UNIVERSITY PRESS OF KENTUCKY

Frontispiece: Johnson's graduation picture, College
Hill High School, Columbia, Tennessee, June 1924.

Copyright © 1988 by The University Press of Kentucky

Scholarly publisher for the Commonwealth,
serving Bellarmine College, Berea College, Centre
College of Kentucky, Eastern Kentucky University,
The Filson Club, Georgetown College, Kentucky
Historical Society, Kentucky State University,
Morehead State University, Murray State University,
Northern Kentucky University, Transylvania University,
University of Kentucky, University of Louisville,
and Western Kentucky University.

Editorial and Sales Offices: Lexington, Kentucky 40506-0336

Library of Congress Cataloging-in-Publication Data
Hall, Wade H.
    The rest of the dream : the Black odyssey of Lyman Johnson / Wade
Hall.

        p.   cm.
    Includes index.
    ISBN 0-8131-1674-0
    1. Johnson, Lyman T., 1906-   . 2. Afro-Americans—Kentucky
—Biography.   3. Civil rights workers—Kentucky—Biography.
4. Kentucky—Race relations.   5. Afro-Americans—Civil rights
—Kentucky.   I. Johnson, Lyman T., 1906-   . II. Title.
E185.97.J693H35   1988
976.9'0049607302—dc19
[B]   88-22660

This book is printed on acid-free paper meeting
the requirements of the American National Standard
for Permanence of Paper for Printed Library Materials. ⊛

For the thousands of black and white southerners of goodwill who have fostered just and amicable race relations and made it possible for all of us to endure and prevail . . . in particular, Tressie Grider Waters and Dyer Johnson

Contents

Illustrations follow page 144

Preface

> Muhammad Ali didn't live on Muhammad Ali Boulevard when he
> was growing up in Louisville as Cassius Clay. He lived on Grand
> Avenue. But we had to name something for him. When the aldermen
> settled on my street, Walnut Street, I said that's all right with me. I
> even went down to City Hall and spoke for it.
>
> —Lyman Johnson

MUHAMMAD ALI Boulevard is not a boulevard at all. It is an ordinary,
sometimes seedy, street that runs about five miles from Louisville's East
End through the heart of the old downtown area into the West End,
stopping near the Ohio River. Along its way you'll pass windowless,
boarded-up commercial buildings, dormitory-style housing projects for
the (mostly black) poor, a block or two of new townhouse developments
for yuppie urban pioneers, an exclusive businessmen's club, a grand hotel
restored to its 1920s elegance, a shiny new Greyhound bus station and
blocks of shotgun houses—so called, according to folklore, because if you
shoot a gun through the front door the shot will pass through all the
rooms before it exits at the rear.

Some parts of Muhammad Ali Boulevard used to be fashionable
addresses, but their owners have moved to the suburbs or to rehabbed
enclaves in other sections of town. In the 2200 block, you'll pass Zion
Baptist Church, where a brother of Martin Luther King, Jr., was once
pastor. By now you're in the nearly all black West End, where many of the
houses are abandoned and vandalized. The house at 2340 is an exception.
Its red brick facade looks freshly scrubbed. The painted trim is bright. The
postage-stamp yard is carefully tended. This house still looks like the
cared-for home of a thrifty, lower-middle class family. Indeed, for some
thirty-five years it was the home of the Lyman T. Johnsons. Now Lyman
Johnson lives here alone, his wife dead, his son and daughter married and
raising their families in Philadelphia. He lives with memories of a life that
started in 1906 in Columbia, Tennessee, a beginning that sometimes
seems to him light-years away. It has been a life spent teaching public
school history for some forty years, almost all in a segregated black school.
Because of Johnson's civil rights involvements, it has also been a life that
has *made* history. It is a life of startling, ironic contrasts.

All four of Johnson's grandparents were slaves in Tennessee. One of
his grandfathers bought himself and his wife out of slavery. Yet Lyman
Johnson lived to know mayors, governors, and presidents. He was a
product of Jim Crow education. When he became the first black student to

enroll at the University of Kentucky in 1949, crosses were burned on campus. Yet thirty-one years later the university that fought to keep him out awarded him an honorary doctorate.

Revolutionary changes have indeed swept over the American racial front during Lyman Johnson's life. And he has held an important position in the movement's vanguard—not as a general in the conflict, but as a company commander leading local operations. He has selected targets, devised strategy, and led his troops from the trenches to a constantly shifting front. One day it was a drugstore lunch counter that refused to serve blacks, the next a whites-only public library. Another day it might have been the "Colored Only" waiting room at the train station, or the segregated park system, or a public school where "Colored" over the entrance really meant "Second Class," or a hotel open to blacks only when they were dressed as waiters or maids. Most of Johnson's life has been lived in a society in which the American dream was labeled "White Only," but it was a society he was determined to help change.

Conditions during Johnson's early years were not favorable for bright, ambitious blacks. As a boy he suffered the stifling humiliation of segregation and the crippling effects of inferior education and cultural deprivation. He was born a full generation after the end of slavery, but opportunities for blacks had hardly improved in the forty years since the Civil War. Most blacks lived in poverty and terror and under conditions that defined a new kind of economic and social bondage almost as brutal and confining as slavery. Few blacks had been touched by the progress and reforms of the late nineteenth and early twentieth centuries. Most blacks worked at menial, low-paying jobs. Unable to join a labor union, they could not benefit from labor advances. Unable to vote, they could not demand legal redress. Segregation, whether by statute or custom, was the law of the land. To survive, blacks had to move cautiously. If accused of a crime, they could expect scant justice from courts composed of white judges and juries. If jailed, they could expect to be abused and exploited as laborers. Finally, there was the lynch mob for blacks who even appeared to cross social lines. Small wonder that Johnson calls his birth year a time of "dark days for black people."

Southern blacks could not expect justice and could find no place to escape. As a youngster Johnson saw thousands of black farmhands pass through the Columbia depot on trains headed for the Promised Lands of the North. As Johnson himself was to learn later, these blacks were unknowingly trading southern forms of servitude and exploitation for northern ones.

Conditions didn't improve much until after World War II, when black veterans (Johnson calls them "a rough bunch of cats") decided that if they could face foreign enemies like Hitler, Mussolini, and Tojo they could certainly face racist enemies at home. Johnson describes vividly, for example, the near insurrection that occurred in his hometown in 1946 after a fight between a black veteran and a white businessman who had mistreated the black's mother.

Like his ancestors who had been wrenched from their African homes and brought into a strange new land and an alien culture, Johnson learned that in order to survive he had to endure compromise. Frequently, he had to bite his tongue and suffer taunts and second-class treatment, whether he was wearing the uniform of the U.S. Navy or the coat and tie of a schoolteacher. But whenever he was forced to ride at the back of the bus, or attend a crowded all-black school, or supplement his meager teacher's salary by serving as a part-time waiter at white banquets, he knew the status quo was unfair, and he never accepted it.

As a student in Tennessee, Virginia, and Michigan, and later as a young history teacher in Kentucky, Johnson was preparing himself to attack the system that brutalized and victimized his people. The lives of such black rebels as Nat Turner, Frederick Douglass, Harriet Tubman, and Sojourner Truth taught him that not all slaves had accepted their status with meekness and resignation. He also knew the writings and stated positions of the two great black leaders of the early twentieth century, Booker T. Washington and W.E.B. Du Bois. Neither man, he concluded, spoke satisfactorily to the blacks of his generation. Washington preached a gospel of hard work, skilled labor, and social accommodation. On the other hand, Du Bois's radical demands for immediate racial equality sometimes seemed impetuous, even suicidal. Young Johnson could look to neither one as a viable model. Nevertheless, as this book demonstrates, Johnson borrowed from both men in forging his own philosophy and developing his own tactics for racial justice. Like Du Bois, he insisted on color-blind justice and fair play. Like Washington, he understood the value of earned rewards and how to use southern mores for black advancement.

An important influence on Johnson's developing attitudes and strategy was his father, a school principal who taught his son by example and precept how to maintain his human dignity despite the confines of a segregated society. The elder Johnson would not allow his son to attend the Columbia movie theater because he would have to sit in the "crow's nest," the balcony restricted to blacks. At first, it seemed to young Johnson that his father's prohibition was unreasonable and unfair, but from it he learned that self-denial and passive resistance can lead to greater rewards. His father thus taught him the value of patience and timing and the importance of withholding support from an unjust system. Like the sly rabbit in the African-based folktales told by Uncle Remus, Johnson was learning that attacking injustice at the wrong time and the wrong place could bring a lynch mob and a noose. Dead men, he knew, do not win victories. But Johnson never ran from a meaningful confrontaion. Conflict has been the constant keynote of his life. His black skin put him in permanent opposition to all racially constructed barriers. Every door marked "White Only" was a challenge and an invitation to be forced open. He never asked *whether* such doors should be opened, only *when* and *how*.

Like Henry David Thoreau, Johnson has lived most of his life "in native pastures." Despite occasional national exposure, his fame has not spread much beyond his city and state. Had he pursued the ministry, as he once considered, he might have been pastor of Dexter Avenue Baptist Church in Montgomery, Alabama, in 1955 when Rosa Parks refused to give up her bus seat to a white man. Johnson had attended that church many times in the 1930s when his brother-in-law was pastor there. But Johnson chose to become a teacher, and Martin Luther King, Jr., was pastor of that strategic church, located ironically within a stone's throw of the spot where Jefferson Davis took the oath of office as president of the Confederacy in 1861. So it was King who was in fame's way. It was King who was in the right place at the right time with the right leadership abilities, and it was King who caught the brass ring of fame, martyrdom, and immortality. The work of Johnson and thousands of other blacks and whites at the local level, however, has been equally important in the civil rights revolution. Lyman Johnson's homefront perspective therefore chronicles the largely untold story of the front lines in America's war for equality.

Moreover, Johnson's life has a special dimension because of his career as a historian. He sees himself in the context of the larger black American experience. It is a unique perspective that sometimes leads to surprising conclusions. Johnson holds, for example, a genuine sympathy for poor whites, even those stigmatized as rednecks. He maintains that from slavery days to the present, poor whites, like poor blacks, have been victims of a labor system that has pitted race against race. Plantation owners and factory owners alike, he says, have cultivated racial animosity to keep wages low and profits high. Johnson does not spare his own race. He castigates eighteenth–century Africans who collaborated with white slave traders, and he lashes present-day blacks who make welfare-taking a career. Indeed, here are the balanced and reasonable views of a black man whose life is ending in a world no longer dominated by whites. His book has much to say to people of all races who must learn to live in harmony in the brave new world of tomorrow.

Johnson has been forced to live most of his life within the limitations imposed by a racist society; nevertheless, by his own reckoning, he has lived a good life, supported by his wife and family and by friends of both races. He now has the peace of mind that comes from knowing that he has been guided by principles, that he has run a good race, and that he has lived to see his attitudes and actions vindicated.

With honors and awards and accolades arriving almost daily, Dr. Lyman Johnson finds it hard to believe that he is the same person who saw the light of this world in the racial darkness of 1906. "I sometimes wonder," he muses, "just who I am today. Am I the boy who played basketball on a crude, dirt court in Columbia, Tennessee? Am I the young man forced to ride a Jim Crow train to see my sister in Alabama? Am I the son who bluffed his way through the National Guard lines to see my father during a race riot in my hometown? Am I the 'nigger' refused admittance to the public library in Columbia? Am I the college student almost seduced by a white woman in Virginia? Am I the young teacher who worked in a high school with 'colored' in its official name? Am I the traveler who had to eat in the kitchen of an eastern Kentucky restaurant? Am I the man who could not enter the front entrance to the Brown Hotel in Louisville? Am I the graduate student who had to force his way into the University of Kentucky? Am I the husband whose wife never knew when I'd be home from a demonstration—or if I'd call her from jail? Am I the father whose children couldn't play in Louisville's Cherokee Park? I can't believe I've been all those people."

Because he *has* been all those people—and more—Johnson now holds three doctorates, degrees he has earned the long and hard way—by saying no to the "crow's nest" in its many and widespread forms. Today Americans of all races can sit where they please in movie theaters, in classrooms, on buses, and in restaurants. Doors and water fountains and executive offices no longer say "White Only." Lyman Johnson helped make that happen.

But this engrossing account of one man's fight for racial justice is more than a civil rights document. Johnson's graphic recall of people and incidents, his ability to reconstruct scenes, and his natural talent for swift narrative make this book the record of a special American life. It is a flesh-and-blood story filled with suspense, humor, tragedy and triumph. It is the drama of a nightmare that slowly and painfully becomes the American dream.

This oral autobiography is based on some fifty-five hours of conversations and taped interviews conducted with Lyman Johnson from 1979 to 1987, the bulk of them in the spring and summer of 1979. Johnson's gracious, soft-spoken manner belies his toughness, his tenacity, and his dedication to fair play, qualities expected in a life that touches on the full range of black experience in this country.

"My grandparents represent the last stages of slavery. My parents represent the period from the Civil War to around 1920. My brothers and sisters and I represent the period from about 1910 down to the present.

Our children and grandchildren are now taking up the new opportunities—as well as the old burdens—of our race. From my grandparents
to my grandchildren, we have covered American black history."

And so in this book an educated, articulate, grass-roots black leader
profiles himself—his background, his career, his views—with the honesty
of a Diogenes and the graphic precision of a Chaucer. Here is a black man's
life that began in a nightmarish period of American history and is con-
cluding closer to Martin Luther King's dream of the Promised Land. Here
is an American life that rings as true as the Liberty Bell—the life and words
of Lyman T. Johnson.

During the preparation and writing of this book, aid and encouragement have come from a number of people, especially John Oppelt, Eileen
Whalen, Pat Allen, Clyde Stallings, Gregg Swem, and Agnes Crume—
and above all, Lyman T. Johnson, whose life is *The Rest of the Dream*.

WADE HALL

The Rest of the Dream

2340 Muhammad Ali Boulevard

Don't pity me because I live in the slums. Pity yourself that you
permit a slum to be.

I'VE LIVED HERE in this same house for almost thirty-five years. When
we moved here, the people who lived across the street and up and down
the street were just about our class of people. One of the best Negro
doctors in town lived a few doors away. A newspaper editor lived right
over there. Nice people lived all around us then. Gradually, the old people
died out, and the younger people married and settled somewhere else.
This part of town became a fading culture area.

My wife used to beg me to get out of here. She'd say: "Why don't we
move? Why do you want to stay here?" Then one day she said: "Well,
we've stayed and stayed and now we're stuck. Now we can't ever move."
I'd say: "Now, honey, you know if we had moved, some of my friends
who have moved from down here would say: 'Ah ha, Lyman, you finally
have to grant us our point. We moved because we couldn't stand it any
longer. Now you've caught on and moved too.' "

But it's hard to sit here and listen to that woman across the street use
her vulgar language. She goes inside and gets her a bottle of beer and
comes back on her porch, and she will curse and swear and use all sorts of
profane language. The next day when she's sober, she repents. "Hi, Mr.
Johnson," she calls out, "I'm going to behave today. I'm not going to drink
today. I'm not going to talk bad today." I will give her credit for being
considerate when I have visitors. "Now, Mr. Johnson is having some
company today," I've heard her say to her drinking buddies, "so let's go in
the house so we won't embarrass him." But just wait till my company is
gone!

Today I couldn't sell my house for what I have in it. Nobody wants to
buy in this neighborhood. The people who live here are no longer owners.
They are renters. And when you put two or three poverty families in one
house, that's the end of that place. They will tear it to pieces. They don't
feel any responsibility to keep it up. If a board falls off, they say: "Hell, I'm
paying rent. I'm not paying much rent, but I'm paying enough to have the
owner come down and fix it. If he won't do it, it won't get done."

The owner is mostly after profit. If he's going to take the little rent he's
paid to repair the place, he won't get any profit. We have a new kind of
owner now. He says: "There's the house. I'll rent it for so much. If it leaks,
you get up there and fix it. You don't pay me enough to do it for you."
Well, it leaks or something else is wrong. The renter refuses to pay his

rent, and the owner puts him out. The landlord doesn't fix it up for the next renter, who is hard-pressed to begin with or he wouldn't come in and take a house that someone else has left in shambles.

Let me give an example of what has happened in this neighborhood. One day the lady who lived in the third house from here came to see my wife. "Mrs. Johnson, I hate to leave you and Mr. Johnson, but I can't take it any longer. In three weeks I'll be gone." She sold her house to an absentee landlord and moved out. The house wasn't very elegant, but she kept it neat and clean. I enjoyed living in a neighborhood where people kept their houses like that. The new owner thought he was going to make some money on the house. It was in good repair and large enough so he could put one family upstairs and one downstairs. That was the beginning of the end. If one family is unable or unwilling to keep up their half, the other one lets its half go down too. Neither one feels responsible. The house falls to pieces.

The absentee landlord doesn't know what's happening. He, in fact, doesn't give a cuss. "Have you paid the rent?" he says. "If you haven't, get out." That's his only concern. Soon both families moved out. By the time the landlord came down to see his property, thieves had broken in and taken out all the plumbing upstairs and down. Then he got mad. "Hell, I won't put another cent in till I get a new tenant." Nobody would move in till he fixed it up, and he wouldn't fix it up till somebody moved in. It went on that way for about a year. In the second year, all the windows got plugged out. Then he boarded it up. Soon the boarding came down. And that's the way it is now. It's still vacant. I hate to be living three doors from it. But I'm stuck here. I don't know why I'm still here. Am I philosophizing? Am I rationalizing? Am I taking principle too far? Am I kidding myself? Are my friends who say I'm off my rocker right? Sometimes I wonder if I'm just whistling in the wind.

The other night a young white lady said to me: "Mr. Johnson, do you think you are staying in that neighborhood to be a model for the rest of the people? Do you think if you moved out, it would be an image drain on the community? Are you staying there just to fight?" I said: "I don't know. I don't know why I'm still here." No, I don't want to give my principles too much credit. I know I'm stuck here. I know it's too late to think about moving now. I used to tell my wife: "Well, we've spent more remodeling this house than we paid for it. The only way we'll ever get our equity out of it is to stay here and use it up."

Sometimes when I invite friends down here they have a reluctance to come because I live in the ghetto. They feel sorry for me. But I say: "Don't pity me because I live in the slums. Pity yourself that you permit a slum to be."

This neighborhood is all black. But it's gone down not because of race but because of economics. If people can't get a job, they can't buy a decent house or pay decent rent. If the landlord can't get a respectable rent for his property, he can't keep it up. The culprit is unemployment. How can anybody put paint on a house when they don't have money to buy dry beans? People get to the point where they don't care about themselves or about where they live. They don't give a damn about anything!

Most of these poor people are not the black equivalent of poor white trash. I don't call them poor black trash. Even if a black man can improve himself, get a good education and a fine job, he will still find out the truth of Booker T. Washington's old saying: "Last hired, first fired."

Certainly, we have blacks who are down and no good. But we don't know whether it's because they are black or because they are good-for-nothing. With proper sociological conditions, poor whites—even poor white trash, so-called—can be retrieved and redeemed. I wish that black people had the same opportunities. I don't believe that God intended for anyone to be just one step above the beast. I believe he intended for human beings, of all races and colors, to look up—not down.

If a person looks down, I think you can find the reason in history. As a history teacher for forty years and as a black man for over eighty years, I know what I'm talking about. But most people don't know the full range of history—the good and the bad, the ordinary and the spectacular, the sordid and the grand, the joyful and the sad, the little terrors and the epic tragedies. Few people know the true history of black Americans—or of a single black man.

I'm not sure how to introduce myself. When I look at myself, I see about five or six personalities. It's easier to describe myself physically. I've always been underweight and slight. Now I weigh 135 pounds, down from my usual 144. I'm five feet eight inches tall.

In the navy I tried my best to get hefty. We were eating on Uncle Sam, who said: "Here, have a steak. You might go over there and Hitler or Mussolini might shoot the hell out of you. Until then you may as well enjoy yourself." That put us in a good frame of mind not to resent the damn service so much. I ate so much I made myself sick. For about six months I got up to 155 pounds, but I was uncomfortable and dropped back to normal. It was more comfortable for me to eat about half what I saw some of my friends eat. I saw one fellow load up his plate one morning and I thought, "Good God, what are you going to do with all that food?" That guy sat there and ate five biscuits, three sausages, and three eggs in about fifteen minutes. He really stored it away. I took about a biscuit and a half, a sausage and a half, and one egg, and I had enough to run all morning.

When I was a boy, I had the usual diseases: measles, mumps, chicken pox. I had them all. Most of my life I've had good health. I finished forty years of teaching without one day's sick leave. The one time I would have missed school because of illness happened during summer vacation. It was back in 1943. I was out painting one summer afternoon when all of a sudden I felt a sharp pain in my side. I was working up around the third floor with a bunch of union painters. They kidded me. "You're a professor. All you know is books. You can't keep up with us." I told the foreman: "You give me the tools, put me up there beside a regular painter, and if I keep up with him, you pay me union wages. If I don't, then you pay me whatever you think I'm worth." I kept up with them, and they paid me union wages.

But this particular day my side was killing me. I said to my partner on the other end of the scaffold: "You'd better hang on. I'm going down before I topple this thing." I slid down the ladder as fast as I could and rolled around in the weeds like a maniac. My partner came down to see what was wrong. I told him to call Dr. Laine, a Negro doctor and a friend of mine. He came out, examined me, and carried me to the hospital, where he found out that I had acute appendicitis. Late that afternoon they put me to sleep and took out my appendix. That held me up for about two weeks.

In the summer of 1941, I had an automobile accident that broke my nose and knocked out all my front teeth. But I was all back together by the time school started. I guess they would have shot me if I had tried to teach school before I got my new teeth. Other than this accident and my appendicitis, I've never had any physical hold-ups in all my life.

I was almost seventy before I had any serious aches and pains. Then I began to get arthritis, which has grown on me more and more since. If I sit too long in one place now, I get stiff. But I still get around very well. My hearing is still good. My eyesight is not improving, but I can still manage to walk by myself, though I don't drive any more. I kid the young ladies when I go out with them. "My eyesight is failing, and my optometrist advises me from here on in I'll have to *feel* the rest of the way!"

When I think of all the people who have been cut down at eighteen or twenty-five or thirty by war or disease or accident, I realize how fortunate I've been. I know a young lady who finished medical school and her internship in surgery and was out on her own for two years making a good reputation for herself when she was afflicted with so much arthritis that she was afraid to take her tools and chop on anybody. She was only thirty-four and had to give up the profession she had spent her life preparing for. She had such great promise and prospects as a surgeon. Now, unless a cure for her can be found, all she can do is lecture. Even in that she is robbed. She can't say, "You do it this way." She's been robbed. So why should I complain about arthritis at my age? My work is done, and my life is almost over.

I'm trying to maintain my sense of humor to the end. It's been a good piece of equipment all my life. Sometimes when I'd try to get across a sensitive point to my students, I'd resort to humor. In the middle of Greek history, I might put in a plug for sex education. "Now, young people, be careful with your equipment. Some of those things God gave you work." They'd say, "Oh, Mr. Johnson, so you know." I'd say "yeah" and go on and talk about Alexander the Great. Now I try to see my present situation with humor. I'm old. I have bad arthritis. I get around by limping and hopping. I'm here by myself most of the time. My wife's dead. My children are gone. When young women get too sympathetic, I say: "Now be careful. Not all of me is arthritic."

My wife, Juanita Morrell Johnson, has been dead since 1977, and I still miss her. She was an attractive woman—graceful, with an elegant bearing. She was five feet, five inches tall and never weighed more than about 120. I expect the things I liked best about her were the very things that disturbed me most. Sometimes, for example, she was a little too delicate and sophisticated for me. We were both from the same town, but she said she came from the "city" part and I came from the "country" part. Sometimes she would say: "Oh, Lyman, you are hopeless. You were born on a farm, raised on a farm, and have the polish of a clod." She liked aesthetic things. She always complained because I didn't take her to enough operas, ballets, and concerts. After they were opened to blacks in Louisville, she would say, "Why in the world did you open up these places, Lyman, and now not go?"

She graduated from college two years ahead of me because she didn't have all the stumbling blocks I had. When her daddy found out that our black school in Columbia wasn't fully accredited, he sent her to boarding school. She spent four years in the high school department of Tennessee State College in Nashville. It gave her a two-year jump on me. She finished college in 1928, and I finished in 1930. She got a job as registrar at Tennessee State before the Depression started. People like her who had jobs with institutions that didn't fold almost didn't know there was a Depression.

I knew her parents, and they thought a lot of me. But she didn't. I used to tell boys out courting: "Young man, be sure you make a hit with the young lady. I know from experience. If you don't lay your racket with her, laying it with her mama and papa won't do any good." That was my problem. Her mother and father would just do anything for Lyman. They thought I was the nicest person around. But I would say: "Well, why don't you tell your daughter that? Can't you get her to see that?" She said I was too sincere, too serious. She'd say: "Relax, Lyman. Let your hair down. Enjoy life. You can do that without being a caveman."

But I finally won her over—with the help of a snappy red Pontiac

Roadster, which I bought in 1936. It was used but sporty. It had a fold-back top, so when it started to rain you had to stop and pull it up over you. When I bought that car, I didn't know too much about driving because my father had never owned a car. I had it for about a month before school was out, and I was beginning to drive it up to about thirty miles an hour. When school ended, I decided to drive it south. I soon found out that I'd have to learn to drive faster. Several times on that trip I even got up to the speed limit of fifty-five miles an hour. I visited relatives in Tennessee and then drove on down to Montgomery and Tuskegee. By the time I got back to Louisville, I considered myself an accomplished driver.

The next summer when I headed south I decided to visit Juanita when I passed through Nashville. I stopped by her office, and she began to warm up nicely. "Are you driving your own car?" she said. I said I was and pointed to my red roadster outside with the top down. "Oh, that's pretty," she said. "I have an hour and fifteen minutes for my lunch period and need to go to the bank. Will you drive me down?" I said I sure would. We drove across campus and scooted downtown in my pretty, little, red car. She was feeling good and I was feeling kind of gay and the car was looking splashy.

When we got back, she asked where I was headed. I said I was going home to see my father. By that time my mother and both of Juanita's parents were dead. She said, "Could you wait till after dinner?" I said, "Why, I could wait till after breakfast. . . ." So I stayed. We drove into town that evening and had dinner. I spent the night with my aunt who lived in Nashville. The next day we had lunch together and dinner again. Then I went on down to Columbia to see my father. When I got back to Louisville, I wrote Juanita and told her how much I had enjoyed being with her. She wrote me. I wrote her. That fall I went down a couple of times to see her, and she came up a couple of times to see me. At Thanksgiving I took her to see Central High School, where I taught, play Sumner High School from St. Louis. It was the first time she'd ever seen big-time school football, and she was amazed.

Our relationship got warmer and warmer. We knew if we got married that one of us would have to move. I was offered a job at Tennessee State, but I turned it down. I wouldn't have made any more money teaching in college there than teaching in high school in Louisville. I also knew that without a Ph.D. I would be a flunky for younger faculty coming in with Ph.D.'s. So I chose to stay in Louisville, and I told her that if we married she'd have to move here. She agreed. We married at Christmas in a preacher's house in Nashville. She finished out the year at Tennessee State and moved to Louisville the following June. We had a wonderful life together. But I used to joke with her. "Honey, you weren't interested in me. You didn't marry me but for one thing. You liked my little red roadster. You took me as a part of the luggage that came with the car."

There were some problems, of course, though not all of our own making. She didn't always understand my actions and my involvements, but she always supported me. I only wish she could be with me now to enjoy some of the rewards we've earned. We could sit here and think about the old times—the good as well as the bad.

Dark Days in Columbia

Don't scratch me too hard. The scars are still there. The scars will bleed right now. I'll try my best to let bygones be bygones. But if you scratch one of my bad scars, goddamnit, I'll unload on you. I've done a lot of self–disciplining to get me to the place where I can talk about it. But I don't intend ever to forget till senility or death wipes it all out.

IT WAS DURING dark days for black people when I was born into this world in 1906. It was a rough time that didn't get much better till the end of World War II, when Negro soldiers came home from the war and said, "Hell, if we've got guts enough to fight the Nazis and the Japs, we can certainly fight these racist rascals here in the United States."

I was born in Columbia, Maury County, Tennessee, on July 12. I was the eighth child and last son in a family of six boys and three girls. I was near the tail end of my family, and I got along easier than the earlier children. My father had fewer children to support and was making a little more money when I came along. He was a schoolteacher for twenty years and a principal for twenty-two years in the "colored" school system. It was standard practice in those days to pay Negro teachers half the scale for whites. Except for one year, my daddy never made over $100 a month during all the forty-odd years he worked in the school system. In 1930, his last year, he got up to $105. I don't know how he fed, clothed, and educated a family of nine children as well as he did.

Eight of us grew to adulthood. My papa's first child, Dyer Johnson, died of some disease six weeks after he was born back in the early 1890s. We were lucky to be born into a family with a mother who had gone to high school and a father who was a college graduate. My father and mother were two of the best-educated people in Columbia, black or white. My brothers and sisters started going north when they got old enough to work. Two of us—my sister Cornelia and I—settled in Louisville; the rest went to New York and Chicago. I almost don't have any relatives living in

Columbia now. A few years ago one of my sisters died in New York. We had the funeral there, and twenty-nine of her closest relatives sat at her table for dinner that night after we buried her. Most of them came from right about there—New York, Hartford, Boston, and New Jersey.

My mother died when I was thirteen. At that time there were three of us children at home. My sister Mary was ten and brother Charles was fifteen. One of my sisters was single and teaching in a boarding school in Memphis, Tennessee. Another sister was married to a Congregationalist preacher who had a church in Montreal. We had a family council and decided it was not appropriate for Mary to be stuck at home with her father and two brothers. So we sent her to Montreal. Before long they all decided it was too cold for them, and they moved back south. My brother-in-law located in Savannah, Georgia, became a Baptist minister, and was later pastor of Dexter Avenue Baptist Church in Montgomery, Alabama, the church Martin Luther King, Jr. came to twenty years later.

When I was a college student in the late 1920s, I used to visit them. His church was right across the street from the state capitol, one of the most flagrant symbols of slavery and segregation in the country. From my brother-in-law's church, you could see the spot where Jefferson Davis took the oath as president of the Confederate States of America. On my visits I could look out from the church windows and see black convicts dressed in striped prison clothes mowing the grass and picking up trash on the capitol grounds. They were hot and sweating, but they knew not to complain or try to get away. They were watched by white men with loaded guns. If they stepped out of line, they knew they would be shot or whipped like hell when they got back to camp that night.

There were, of course, white convicts too, but they were not displayed so pitifully as the blacks. The vicious thing about so much of the South's racial practices was that they were intended to degrade the black man in the presence of the black community. Putting the black convicts out like that was a way of intimidating black people and stamping in their minds a pattern of culture that said: "Don't misbehave. Look what will happen to you if you do. And you might even get lynched. We'll hang you from a cedar tree and let you swing there a couple of days as a warning. And we'll cut off your genitals just to show what we do to a damn nigger that gets out of place."

One of my brothers couldn't wait to leave Columbia. He said: "Hell, I'm not going to spend my life down here plowing. I may not have much brainpower, but what I've got I'm not going to burn out behind some old mule." When he finished high school, he took a job as a white man's chauffeur. That almost broke Papa's heart. He said, "I didn't raise any of my sons to be a lackey for rich people, and that's all you are now." My brother lived on the estate where he worked, and that also broke Papa's heart. "Son," he said, "you might as well be in slavery. You don't get paid much, and you're always at the beck and call of white people." Finally, Papa talked him into going to college. When he finished, he left for New York and married there.

My brother Neill didn't take much to book learning. He took up house painting as a trade and lived for a while in North Carolina. After all of us had moved away, we got him and his family to move back to Columbia to look after our father and our Uncle Will. Neill drank too much, but Papa and Uncle Will were teetotalers and never allowed any liquor in the house. Papa gave him a house about five blocks away so he could drain the keg all he wanted to without tormenting those two old fellows.

My brother Rob was the most sincere, honest, intellectual member of the family. He was a man of principle and religion, but he didn't want to be a minister after he graduated from Virginia Union University in 1919. Instead, he married his college sweetheart and left for New York, swearing that he'd never live another day in the South. I'm not sure he bettered his condition very much, but he thought he did and made it possible for his children to do better. In the South there weren't many professions and decent jobs open to Negroes in those days—mainly teaching and preaching—but in the North there was also the post office. So Rob worked in the post office all his life and raised a large family. When he died several years ago, I thought at first I couldn't go to the funeral because of commitments in Louisville. But at the last minute, my fraternal instincts took over, and I flew to New York and went directly to the church. The ushers took me down to the section where the family would sit and handed me a church bulletin with Rob's obituary. It read something like this. "Today we celebrate the life of one who has lived among us for fifty years, one who has served our church as deacon for thirty-five years, one who has been a trustee for fourteen years—and one who has reared nine children on the sidewalks of Harlem. Four sons and two sons-in-law are serving as active pallbearers. All nine of his children are attending the service today." One line in particular struck me, and I read it over and over. "One who has reared nine children on the sidewalks of Harlem."

As I sat waiting for the family to arrive, I thought of what had become of those children. One daughter has a master's degree and teaches in New Jersey. Another daughter is a school counselor in Connecticut. Another daughter works in the Los Angeles school system and is married to a prominent physician. One of his sons is a successful dentist with an elaborate suite of offices where he helps young dentists get started. Another son is a professor of dentistry at Columbia University. He was recently invited to set up a dental program for Harvard University. So he commutes between Columbia and Harvard in a car as long as from here to the other side of town. One time I said: "Young man, I can't believe you.

Are you really my nephew or not?" He said, "Yes, Uncle Lyman, I am."
Another daughter graduated from a New York law school and was elected
a superior court judge in New York. Then in 1978 President Carter
appointed her to a federal judgeship.

With all those children going to college and getting ahead in the
world, their mama decided she'd go back to school too. So when her
youngest daughter was about to start her junior year in college, she said:
"Now, darling, would you be embarrassed if Mama tagged along and sees
what she can do in college? All you children are college people now and
have gone beyond me. I need two more years to get my degree." So
mother and daughter teamed up and graduated the same year. Then they
both received master's degrees from Columbia at the same time. The
mama couldn't get a regular teaching job because she was over sixty, but
she was a substitute teacher for seven years and hardly missed a day. Yes,
brother Rob was so proud of his family. He gloried in what those children
had done—those children he had raised on the sidewalks of Harlem.
That's why when I see young black people today discouraged and in
despair, I say: "You can make it. Yes, you can. Even if you have to live in a
ghetto, you can make it. Look what others have done with less." My
brother Rob had done well in New York. His children were celebrating his
life at his funeral.

After my mother died, I did most of the housework because my
brother Charles had a weak heart and couldn't do much work. I also
carried papers in the afternoon and milked the cow every morning and
evening. I was a pretty good cook with basic foods. I could handle beef
and pork and chicken and fish as well as vegetables. We raised our own
chickens, and I learned to kill chickens, pick them, dress them—and eat
them. I'd kill them one or two ways: either wring their necks off in my
hands or hold their heads on a block and chop them off with a hatchet like
old King Charles's head. I learned that I didn't have to wring the head
completely off. All I had to do was wring till I could feel the neck breaking.
Then I'd drop him to the ground, and he'd flop around a minute or two.
But I didn't have to worry. He wasn't going to get up and walk away.

I learned to make good biscuits, and my cornbread was out of this
world! But I never learned much about pies, cakes, and desserts. I made
one lemon pie in the three years I was running the household and after
that decided not to try any more. In those days there were no ready mixes
so I had to make everything from scratch. We didn't have gas or electricity,
and I had to cook on a wood stove.

My family had long before learned to be self-sufficient. We always had
a big garden behind the house, and then we'd have little patches of
vegetables on the vacant lots Papa owned around town. Out of his salary,
he'd managed to save enough to buy little pieces of property from time to

time. In those gardens we raised just about every kind of vegetable—English peas and field peas, beans, corn, sweet potatoes, white potatoes, turnips, okra, popcorn—even peanuts. Long before Dr. Carver down at Tuskegee became famous for his peanuts, my papa was raising them. To us they were a novelty. Late in the fall, before the first frost, we'd pull up the whole vine with the peanuts still hanging to the roots and stack them on racks in the barn loft to dry. I remember many times at lunch period four or five of my little friends would go home with me—we lived about three blocks from school—and we'd go up into that loft, pull off peanuts, stuff our pockets, and eat them raw all the way back to school. I've thought a lot about those peanuts since I was a boy. I think raising those peanuts was one of the things my daddy did as compensation for us because we were shut off from the freer life the white children had.

I don't mean to say that Papa did all the work himself in those garden plots. He had five boys whom he managed to keep busy most of the time. He had a vicious horror of weeds. It seemed that those little plots could grow weeds when nothing else would grow. Papa would say to us boys: "Get those weeds out. And don't chop them down. Dig them up by the roots! Burn them so there won't be any seed to come back next year!" But the next year there would be as many weeds as ever! Those little gardens all over town kept us busy, but when we ran out of work to do in town, he's send us out to our farm in the country. Papa hired a Negro farmhand to help with the farm. He was named Jim Smith and lived nearby. He also worked for white people. When they wanted him, all they had to say was, "Jim, I want you to start plowing my corn tomorrow." And Jim would say, "Yassuh, I'll be there." He'd be over at the white man's house, have the hogs fed, the cows milked, and the mules hitched up to plow by seven o'clock in the morning. He would plow till noon, take half an hour to eat, and plow till almost dark—for about seventy-five cents a day.

When Papa wanted him to plow for us, we'd say, "Mr. Smith, can you help us plow our corn this week?" We were told to call him "Mr." even though he was only a farmhand. It never got into our family cultural pattern to look down our nose at anyone, regardless of how humble he was. And Mr. Smith would say: "Well, lemme see. I've got to work for Mr. Charley on Monday, Tuesday, and Wednesday. I'll come plow for you on Thursday." He'd arrive about seven o'clock, take an hour for lunch, and quit at five o'clock. And we had to pay him $1.25 and call him Mr. Smith. When I was about eleven years old, I said to Papa: "Papa, why do you call him Mr. Smith when that white man down the highway calls him Jim? And why does he come to work for you later, quits sooner, and charges you more?" My father said: "Son, if you live long enough, it'll come to you. I need him because there's no one else I can hire, and I've got to pay what he charges me."

We also had to get other Negroes to help us when we killed hogs.

Papa never had any trouble getting them to help "professor" when we had a couple of hogs to slaughter and dress. They said: "We gonna work for you, professor, because we like you. You're our leader." Of course, they charged us more than they charged white people. They would work for the white man at hog-killing time for two dollars a day. Papa paid them five dollars. Sometimes they didn't make anything when they helped white people slaughter their hogs. It was a part of their regular work. They were usually given some of the less desirable parts of the hog to take home—the feet, the intestines, and such like. Later when the meat was all hanging in the smokehouse, the white people expected their black servants to take some. White people would say: "It's all right if you want a little piece of bacon to eat. But if we catch you stealing any of our hams out of the smokehouse and running a little black market off to the side, we'll chop your hands off." Some of the best bacon and hams I've ever eaten have come from those Negro servants who "borrowed" a little piece of meat from the white man's smokehouse. But they knew not to sell any of it. They'd give it to me.

The son of one of the Columbia bankers went to New York and became a rich member of the stock market. He bought a thousand acres of prime farming land back home and raised hogs that he made into sausage for his choice clients. One day the black man in charge of the sausage operation said to me: "Mr. Johnson, I can't sell this sausage to you. It's the finest sausage made. It's a delicacy made with the best pieces of pork. I can't sell it, but here's three bags I want you to have." It was the best pork sausage I ever tasted.

We got along very well with other black people, even though they sometimes took advantage of my papa's goodness and generosity. Most of the Negroes in Maury County—they made up about one-third of the population—worked hard and barely made enough to eke out a bare subsistence. Most of the country Negroes were sharecroppers, while most of the city Negroes worked in domestic service or in janitorial jobs in small factories, stores, and hotels. A white woman would hire a black cook for two or three dollars a week. For that pay the Negro woman would not only cook most of the meals and clean up after them but also do the white family's washing and ironing and housecleaning. It was a hard life for black people. Sometimes a man would crack under all the pressures we Negroes had to live under.

Maybe that's what caused Elijah to go crazy in the first place. I don't know. I do remember that we called him "Elijah with a crowbar." People said he was too crazy and mean for anybody to live with, so he lived alone. When we boys used to taunt him and call him "Elijah with a crowbar," it made him mad as hell. According to the stories we heard, he got that name one time when he killed a man. This is the way I heard it. Elijah said one day to another man he didn't like: "Sam, if you take this glass out tonight to where cousin John was buried last week and hold it over his grave, you can see through the dirt and see what John is doing. For all you know, he may be shooting craps." That poor dumb man had no better sense than to go out to the graveyard at night and start looking through the glass Elijah had given him. While he was there, Elijah slipped up behind him, cracked him across the back of the head with a crowbar, and killed him. The law did nothing to him. The man he killed had a bad reputation, so the sheriff said: "Good riddance. Elijah got rid of him for us. He saved us the trouble." I was just a kid, but I remember so vividly old "Elijah with a crowbar." He was a town character.

I don't remember what Elijah did for a living. I don't think he held down any kind of permanent job. He lived off the things people gave him. I imagine he lived about as good a life as those Negroes who continued to slave themselves to death years after slavery was outlawed. Most of the county Negroes raised corn and hay on farms owned by white people. The corn and hay were fed to hogs, cattle, mules, and Tennessee walking horses. When I was a boy, stock raising was an important industry in the county.

Columbia was called Muletown. It was the greatest mule market in the world. Farmers all over the county bred mules for sale. People from all over the country—and especially from the cotton plantations farther south—came to Maury County the first of the year to buy mules to work on their plantations. On Mule Day—it was the first Monday—you couldn't get within a block and a half of the courthouse in all four directions. Mules were everywhere—all over the streets, on the sidewalks, from one building to another. There were mules and mules and more mules. For four or five weeks after Mule Day, the stench of that town was stifling! There was no way it could be cleaned up quickly. Everybody just put up with it. If you wanted to live and work in Columbia in those days, you simply had to put up with the smell because mules were the biggest revenue-producing industry in the county.

A good, trained, three-year-old mule would bring a handsome price, and they were in great demand on the big plantations down in Mississippi and Alabama. "A good mule and a good nigger for a dollar a day"—that's all a white farmer needed to make money. The mule and the nigger would plow from seven o'clock in the morning to six o'clock in the evening, with maybe an hour off for dinner at noon, when you'd feed and water the mule and the nigger. You paid the nigger one dollar. You owned the mule, so you didn't have to pay for him daily. But he cost more in the beginning—up to two or three hundred dollars. The poor old nigger wasn't worth much, even after he got to be free! In Mississippi Senator James Eastland and the rest of those rascals grew fat and rich off that kind of business. They thrived off the mule and the nigger. It was a combination that made a lot of white men rich.

On our farm outside town, we raised mostly corn. When we caught up with our work on Papa's little vegetable patches around town, he'd send us out to help with the corn crop. I'll never forget the old mule I used to plow out there. We named him Jack. He would be so nice and kind, but then all of a sudden he would decide to balk. Then you might as well take him at his word. He'd kick you. He'd bite you. He'd butt you. Papa always warned us: "Now, look out. Look out for the mule. Don't let old Jack kick you!" We knew that when old Jack kicked you, you were truly kicked!

But old Jack was a worker. We figured we were imposing on the horse to give him the hard work, so we'd give it to Jack. He didn't mind at all. You couldn't hurt his feelings. He would plow all day long without stopping. Long as you were able to follow the plow, he'd pull it; I mean, he'd pull it till he decided he wouldn't pull it any more. Then we'd have to unhook him and carry him back to the barn. He was finished for the day. If you tried to work him after he decided he was through, he'd break up the plow, break up the harness, and plow up half the corn. And he'd kick the hell out of you if you got too close to him when he was acting up. In other words, when old Jack decided to quit, he quit—then and there—and without asking our permission.

When I'd be out on the farm plowing with Jack, I'd have a lot of work to do and would try to get it done as quickly as possible. And when Jack balked, I'd try to coax him into a change of mood. I never hit him, but I'd beg him. "Please, Jack. Now, come on, Jack. Get up, Jack." But if his mind was made up, I could never do anything to change it. I'd have to take him back to the barn, put him in his stable, hitch up the horse, and go out again to finish the day's work. I'll tell you the difference between a horse and a mule. You can yell at a horse. You can beg a horse. If you need to, you can even take a whip and tap a horse with it, and he'll do what you want him to. He couldn't do as much as the old mule, but he'd try. The old mule wouldn't pay any attention to anything you did to him.

Sometimes I think about how mean I was to that old mule when he got stubborn. At the end of the day, I'd go up to the loft and throw some feed down for the horse in his stable but nothing for the mule. I'd let old Jack stand in his stall for a couple of days and wouldn't feed him. Then maybe on the third day, the old mule would stick his little head out over the gate of his stall and look like he was begging for something to eat. I'd go up and put my hand on his head. He'd lay his head on my shoulder and seem like he was pleading for something to eat. "Jack," I'd say, "will you plow for me now? I'll feed you if you'll plow. Will you do your work now?" I'd talk to him like that for several minutes. Then I'd feed him and maybe give him too much to make up. After he'd eaten, I'd hitch him up, and that mule would plow all over creation—until he decided to balk again. No question about it, though. That mule was the most efficient animal on our farm—on anybody's farm. He could do more work with the least upkeep. The mule is the South's great unsung hero.

Even though Papa worked us boys pretty hard, there was always some time for recreation. We played baseball and tennis but no football. Papa thought football was too brutal. Sometimes we'd make our own softballs, which we'd bat to pieces quickly. Then we'd scrape around and save our change to buy us a store ball. But it was so cheap that after we'd knocked it around a couple of days the cover would come off, and it would soon fall to pieces. I also had a bicycle, but since I was the youngest in the family, I never had a new one. That was one of my little bellyaches.

Papa did his best to provide amusement for us. He turned our backyard into a veritable zoo. It was as big as a small farm, and we raised all kinds of animals in it: Bellingham rabbits, pigeons, chickens, guineas, geese, and ducks. We always kept at least one cow—sometimes three cows. We had one or two horses all the time and usually a pony. We built two big cases back there made of chicken wire. In one we kept as many as 100 pigeons at a time, and in the other we kept the rabbits. I enjoyed feeding and playing with the rabbits and watching the pigeons. We had so much space that there was a section for each species. "This is the pigeon corner," we'd say. "Here are the hogs, there the cows, the goats, the mule."

Our pony was named James. Mama and Papa got a kick out of snapping pictures of three of us children astraddle that pony. We played all sorts of little pranks with him. I can remember running from the rear, throwing my hands up on his hips, and leapfrogging myself up to the saddle. We would ride him backward. We would ride him without a bridle or a saddle. It was a show-off thing, especially when we were putting on a show for the white kids. After we'd done some tricks on the pony, we'd hold out our hands and feed him an apple or some sugar. When the other kids wanted to ride James, we would tell them very carefully, "Now, when you get to the corner, you must lean toward the right or toward the left because if you don't guide that pony, he's going to hit the corner so fast he'll turn, and you'll keep on going down the street." But always some of the kids would fall off. It was such a sight: the pony galloping down the street, turning the corner suddenly, and a kid tumbling onto the street. Sometimes we'd hitch up James to our two-wheeled cart, load into it, and drive around the neighborhood. It was always so much fun to have little white kids come over and admire our zoo, ride our pony, and play with our rabbits. Papa even had a red and white pet rooster that he showed off. He'd go out in the yard, and the rooster would come up, jump on his hand, and then onto his shoulder. Then Papa would hold out a handful of corn, and the rooster would eat it. Some of our neighbors had pigeons or rabbits or other pets, but we seemed to have a little bit of everything.

We raised those animals mainly for recreation, not for food. I don't remember ever eating any of the pigeons or the rabbits. They were our pets and a part of our backyard menagerie. We seldom even ate our chickens. We ate their eggs, but they were pets. Even our crazy, old mule was a pet. I won't say we idolized or worshipped our zoo, but we certainly didn't want to eat it.

There weren't many opportunities for culture and recreation for anybody in Columbia, and we Negroes had almost none. When a New York theatrical outfit came through to put on a play, we weren't allowed to go. One time my father made such a stink about it that they finally set aside about twenty-five seats way back in the tent on the left side and marked it "Colored." They may have been fine cultural programs, but the degradation that Negroes had to suffer to attend them caused only a handful of us to go. The traveling troupe would put on a play or a musical program or a recitation or a combination of acts for, say, six days straight. I went to several of them when I was a boy, and I rather enjoyed them. I know now that it must have been the third or fourth-string people who came on those tours, but we didn't know any better—we hadn't heard any better—and we thought they were good. Circuses also used to come through town, and they had the same racial arrangement—a separate section for colored. I couldn't go to anything of a cultural nature in the community unless it was segregated, and to me it was embarrassing. It was kind of like Renaissance Europe when there was culture and art only for rich families. Columbia had no orchestra or ballet or opera or museum for any color. Well-to-do white people made their own culture. They had their own cultural entertainments, and they could go to Nashville and other cities to art shows, concerts, and museums—places we Negroes were not allowed to go. Blacks were not even allowed to use our little public library in Columbia, which was operated by the United Daughters of the Confederacy.

The summer after I received my master's degree at the University of Michigan, I was visiting back home and went by that little library and asked for the use of some books. The lady at the library desk apparently didn't recognize me as a Columbia boy or as a Negro. I told her I was doing research in southern history at the University of Michigan and showed her my card. I said, "I hear you have a good collection of books on the Old South." She said: "Oh, yes, we have one of the best anywhere. Just make yourself at home and use any book you want to." I said: "Would it be all right if the university should want to microfilm some of your materials? It would be a boost to their collection." She said: "Oh, yes, of course. We'll do anything we can for the university." So she turned me loose in the stacks, and I found a lot of good stuff. After a while the lady walked back to where I was working and asked, "Oh, where are you staying, Mr. Johnson?" I didn't answer her directly. "I'll be here for about three weeks before school starts again," I said. She said: "That's good. Now, where are you staying? Before I can charge a book out to you, I have to have your local address." I said, "I'm staying out on East Ninth Street." She said, "Where on East Ninth Street?" I gave her the block number and said, "I'm staying with some friends out there." Well, my father was a good friend. "Oh," she said, "I know some people out there. I know the Roberts." I said, "Yes, I've met them. They live just two doors from where I'm staying." At that time the Roberts were pretty high-class white people. The librarian didn't know that there was one black family living on the street—my family. I decided not to tell her.

She apparently had enough information to trust me and said: "I'll tell you what. I'm not supposed to do this because you're not a resident, but if you'd like to take out any of these books with you to read at night, you're welcome to. You can even take some of the restricted books out and keep them for three days." So I checked out an armload of books and kept them for three full days. At the end of the third day, I went back to the library to return the books I'd borrowed. I started to open the gate leading up the walkway to the library door when the door opened and the same lady called out sharply: "Wait right there. Don't come in that gate." I said, "But I'm returning your books." Already I knew what she'd found out. "Nigger," she said, "don't come any farther. We don't allow niggers in this library." I said, "But you were so kind and helpful the other day." She said: "Yes, but I didn't know you were a nigger then. I called the Roberts, and they told me who you were. You grew up here. You know better than to try to use this library. Don't ever try that trick again. Stay right where you are and hand me those books over the fence." I said: "Thank you, madam. I have found all the material I need. When I get back to the university, I'll see that you get a letter of thanks." She said: "I don't want their letter of thanks. That was a dirty Yankee trick you pulled. They sent you down here to torment us, and we don't appreciate it at all."

That was a long time ago. Columbia has a first-rate library now, and it's truly public and open to everybody. Now I can walk in as big as anybody and check out books.

We Negroes, of course, had a social life within our own community. Girls and boys went courting. Papa was very protective and never allowed me much freedom to call on the girls. "Son," he'd say, "some of these girls are loose. Some of them are jealous of us because we have a little more than they do and will do anything to embarrass us—especially if a girl came up pregnant. They would say, 'Now Professor Johnson's son's got to marry that girl.' You've also got to watch, son, because some of them have diseases, and you don't know which ones. And you've got to be careful because you might get into a fight over a girl, and you'd come home all cut up. Son, just be careful with the girls." Despite the warnings from Papa, I had a number of little girlfriends.

I never had a real date all the time I was growing up. I never carried a girl to a party or carried a girl home from a party. Sometimes I would go to parties by myself. I remember one high school party I went to. It was a house party where there was a gramophone—a music machine—and I knew they'd be dancing the Charleston and the Fox Trot and all the latest steps. And I knew Papa was as opposed to dancing as he was to drinking and cardplaying and other such stuff. But I was next to the last one of his children to come along, and he was beginning to get adjusted to such things. I told him I wanted to go over to Roosevelt Barton's birthday party and added, "Now, Papa, you know I don't drink or play cards, and I don't know how to dance, but I just want to go to the party and be with my friends." He said: "All right, son. Roosevelt is a nice boy. I know the Barton family, and I know nothing will go on at their house that won't be good. You go ahead."

I put on my best Sunday clothes, and when I got there about nine o'clock, the party was jumping. It was in a little house, and the party was in the front room. It was crammed full of boys and girls jumping up and down, dancing, carrying on, and having a good time. About ten o'clock somebody said to me, "Shag's out there on the front porch." Shag was what the kids called my father, though not to his face. If they had, he'd have torn them to pieces. He used to let his hair grow down on his face, and he had sideburns. When the wind blew his sideburns and his whiskers, they said he looked like a "shag." I said, "What's he doing out there?" But I knew he was out there talking to Mr. Barton and would be there till the party was over. Sure enough, he stayed outside till the end. Then we walked home together.

Papa kept such close tabs on me I guess I was intimidated into being good. I can't say I *intended* to be as good as I was. After I went off to college and came back home, people used to tell me: "Lyman, you were such a fine little boy. I tried to get my children to be like you." My reputation followed me even into the navy. Many years later I was out in California and went into a base barbershop to get a haircut. By that time the government had scrapped segregation in the navy, and when you'd go into a barbershop, you'd take a number so there would be no opportunity for racial prejudice. In this barbershop there were five white barbers and two black ones. I was reaching up for a number when one of the white barbers said to me, "Say, could you be from Columbia, Tennessee?" I said, "Yup, I sure am." He said: "I know you, then. You're Lyman Johnson. You don't know me, but you knew my parents. My daddy was Joe Troop, who used to cut hair. You delivered papers to our house. When you would come by to leave the paper or collect or when you'd be walking by on the way to church or going to town, my mother used to say to me, 'Joe, why don't you be like Lyman? He's trying to make something of himself. He never misses a day of school, and he makes As and Bs.' I was about six years younger than you, and she held you up as an example all the time you were in high school and college."

By this time everybody in the barbershop was listening. He said to the fellow who was supposed to cut my hair: "I know it's a violation of regulations, but I want Lyman's number. I want to cut his hair." He had me sit in his chair. He said: "You know, Lyman, back in Columbia my daddy couldn't—and probably wouldn't—have cut your hair. But here I can. And I want to. I want you to know how much we thought of you." Now, that was all well and good, and I appreciated that man's show of respect for me and my family. But I don't really deserve any special reward for being good. I was afraid to be bad.

Some of my "goodness," I guess, came from the fact that we were a church-going family. The church was the center of community life for all Negroes in Columbia, but in our family we had to at least try to practice what the preacher preached. We went to Mt. Lebanon Baptist Church, a church started by a handful of free blacks in 1843. It was one of the first separate churches in Tennessee for Negroes. Most of the slaves attended their masters' churches or were given religious instruction in their quarters. Slaveowners were afraid to let their slaves have their own churches where they could plot insurrections. A few masters allowed their slaves to attend Mt. Lebanon, but most of its membership was made up of free Negroes.

Like most Negro churches, Mt. Lebanon was a plain building with rough benches for pews and a simple platform for the preacher. But we did have a brick sanctuary. Originally, the church had been a plain wooden building, but around 1900 the church had a pastor who was also a brick mason, and he talked the members into tearing down the old building and putting up a brick structure. I remember very well a number of the pastors at Mt. Lebanon. Several of them had good educations and set a fine example for their people. One of our pastors grew up in Columbia and then lived in New York till his mother got ill and he came back to take care of her and to be pastor of our little church. He said: "I think every person owes something to his hometown. I know you folks can't afford to pay me much, but I'll be your pastor for whatever you can pay me."

We had a revival every summer that would last about ten days or until the preachers gave out or the people stopped coming. Preaching was every night except Saturday. When the revival was over, we'd have a mass baptism in a nearby river. I was baptized in the Duck River. The deacons led me down to the river and out to where the preacher was standing. He threw me under that water, stood over me, and held me down until he was sure all my sins had been washed away. Then he let me up.

The church offered a change of pace from the Negro's hard, dull routine during the week, and it gave him great promises for the here-after—a life free of toil and mistreatment and filled with comforts and delights. My family was better off than most black people in Columbia, but there were a lot of earthly pleasures we never had. One thing I always wanted as a young boy but never got was a record player. I'd go over to other people's houses and listen to their jazz records. I'd say, "Papa, why can't we get a record player?" And he'd say, "Son, a record player isn't something we need." There was no appeal from my father's decision. It was final.

Until I was in the ninth grade, we didn't have electricity in our house. Through the eighth grade, I did all my homework around the dining room table with a kerosene lamp for light. It was a pretty lamp with a big white globe, but it didn't give off much light. When we got wired for electricity, Papa had seven drop sockets put in our seven rooms—and that was it. There were no wall plugs. And we had no electric appliances, no frills—no fan, no electric iron, no electric churn. Just lights hanging on a cord from the ceiling. Papa was really a sort of tightwad, always saving for a rainy day. Of course, he had no retirement plan to support him in his old age, and he didn't want his children to have to take care of him. His philosophy was that each generation should give the next one a good start. He didn't want his children robbing their children to take care of their father. But papa was probably too cautious and frugal, and he died leaving money and property he should have spent on himself.

We had no luxuries and very few conveniences at our house. Our toilet was at the far end of the backyard. It was, in fact, so far away from the house that it was terribly inconvenient. As we got older, it got to be embarrassing too, especially for my older sisters. My sister who lived for a while in Montreal, Canada, had entirely gotten away from the habit of going to a toilet in the backyard. But when she came home to visit, that's where she had to go. Summer and winter, day and night—we all had to go to that outdoor toilet. Sometimes my sisters would be afraid to go back there at night, and I'd carry a lantern and go with them almost to the toilet door, then wait. We didn't use commercial toilet paper—we used old newspapers—but we never used corncobs, though I've heard of country people who did. Going to the toilet in my family was never considered a bodily function to hide. It was a natural part of life. In fact, if I had a headache, Mama might say: "Son, have you been to the toilet today? If you haven't, you may need to take a laxative." And I'd have to take some awful-tasting medicine like castor oil, which really opened up the works! When I took a strong laxative like that, I tried to stay as close to the toilet as I could.

Despite such deprivations, the Johnsons had a good family life. We had a shelter over our heads, clothes on our backs, and enough good food to eat. Our family dinners were almost as large as boarding house dinners. There were times when eleven of us would be at the table—eight children, Mama, Papa, and our Uncle Will, Papa's brother. We always had a prayer and a blessing before we could eat. We stood behind our plates for the prayer and sat for the blessing. And Papa's prayers seemed endless, especially when we were hungry. It seemed he wanted to ask the Lord to bless everybody in the world individually, country by country.

One day we were going to have soup, and our soup bowls were all turned upside down on the table till the blessing was over. Mama didn't trust me with a good china bowl, so mine was an old cracked one. I bowed my head, and Papa started to pray. And he prayed and he prayed. He kept on praying till finally I gave up, put my head down on my bowl, and almost went to sleep. Suddenly, the weight of my head cracked my old bowl to pieces, and it popped to the floor right in the middle of Papa's prayer. He opened his eyes, saw what had happened, gave me a backhand left with the palm of his hand, caught me under the chin, lifted me up and right out the back door—and went right on praying. When I slipped back in, he was still praying. I don't think he missed a single one of the children in China—plus at least one of the Johnson children!

Papa believed that if you spared the rod you spoiled the child. We Johnsons were not spoiled children! Any infraction of a home rule or regulation and he took out his strap. If he was outside close to a peach tree, he'd break off a switch. Mama used a ruler. But neither one ever gave us cruel whippings. Both of them used physical punishment to nudge us back on the path that to them was straight and narrow, and neither allowed any shortcuts or detours.

Like all parents Papa sometimes made a mistake and whipped one of us when we weren't guilty. One time I was playing with my brother Charles, who had a weak heart. He couldn't exert himself much or he would have to rest in bed for several days. We were running through the house, that is, I was running through the house, and Charles had stopped by the water bucket stand. Mama was uptown somewhere, and Papa was out in the yard working. Charles filled the dipper full of water, and as I raced past, he threw it at me. It was a lot of fun, we thought, and I kept running by, and he kept throwing water at me. He'd usually miss me and splash water all over the wall and floor. Papa heard the commotion and came in. My sickly brother said, "Papa, Lyman kept running through here." That was all Papa needed to hear, and before I could explain that *I* hadn't thrown the water, he had whipped the hell out of me. I know he wouldn't have whipped Charles because of his weak heart, but I thought Charles should have at least shared the blame.

Another time he gave me a whipping over a missing handsaw. Papa had all sorts of tools—hammers, saws, chisels, levels, squares—anything you'd need to do carpenter work. He taught me carpentry as his father had taught him. One day Papa said: "Lyman, I can't find my saw. Have you used it?" I said: "Yes, Papa, but I don't know where it is. I thought I returned it." He said: "Lyman, it's not where it's supposed to be. You must learn to return what you borrow." I knew a whipping was becoming more and more likely, so I tried to remember where the saw was. Maybe, I thought, I did leave it where I had used it. I looked everywhere but couldn't find it. Finally, Papa gave me a terrible thrashing for using his saw and not returning it.

About ten days later, after we'd had two heavy rains, Papa was out in the garden picking up leaves and limbs scattered around. As he was bending over next to the paling fence, he found his saw. The rains had rusted and warped it. He picked it up and came looking for me. "Lyman," he said, "remember the whipping I gave you for misplacing my saw?" I said uneasily, "Yes, Papa, I remember it very well." When I saw the rusty saw he was holding, I just knew I had another whipping in store. "Well," Papa said, "I want to apologize for that whipping. I was the one who misplaced the saw. I left it where I was working on that paling fence. I was wrong. I want you to forgive me." I looked up at him and said: "Papa, I'll forgive you. But you can't unwhip me!" I know most of the whippings I received were well earned, but I happen to remember the undeserved ones.

My father's father was a carpenter and a slave. He never learned to read or write, but he was an excellent carpenter so he must have known how to figure. He had to have a lot of native ability to pick up a trade like that and excel in it. People could tell him what they wanted built, and he could build it. He was a smart man—smart enough to buy himself out of slavery.

He did such good work that his master hired him out to work for other people repairing and building houses. When the master got paid for my grandfather's work, he would sometimes share part of it with him to keep his incentive up. My grandfather quietly saved what he was given. Of course, he didn't have access to banks, so he must have hidden it in little cans under the apple trees or some place like that. One day, apparently kidding his master, he must have said: "Massa, would you sell me? If somebody offered you a good price, would you sell me?" The master said, "Oh, yeah." My grandfather said: "I thought you liked me. I didn't think you'd sell me." The master said: "Oh, yes I would. If the price was right, you'd go like all the rest of my slaves. But don't worry right now. As long as you satisfy the people you're working for and as long as you behave yourself, I won't put you on the block."

My grandfather brought up the subject several times, and finally the master admitted that if anybody offered him $1,300 he would sell him. This was around 1849. One day my grandfather walked in and said to the master, "There's a fellow I know that wants to buy me." The master said, "Well, tell him to send me $1,300 and he can have you." My grandfather was all set. In a few days, he came to the master and said, "That man I told you about that wants to buy me, well, he sent you $1,300." So he counted out $1,300 that he'd picked up out of those cans under those trees. The master took his money and said: "Well, if he trusted you with this much money, I'll trust you to go on over there and turn yourself in to him. You're through here. Get going." "Yes, sir," my newly freed grandfather said, "but the man said he'd like to have a receipt." So the white man sat down to write a receipt. He looked up at the freedman. "Now, whose name do I put down as your new owner?" My grandfather said, "Put down 'Dyer Johnson!'" The man started to write it down, then looked up suddenly and said, "But that's you." "That's right," Grandfather said. "Put *my* name down as my new owner!" So the slaveowner said, "Well, I said I'd sell you for $1,300 and so I will." He wrote "I sell Dyer Johnson to Dyer Johnson" and signed his name. My grandfather reached down for the document and was a free man from then on.

But he wasn't finished with his buying. Three or four years later he bought his wife, my grandmother, whom he had married while he was a slave. After he became a free man, he wasn't allowed to see his wife. Slaveholders were suspicious of free blacks. I imagine Grandmother's owner said to him: "Don't you come around here any more. You're a free man, and you might give my other slaves screwy ideas about freedom. You'd bother them." Grandfather said: "But you let me marry Betty. She's my wife." Her owner said: "Yeah, but she's still a slave. She's still my property. I can't let her off the place. Don't come back to see her." Finally, however, he talked her owner into selling her to him. Before he could claim her, the agreement was that he had to buy a little piece of property and build a house on it. Within a year he had bought some ground and built a one-room log cabin. That cabin is still standing. It's part of the house I was born in and grew up in.

So Grandfather bought Grandmother from her mistress and took her to live in that log cabin—both of them free people of color more than ten years before the Civil War freed all the slaves. They were impatient to be free. They couldn't wait. Maybe that's where I got my own sense of justice, my own impatience with the law's long delay. Because my grandmother was an invalid, my grandfather bought her cheap—for only $300. The bill of sale does not warrant that she is sound of body. This is the way it reads.

State of Tennessee. Maury County. Know all men by these presents that I, Nancy White, of the state and county aforesaid have this day sold and do hereby convey to Dyer Johnson, a free man of color, to his heirs and assigns forever for the sum of $300 to me paid one Negro slave named Betty, age about thirty years, of mulatto color. I warrant the title of said slave to said Dyer Johnson, his heirs and assigns against the lawful claims of all persons but I do not warrant the said slave Betty to be a healthy and sound woman. May 10, 1852. My hand and seal. Nancy White.

Below this she drew a little seal and wrote in the middle of it "seal." The sale is attested to by somebody named I.B. Hamilton and W. Watson. They were the witnesses. It was important that Grandfather have this bill of sale. Technically, she was still a slave. The bill of sale simply transferred her ownership to another person who happened to be her husband and my grandfather. She was legally a slave till she was freed by the Thirteenth Amendment to the Constitution. Till then, anyone owning this document could have legally sold her.

I imagine my grandfather must have kidded her about how cheap she was. He had cost $1,300 while she had cost only $300. Despite the refusal of her owner to warrant that she was "a healthy or sound woman," she was quite a bargain! She lived to be almost eighty and had three healthy children. Her daughter lived to be eighty-three, and her two sons reached ninety and ninety-two.

How do I feel about this piece of paper in my hands? How do I feel about the fact that my grandparents—on both sides—were slaves? My mama and papa taught me that a person should never be ashamed of where he comes from. It's not my fault that my grandparents were slaves. I make no apology for it to anybody. It's the other side that should be apologizing. I tell other black people not to pity themselves because they once were slaves. "Many whites were slaves too," I say. "In the days of ancient Rome, many Greek scholars were enslaved by Roman generals who would take them to Rome to teach their children. So don't feel sorry for yourself. White intellectuals once were slaves to their inferiors." So I remind black people that Rome was a drop down from the Greeks in culture. But when Caesar got to England and saw those little stringy-haired, blond, pale-faced English children, he almost cried to see how backward they were. "It is a disgrace that these children are so dirty and dumb," he said. I tell black people that history makes the whole racial eugenics argument absurd—the idea that black people are inferior because they can't help it.

Slavery, of course, wherever and whenever it existed, was an evil. But American slavery was a compounded evil because it was based almost exclusively on race. In other parts of the world, slavery was not racial. The Arabs took black and white slaves. Indentured servants in early America lived almost in slavery, but they were at least term slaves. They agreed to serve a man for a period of time, usually seven years, in return for passage to America and maybe other considerations. On the other hand, to be a life slave in this country was to be black. The life of a white indentured servant was often not any better than that of a black slave. Sometimes their indenture was arbitrarily extended by their masters on some flimsy excuse. Then when they were old and worthless, they would be thrown out. Nevertheless, their children weren't handicapped by a black face. It's taken a long time to get Negroes themselves to believe that they are not inferior simply because they are Negroes. That is the legacy of slavery in this country.

Fortunately, my grandfather and grandmother didn't let their black faces discourage them. They set an example for my father, who then set an example for my generation. Grandpapa worked hard to make a good life for his wife and their three children born after she left the plantation. But when he died in 1873, he had nothing to leave them, except that one-room cabin and the ground it was on. I never knew what made Grandmother Johnson an invalid. I was told it was a frailness, but I never heard its source.

So Dyer Johnson died and left an invalid wife, three children ten to thirteen years old, and whatever was in that cabin. They had no Social Security, no food stamps, no retirement funds. The children were too young to do steady work, and Grandmother was unable to. They were in utter, dire poverty. I'm sure they scratched around in the dirt and grew what vegetables they could. Maybe they had chickens and a milk cow. Neighbors—black and white—helped too. They would come by and leave little sacks of food. "Here, Aunt Betty," they'd say, "here's a little something to cook." And they'd give her a handful of sweet potatoes or beans or collard greens, whatever they had to spare. She'd cook whatever she had and whatever she was given, and she and the three children would sit around the table and eat till it was gone. It usually wasn't very much. Then she'd say: "Children, that's all we have today. Now, go on out, but don't tell anybody you're hungry."

When my Uncle Will was about twelve, he got a job as a handy boy in a wholesale grocery store. He swept the floors, helped move the goods around, and stocked the shelves. He'd go to work right after school and would work till closing time. He and the owner were usually the last two people to leave the place at night. As they left, the man would say: "Well, Will, we put in a good day today. You've done a good job. Now, Will, what do you think Aunt Betty wants for tomorrow?" Uncle Will would say, "Mr. Sloane, Mama says can you spare a little piece of bacon?" Mr. Sloane would say, "Yes, Will, and you tell Aunt Betty how much we think of her and hope she's feeling better." All the time he'd be getting out his big butcher knife and reaching up and cutting off a little slab of bacon. And that was Uncle Will's pay for the day. The next day they'd go through the same little act. Mr. Sloane would say: "Will, you did a nice job today. Tell your mother what a good workman you are. What does Aunt Betty want tomorrow?" And Uncle Will might say, "Mama wants to know could you spare a few beans?" And the white man would get out a little bag and put some beans in it, and that would be Uncle Will's pay for that day. In that way Uncle Will provided the main foodstuffs for the family—a little meal, a little flour, some beans, a piece of bacon.

Uncle Will was the youngest of the three children—two years younger than my papa—but he could do more hard work than Papa. As a boy father was kind of frail, though he eventually grew more vigorous. Uncle Will was the mainstay of the family. A white man out in the country furnished him a mule, a plow, a wagon, the seed cane, fertilizer, and the land. My uncle furnished the labor, and when the cane was cut, they split it in half. That was usually the way sharecropping worked. The cane crop was big that year, and it was backbreaking work. My papa helped with some of the labor, but he couldn't do much or he would be laid up for weeks. Uncle Will wouldn't let his mother or sister help. "You can't go to the fields," he's say. "That isn't your place." So my uncle raised the sorghum, cut it, and hauled it to the mill. He was a man who had muscle *and* brains. But for the grace of God he might have stayed a sharecropper all his life. He might never have bloomed out.

But he had brains, and they helped take him to college. This is how he got there. Uncle Will's share of the syrup made from the sorghum crop was one-fourth. He had given one-half of the cane to the landowner. Then he took his half to the sorghum syrup mill and had it squeezed and the juice cooked down until it became molasses. Then he had to give half of the syrup to the mill owner. So he wound up with a fourth of the original crop. Still it was a lot more than he, his mother and brother and sister could eat at home. So he started to college on the excess.

In those days it was about forty-eight miles from Columbia to Nashville on an old dirt road. I imagine Uncle Will hitchhiked to Nashville by wagon. There were buggies on the road too, but I don't think anybody in a buggy would have picked him up. He probably hitched a ride on a wagon being sent to Nashville to pick up supplies. One more little Negro boy on a supply wagon wouldn't have overloaded the mules. So Uncle Will arrived at Roger Williams University in Nashville, one of those schools set up in the South by northern churches after the Civil War to educate the freedman and his children.

When he got to the campus, he went to the president's office and said, "Professor, I want to go to school, but I don't have anything but molasses." Uncle Will must have had rags on his back, but he had a beautiful countenance and light shining through his eyes. The president didn't know whether he was naive or just bold, but he was apparently impressed with the young man before him. And he said: "You are the kind of person we want here at Roger Williams. I think we can find enough money to take care of you." And that poor country boy who could only offer a few gallons of molasses to pay his tuition and board went to college—and finally became a college president. That story has been in the recesses of my mind a long time. It's one I've wanted to unload on blacks and whites. Young men like Booker T. Washington and my Uncle Will rewarded those dedicated teachers who came down from the North to teach the illiterate freed slave and his children. And such rewards they were—the awakening of a whole race of people!

I don't know how many buckets of molasses got transferred from Columbia to Nashville to pay Uncle Will's expenses. But I do know he got a good education at Roger Williams, good enough that Brown University validated his work there and took him into graduate school. He later returned to teach at Roger Williams and was president when the school folded about 1915. At that time one of his former students, who was president of Morehouse, said: "Professor Johnson, I want you to move down here to Atlanta and teach our students. I've worked under you. Now would you mind if we turned things around and have you work for me?" My uncle taught there till he retired and moved back to Columbia to live out his remaining years with his brother, my father. He lived to be ninety-two. When I was growing up, he was always a glamorous somebody to me. He never married. He'd say: "I don't need any children. My brother and sister have so many they can't feed and clothe and educate them all, so I'll just adopt some of them." And he did a marvelous job of helping us all.

Uncle Will was an inspiration to me. I could sit for hours and listen to him tell stories about his life. One story he told me the last year of his life shows how much he loved his mother. One time she whipped him for something he didn't do. Something went wrong, he said, and his mother satisfied herself that neither of the other children had been responsible. So she called Will in and said, "Now, Willie, you know you did it." He said, "No, Mama, I didn't do it." She said: "Willie, it has to be you. You must be lying, and I will not tolerate lying from one of my children." They went round and round for a few minutes. She accused him, and he denied it. Again and again. The more she accused and he denied, the more convinced she became that she was right. Finally, she said: "All right, Willie, I'm not going to punish you for doing it, but I am going to punish you for lying about it. Hand me that switch over there. I'm going to whip you for lying." Uncle Will said he handed her the switch, but she was so frail she could hardly raise it up, and when she brought it across his backsides, he could hardly feel it. But just to give her satisfaction he pretended he was being hurt. "Even though I was innocent," he said, "I would never reject her effort to straighten me out. So I stood there and she switched—or tried to switch—me good for something I never did."

Grandmama Johnson did her best not only to feed and clothe but to educate her children. She sent them to school in the Baptist church her husband, my grandpapa, had given the land for. It was next door—just across the fence—from where they lived. When it got lunch time, the other little children sat on benches in the yard and ate lunches they brought from home. But Grandmama told her children: "Now, don't stand around when the other children start to eat. You get over that fence and come home. If I've got anything to eat, we'll eat it together. If I don't have anything, we'll all just sit here till the lunch period is over. I don't want you hanging around and begging for something to eat. And when you go back to school, don't tell anybody you're hungry. Just say you went home to eat because you live so close."

The little Negro children went to school in that church on weekdays. The teacher was one of my papa's older cousins named Edmund Kelly. He had been born a slave but had run away, and the underground railroad had got him all the way to Massachusetts. He was found to be a brilliant fellow, and the people there gave him a first-class education. About six years after slavery ended, he came back down to Columbia to live with his kinpeople and to teach in that little school in the Baptist church. The facilities were improvised and primitive. The little children sat on the bare church benches. But that didn't matter. It was a school—the first one for black children in that town. And Edmund Kelly was a dedicated teacher. It must have been ironic and aggravating to the white people who had known him when he was a slave. He came back talking with a northern accent. After ten years in northern schools taught by teachers motivated by the zeal of religion, he was speaking correct grammar, pronouncing his words correctly, putting "r's" in his words, and teaching Negroes right out of slavery to do the same thing. He didn't get any regular pay. He got whatever handouts the black parents could afford. He did what he did out of a love for his people. He is one of the unknown heroes of American history.

My papa was just one of the dozens of black people in Columbia who got their start under Edmund Kelly. When I came along, Papa was one of the three Negro leaders in town. The second one was the Negro doctor. The third was my wife's father, the mail carrier. He was a college graduate but made twice as much money carrying mail as he could as principal of the Negro school. Papa was the school principal and also taught mathematics. When I got out from that little school and started sailing high and wide, I found out how good a teacher my papa was. He was a graduate of Roger Williams but came back to Columbia to live. The white people always called him Professor Johnson instead of Mr. Johnson, just like they called a minister "preacher." They always referred to Papa as a "colored gentleman." Most white people respected him and gave him a qualified acceptance in the white community. But even more important to him—and to us—was his acceptance and respect in the black community. Sooner or later, regardless of how much educated Negroes butter up to white people, there always comes a time when they're shut out and have to come home. Papa knew who his people were and where his home was.

We lived in a white neighborhood. We were the only Negro family on our street. This is how it happened. When Grandpa bought the property back in 1853, it was way back in the woods, off the main highway. A place like that was the only one a free black man could buy. So he bought a pretty little piece of land and built a cabin. From then until my time in the 'teens and 20s, the town expanded till there weren't any woods left. It was all residential. A highway between Columbia and the nearby town of Louisburg had been built right by our door. For five miles up and down that road, we were the only Negro family.

We got along very well with our white neighbors close by. Although I went to school and to church and to social events with other Negroes, I played with the white children in our neighborhood. But they didn't want me to bring other black children home with me to play with them. "Lyman," the white children would say, "tell them niggers to go home. We don't want to play with them." I caught it from both sides. When I went over to the black side of town, they would say: "Lyman, tell them damn yaps not to call us niggers any more. If they do, we're gonna make it hard for you." I had to walk a tightrope.

Occasionally, we'd have a run-in with whites who didn't like our living in what they considered a white part of town. We kept our property up, and it looked as good as anybody's. Papa insisted that as long as we lived on that street, nobody could come by and say, "You can sure tell where the niggers live!" Our place always looked nice. My mother admired pretty flowers, and our front yard was always filled with flowers. But regardless of how much we tried to get along, there were always some whites who didn't like us. One time I remember some trashy-looking white folks passing by and looking over in our yard and seeing Negroes in it. They screamed, "We don't want niggers—niggers!—out on this street with white people!" They kept on ranting and raving from the road. Sometimes my papa got bold and showed his spunk. "Let me tell you right straight off," he said, "we were here first. If you don't want to live around me, you can go wherever you damn well please! When my daddy was alive, out here in the woods was the only place he could buy. You folks came in here later. And whenever you get ready to go, you can go. I'm here to stay! You came around me. I didn't come around you!"

Most of the discrimination we suffered from people outside our immediate neighborhood. And I will never—no, never—forgive the meanness of those white people who mistreated us outside that little handful of our white neighbors. Their meanness gets meaner as the years go by. I don't intend to forget it. Never! I won't hold it against their children, but I won't forget or forgive those people who made us suffer. It was cruel and vicious.

I attended, of course, a separate and unequal "colored" school for eleven years. It was called College Hill School, and my papa was principal all the years I was a student. Our facilities were grossly inferior to those in the white schools. The white school had a lunchroom where hot lunches were served, but we had none. Every little Negro child brought his lunch or waited till he got home to eat. At noon recess the children who had lunch opened their brown paper bags and ate their peanut butter and crackers or buttered biscuits. Little children who didn't have any lunch ran around and played off their hunger. I always got home half-starved and ate up everything in sight, cooked or raw. Usually, my mother had something like a pot of beans on the stove. And naturally, we had eaten a good breakfast before we left for school. Then around six o'clock we had a heavy supper.

We didn't have indoor plumbing at College Hill School till I was in the sixth grade. The water fountains were outdoors, and so were the rest rooms. The toilets were stinking because they were not properly treated or cleaned out. Fortunately, they were way back in the school yard, the boys' toilet on one side and the girls' on the other. Finally, the health department closed them up and made the school system put indoor toilets in.

When I was in the eighth grade, I found out how truly unequal the Negro and white schools were. One day Papa sent me over to the white school with a message for the white superintendent. I was supposed to bring back some papers to my father. I went to the superintendent's office in one end of the white school building. The clerk took my father's report and said she would have the other package ready for me in a few minutes. So I moved over and took a seat next to the superintendent's office to wait. The school janitor—the Negro janitor—passed by the door, looked in, and saw me sitting there. He knew me and my family very well. Suddenly, he went into an awful commotion, which I didn't understand at the time. He came in the door, looked over at the clerk, and, when she was not paying any attention, said to me: "Hey, boy, don't you want to go with me? While you're waiting, don't you want to walk around with me?" I said, "What are you doing?" He said: "I've got to make my rounds now. Come on and go with me." I said: "All right, Mr. Graham. Yes, sir, Mr. Graham, I'd like to do that while I'm waiting." He said in a whisper, "Call me Tom."

I had been taught to have proper respect for everybody and not to downgrade a person because he was a Negro. I was taught to call all grown-ups "Mr." and "Mrs." So I called him Mr. Graham because it was part of my training. He said again: "Don't call me that, boy. Call me Tom." I didn't understand then what he meant. Later, of course, when I got older, I realized that although he was Mr. Graham to us he was just plain Tom in white society, regardless of his age. Six-year-old white children called him Tom. I also realized later that he would have lost his job if he had gone around that white school as Mr. Graham. You called the white teachers and the white superintendent "Mr." but not the janitor—the nigger janitor. You called him Tom.

I was still puzzled as to why Mr. Graham wanted me to go with him, but I went as he made his rounds picking up paper in the halls. Finally, we got to the gym. My eyes were opened. For the first time, I saw that highly polished hardwood floor, and I looked at it in perfect amazement. I said, "Mr. Graham. . . ." He said, "Call me Tom." But I could never bring myself to call him Tom. I said, ". . . , uh, do they play in here all the year?" He said, "Yeah, they play basketball here and have gym classes all the time." I couldn't believe it. I went on with him picking up paper, adjusting window shades, and so on till we got back to the superintendent's office. The package was ready, and I got on out.

I left that school, but I've never forgotten what I saw. Way back in 1921 white children had a pretty polished hardwood floor and an indoor gymnasium to play in. Over on my side of town at the Negro school, we had to play basketball outdoors, year-round, and we had to play around the big rocks that stuck up out of the ground. We had to skip over those rocks to throw the ball in the basket. No wonder Negro boys could play better basketball than white boys! They were trained not to fall over rocks and to put the ball in the basket at the same time. No, I cannot forgive my hometown for not even smoothing off the outdoor court for us so we could have a decent place to play. No, I just won't forgive them. That tour of the white school with Mr. Graham opened my eyes to the fact that something wrong was going on. As I grew older and became more aware of other inequalities of racial discrimination, my eyes opened wider and wider. And I became determined to do what I could to correct them.

What our school lacked in physical conveniences we made up for in dedicated teachers. One of my favorite teachers was Miss Queenie Moore, one of the three first-grade teachers. She was so compassionate. I don't remember her saying an angry word to any of the thirty-five pupils in her room, but she kept perfect order. After teaching for forty years, I can admire her ability to work so well with so many, though I don't know whether she could survive if she were thrown back in the classroom today. Of course, we weren't angels in those days, but she knew how to handle us effectively. She never scolded us, but she knew how to use a switch or a ruler. She'd say sweetly: "Come here, child. What you did was wrong." Or

she'd say: "Now, child, you don't talk to me like that. Now, turn around."
And she'd lay it on us. We'd sometimes protest: "Oh, Miss Queenie, that
hurts. That hurts." And she'd say: "Yes, my dear, I intend for it to. You
promise not to do that any more?" We'd say, "Yes, Miss Queenie." And
we'd still just love the hell out of her because we knew she was loving us.
She punished us in such a nice way that we had to like her even when we
were begging her, "Please, Miss Queenie, please don't hit me any more."

Not all our teachers were as good as Miss Queenie. I didn't like
Samson Brown, who thought he was a good teacher because he could
scare the hell out of us. We didn't respect him, but he got by on his bull-
dozing. But most of my teachers I liked: Mrs. Melinda Frierson, Sam
Howell, Miss Willie Harlem, Miss Norvella Brown. The teacher who
taught me to respect English language and grammar was Miss Bea (Bea-
trice) Gordon. I don't think she ever finished college, but she knew
English grammar. She gave me a good foundation in grammar. She would
have ridiculed so-called Black English, thinking it was a cop-out. And so
do I. I have no sympathy for it. If I want to get a job down at the First
National Bank, I've got to go in there and use the language the president of
that bank wants me to use. And he wants me to use the language of the
people who do business with that bank. He doesn't want me saying "dis"
and "dat" to his customers. I know three people with Ph.D.'s who try to
justify Black English. I say to them: "Ah, go to hell! Don't come here with
that stuff!" I've always tried to teach young people to speak polite,
courteous, elegant English—not some debased variety used by illiterates! I
know a black woman up in Chicago who will not have certain black
babysitters because their grammar and pronunciation are so horrible. "I'll
pay such a girl five dollars," she says, "then dismiss her. I don't want her
teaching my children to talk like her."

I used to do the same thing when my children were coming up. A
couple of times certain black girls would come over to babysit, and when I
heard them talk, I'd just say: "I'm sorry. I guess we don't need you after
all." I paid them for coming, but I didn't want anybody speaking "Black
English" to my children. Maybe I should have told them the reason I
didn't want them to stay, but I didn't have time to go through an explana-
tion they'd understand. I've always taught my students that if they're
going to live in a country where English is spoken and written, then they
must learn to speak and write the best English. Anything less is second
class. And black people have put up with being second class long enough.

Unfortunately, most of my classmates at College Hill School didn't
stay in school long enough to master good English. When I started to
school, there were three first-grade classes, about 100 pupils in all. Of that
100, only nine finished high school, and I was the only one to go on to
college. What a terrible mortality rate! But I can't criticize my dropout

classmates too much. They didn't have the advantage of having my mother and father. They had no one to encourage them or to set examples for them. In addition, the economic system encouraged early dropouts. The jobs that were available to Negroes required little or no education. There was little incentive for most blacks to stay in school. But, oh, what a waste of brains and talent! Who knows what William Summers or Lester Pointer or Chester Green could have amounted to if they had had the opportunity to develop their potentials? I don't know where my old Columbia classmates are now. I imagine most of them are dead.

Even with the advantages I had, there were still problems. Although the white school went through all twelve grades, our black school only covered eleven. I used to study in the kitchen of the little white boy who lived across the street from me, and he used to study in my kitchen. I used to study on his front porch, and he used to study on my front porch. He went to the white school, and I went to the Negro school. He went on to the University of Tennessee without any conditions. But I had to make up the twelfth grade before I could be admitted to college.

I went up to Knoxville College Academy, which had been set up for Negroes like me who had gone to schools that did not prepare them for college work. Knoxville Academy was a no-nonsense school run by northern Presbyterians. They said: "Mail your credits up here, and we will evaluate them. Then you must take an exam, and anything you don't pass you have to make up." Well, I did all right on math and English. But because I went to an unaccredited school, I had to make up two years of high school work. I had to go two years to make up for what I couldn't take in the black school in my hometown. The white boy across the street didn't have anything to make up because he went to an accredited school. I had to pay room and board and tuition to a school away from home as a penalty for having gone to a black school. Even those of us who tried to get an education were penalized at every turn.

My growing-up years were bad times for black people all over this country and especially in the South. We had little protection and very few rights. We lived in fear. My father knew the score and did his best to prepare us for life in a racist society. He'd say, "Children, I must be strict on you here at home so that when you leave you'll be so well behaved you won't get into trouble and there'll be no reason for the police to pick you up." We were always afraid of the police—the white police. We were afraid of what they would do to us. We knew what they did to other blacks in Columbia when they arrested them. They'd handcuff them, beat them on the spot with their pistols or whatever was handy, and then take them to jail.

One day after I was grown and had moved to Kentucky, I was visiting back home when a local, white politician asked me if I would support him. He knew I couldn't vote in Columbia, but he also knew I carried a lot of weight in the black community. I said: "I don't know whether I will support you or not. Before I commit myself, I want to know why, when your police go to arrest a black person, the first thing they do is take out a stick and start beating on him." The politician got mad and said, "Johnson, if you're not careful, I'll put you under arrest and have you beaten." I said, "The hell you will!" and walked away. I didn't have that kind of nerve when I was twenty to stand up to him. When I was a boy and a young man, I didn't have any protection from such brutes. But now my eyes were open, and I knew I could bring in the power of the federal government to protect me. Conditions are better now, but I'm not going to glorify and embellish a society that once used fear and violence to keep Negroes in their place.

When I was a boy and a white boy hit me, there wasn't much I could do about it. If I wanted to take chances, I might argue with him. But I'd better not hit him back. It wasn't cowardice that kept my fists in check. It was just good common sense. The cards were all stacked against me. The boy was white. The police were white. The judge was white. The lawyers were white, even the one I might get to defend me. And the mores were white. White people were in absolute and total control. And their dominant attitude was: "Teach the nigger to take what we give him. Don't ever let him get the idea that he can fight back." It was an attitude of submission, a carryover from slavery that had kept the slaves from rebelling. It was a serious crime when a Negro was brought into court for striking a white man. On the other hand, white people were almost never cited for beating Negroes. So don't accuse me of being a coward. It was how I had to behave if I wanted to keep my brains inside my head. If I had ever struck a white boy, I'd have been whipped with many stripes—if not lynched. We had no right to defend ourselves.

Lynching. I don't like to talk about it, even now. At least thirteen men were lynched down in Columbia in my day. Anybody who says that living in the South in those days wasn't hell—well, he doesn't know what hell is! A boy who had been in my fourth grade class was lynched! I knew him well. He was hanged in a cedar tree between my uncle's farm and my papa's farm. Yes, I knew Willie Cheek. He was not very smart, and I don't think he got much beyond the fifth grade. When he got to be a grown man, he went out to work on a white man's farm. I was a junior in college when it happened.

One evening Willie was driving the cows in from the pasture to milk them. As he was herding them back, he heard noises down in a little ravine he was walking by. It was what we called a dry creek. In wet weather it had water but dried up afterward. Trees and little shrubs and undergrowth screened it on both sides so you couldn't see the bottom. Willie was walking along with the cows when he heard some noises coming from down inside the ravine. He went over, peeped in, and saw a man and a woman, both white, having sex and having a good time at it. Now if he had looked, enjoyed the scene a while, and moved on, maybe he'd still be living today. And maybe the girl would've continued to enjoy whatever sex she was having with the man, and maybe he would have had his fun too, and everything would have been all right.

But poor old Willie Cheek didn't have any common sense. He started laughing and giggling at that white couple and their little sex party. The girl was his boss's daughter. She looked up and saw Willie looking at them and laughing. She was embarrassed at being discovered and jumped up and started to run off toward home, with her clothes half on. The boy went after her. "Don't run," he said. "Don't run. Wait! Don't do that. If you tell on me, I'll kill you!" He must have threatened the hell out of her and got her to come back and agree to accuse the nigger of trying to rape her. They were both afraid that poor dumb Willie would tell on them. So the girl ran toward home, screaming hysterically, her clothes muddy and torn. Her mother ran out to meet her and quickly pumped the lie out of her. The mother told the father. The father started making some calls, and in three hours they had a lynching party. They rounded poor old Willie up and, despite his pleas of innocence, hanged him from that cedar tree. They cut his privates out and left him hanging as a warning. "See," that ghastly, mutilated figure seemed to say, "see what happens to a nigger who tampers with a white woman."

Five years later when I was visiting down home, my uncle told me the rest of the story. "That girl must have gone crazy over the lie she told," he said. "She even tried to tell the truth—that it was her white boyfriend she was having sex with. He was the 'nigger' who had tried to rape her. But nobody would believe her—or would choose to believe her. And she committed suicide. It must have been suicide. In her car by herself, she rammed straight into a six-foot stone wall. People who saw the car coming say there was no way she could have made the curve at the rate she was driving. It had to be premeditated. It had to be suicide." Her death didn't bring Willie back, of course, but maybe it eased her pain. It didn't, however, change the racial climate that provoked such tragedies.

A similar incident occurred when I was a student at the Knoxville College Academy. A Negro politician was getting too high in the ranks, and the white bosses didn't know how to control him. They knew the easiest way to get rid of him was to frame him by saying he was molesting a white woman. Soon they had the opportunity. A political caucus was being held in one of the Knoxville hotels. The Negro went around to the side door, as he was supposed to, and came up the back way and on to the meeting. Then they framed him. They said he slipped away from the meeting and started out the back way when he passed a room with an open door. They said he then went in and began to attack a white woman. Those accusations were all that were needed to end his political career as well as his life. Several years later, when I was finishing college at Virginia Union, I read about a white man in Virginia who had gone back to Knoxville, given himself up, and said that he was the man in the room with that white woman. "It was all a frame," he said. "That nigger never even came in the door. I was with that woman all night." It was too late, of course, for his conscience to save the innocent black man. He had already been hanged.

But most of the injustices and indignities that Negroes suffered were less sensational. They were considered an ordinary part of southern life. Take economic exploitation, for example. I knew a white woman who lived out in the country near our farm. She got a job in town as a bank teller, working eight hours a day and making $1.25. It wasn't much, but don't feel sorry for her. "I got a nigger woman," she bragged, "doing my housework for twelve hours a day for only seventy five cents. When I get up in the morning, my breakfast is ready, and when I get home in the evening, my supper is ready. I don't have to do my own cleaning or washing or ironing, and I'm still fifty cents to the good every day!" This woman's husband was not a member of the landed gentry, but he owned a few acres of land, and, most important, he was white.

Negroes, of course, did most of the farm work on white-owned farms. Since most of the blacks living in the country didn't own land, they either worked on shares or as day laborers. Even the lowest level of white farmer—the ones who had to peddle their produce in town—had most of their work done by Negroes. They would hire Negro hands for maybe seventy five cents a day to work their corn, pea, collard, and watermelon patches, and then they would bring their produce to town on wagons to sell it. Such white people may have been doing the most demeaning kind of work—and peddling was considered near the bottom—yet they considered themselves superior to all Negroes. One day I was out in the front yard playing, and Papa was on the front porch reading the paper. A white fellow, about twenty, from out in the country came by in his wagon selling garden vegetables. It was in the days before supermarkets, and we had to grow our own produce or buy it from peddlers. We raised just about everything we needed except for watermelons and cantaloupes. Papa usually bought a dozen or two melons for our large family. We were one of this white farmer's biggest customers. So this white boy pulled up in his wagon and said, "Need any melons today?" Papa looked up from his paper and said: "Yes, I believe we could use some more. The ones we got from your daddy last week were very good." Papa got up and walked out to the wagon. I was still playing, but I saw everything that went on. Papa looked over the wagon body at the melons, and the white fellow said, "All right, uncle, how many?" Papa must have had his evil hat on that day. He stopped, looked up at the white boy on the wagon, and said: "I'll take a dozen cantaloupes, but don't call me uncle. I'm no kin to you. You're not my nephew. Just call me Johnson. Other white people do."

The white boy glared at him and said: "I know I'm not kin to you. But I've been taught by my people to have respect for you and your family because you're high-class niggers and not to call you by your first name or just plain Johnson. You know we're not gonna call you mister or your wife missus. I've been taught to call you uncle and aunt, and that's what I'll call you." Papa said, "just don't call me anything then." When he said that, the white boy pulled out a three-inch knife, jumped off the wagon, and started chasing my father around the wagon. Finally, Papa got away from the wagon, jumped up into our yard, and ran into the house to get his gun. The white boy was still raving out in the road. "I don't care how educated you Johnsons are," he shouted. "I don't care what kind of jobs you got. You're all niggers! And I'll cut your black guts out with this knife." By this time Papa was back on the porch with his gun. "Come in my yard," he said, "and you're a dead duck."

When the ruckus started, I stopped playing and kind of hid behind a tree. I was sweating like everything. I wanted to dig a hole and hide. I was afraid to go out there and help my daddy. I was afraid of what the white boy might do. And I was afraid of what Papa might do to him. Either way, I knew there was no way we could win. All three of us stayed frozen where we were for a few minutes. I was shaking and sweating behind my tree. Papa was holding his gun on the front porch. And the white boy was cursing out on his wagon. But he didn't make a move to get any closer. Finally, he started up his mule and went on down the street yelling, "Nigger! Nigger!"

We were the only Negro family on our street, but we never had any trouble with our white neighbors. We didn't see each other socially, but the Johnson kids played with the white cracker kids in the neighborhood. That's what they called themselves, but Negroes usually called them Yaps and didn't have a lot of respect for them. Neither did upper-class white people. In those days educated blacks and educated whites didn't have much direct contact, but I knew one wealthy white woman in Columbia who was liberal. There may have been other white liberals in town, but I didn't know of them. She owned quite a bit of property and had money. Sometimes we'd go over to her house. She'd say: "Lyman, you must not play with those poor white trash down at the foot of the hill. Hold yourself above them. They don't speak good English, and they don't have any manners. You can sit here at our table because you and your family are cultured and refined. But we don't allow those crackers in our yard." Even though we were black, she considered us a cut above the ignorant crackers.

White people in our town, in fact, generally thought well of the Johnson family. We were often held up as an example to white kids. White parents would say: "Why don't you be like the little Johnson children? They're finishing high school. They're going on to college." I think we were held up not only as an example but as a threat too. "If you don't watch out," white parents seemed to warn their kids, "one of these days you'll be working for the Johnsons." But I don't think any of the white people in Columbia ever thought those days would come. No matter how much education a black man got, no matter how much money he had—he was still a nigger. Nothing could change that. So they thought.

It wasn't till after World War II that conditions in the South began to improve very much for Negroes. Long before then, a lot of black people got fed up and left. The big black migrations north started right after World War I. When I was a boy, my friends and I used to go down to the L & N station on Saturday afternoons to see the trains come through headed north. We were waiting for Number Two to come in. It was due at 4:50, and we'd get there about half past four. There would be a lot of other people— white and black—there to watch the trains pass through. In those days people worked at least five and a half days a week. Saturday was the day to finish the week's work, take a good bath, get the groceries, and do any other shopping you needed to do. The streets of Columbia would be thronged with people.

Just before five o'clock Number Two would pull into the station—the cars for white people first, then the Jim Crow cars stuffed with black people, hanging out windows, yelling and waving at us, and talking about where they were going. The train was in the station for about five minutes, but we enjoyed kidding around with the Negroes we didn't know. They'd say: "Oh boy, she's a cute chick. Hey, man, you're a sharp cat." A few people would get off, and a few people would get on. The train would take on some water for the engine. Then we'd hear the choo-choo, and the train would shove off. And the poor black men, escaping from the cotton and cornfields of Mississippi and Alabama, would yell back: "Come on up to Detroit. There ain't no Jim Crow up there. I'm gonna get me a good job and make a lot of money. You ain't gone see me behind no mule no more! I'm going to the Promised Land." That bunch would disappear up the tracks, and the next Saturday another trainload would come through. And again, the Negroes sounded like they were being delivered from bondage.

In those days, of course, I didn't understand what I was seeing. It was simply an amusement to go down to the L & N and see the trains come in and talk to strangers I'd never see again. Years later, when I was in college,

I began to realize what they were leaving and what they were going to. Then I understood their desperation to leave the plantations of Mississippi and Alabama. Down there they had been gypped in school. They had been gypped in the work fields. And they had been gypped by society all around. That's why the recruiters had such an easy time when they came down to get cheap labor for the northern factories. They said: "Fellows, up north you can eat where you want to. You can sleep where you want to. We'll give you a job with good pay. You can even go out with a white girl if you want to." Those were powerful appeals to black men who knew that in Mississippi if they even looked at a white girl in a certain way they could get lynched. Up north they could do more than look. They could even work them over! No wonder they thought as they passed through Columbia on the Jim Crow train that the North must be the Promised Land.

Well, it was no Promised Land. That's not the way it was. Years later, when I was in graduate school at Ann Arbor, Michigan, I decided to go over to Detroit to see for myself how those blacks were doing—the ones I had seen heading north with such joy and anticipation when I was a youngster. By 1910 there probably weren't more than 5,000 Negroes in Detroit, but by 1930, when I visited, there must have been close to 60,000. And living and working conditions, which were never as good as they were supposed to be, began to worsen when the Depression came on. From the beginning blacks were not given good jobs, and even those were taken away from them when the Depression hit. Most of the southern Negroes who had gone north to find the Promised Land were living in poverty when I saw them. They were trapped. When they tried to organize and demonstrate for better conditions, they found that northern racial prejudice was just as bad as southern.

They also discovered that they had not even escaped from the racist southern policemen. Gradually, northern authorities began to recruit white police from the South. They said: "You people in Birmingham know how to deal with niggers. Come on up here and show us." One summer when I was in school at the University of Wisconsin, I saw a white policeman in Madison say to a Negro: "Look here, boy! These people brought me up here because I know how to handle you niggers. You parked your car in a no-parking zone, and you yelled at me, 'Whitey, go to hell!' Don't ever do that again. I'm not going to beat you up this time, but I'm going to give you a two-dollar ticket. And the next time I get any lip from you. . . ." I imagine most of the black people from the South wondered how far they had really come from the cotton fields.

My father never left the South. He lived and died in Tennessee. He died in 1950 at the age of ninety, before the time of full civil rights. He lived for thirty years after my mother died and never remarried. He said he had such a high regard for her that he didn't want to dilute it by marrying a second time. Most of that time he lived by himself. When he retired in 1930, he stayed on in Columbia. When my Uncle Will returned from Morehouse College, he came to live in a house he owned next door to my father. There they lived side by side—an old widower and an old bachelor—two brothers who still enjoyed each other's company.

He lived a good life, but it was a life filled with restrictions and off-limits signs. Papa knew where he lived, and he knew what to expect of life there. Near the end something happened that left me with yet another scar. A few months before he died, Papa became seriously ill late in the winter. His Negro doctor checked him out and said he needed an operation. He arranged with a white doctor to have him admitted to the King's Daughters' Hospital, a white hospital in Columbia. The Negro doctor couldn't even go into the building. A white doctor admitted him and performed the operation. I had driven down from Louisville and was waiting at my father's home for the outcome. They wouldn't even allow me to sit in the white waiting room at the hospital.

When the operation was over, they called to say that it had been successful and that my father should come through all right. Then a voice said, "You can arrange now to have him transferred from the hospital." I said: "What? At his age? Just after a serious operation? In his critical condition?" She said: "Yes. We have no provision for Negro patients in this hospital. He's still on the operating table down in the basement hall. It's drafty down there, so you'd better come pick him up before he contracts pneumonia."

I couldn't believe what I was hearing. But why should I have been surprised? After all, this was Columbia, Tennessee, and it was 1949. "Lady," I pleaded, "can't you put him in some kind of room till I can have him taken to another hospital? I can't bring him out here. I don't even live here. He lives alone. There's no one to look after him. I don't have a nurse or anybody. My mother is dead." She said: "I'm sorry. We have no provision for him here. You'll have to come get him now." What could I do? I called the Negro doctor, and he said to have Papa sent over to his office. So my critically ill father was removed from that white hospital and taken to the Negro doctor's office where he stayed overnight. The next morning we hired an ambulance to take him the forty miles up the road to Nashville, where we put him in Hubbard Hospital, a part of the black Meharry Medical School. Papa died a few months later. Of course, he was an old man. Maybe he would have died anyway. That's another scar that will still bleed if you scratch it.

Papa had to wait a quarter of a century before his account was adjusted with that racist, exploitative white establishment. Even then it was only partial payment. Papa died in 1950 and Uncle Will in 1955. I was the administrator of their undivided estate, which I handled for twenty years. They owned four pretty-good-sized stores that fronted on Main Street, the white business area. We rented the space to white tenants for a shoe store, a veterinarian's office, and an amusement hall that had juke boxes and slot machines. In order to supervise the property, I went down a number of times every year. Then in 1975 I sold out because my wife had developed muscular dystrophy, and I had to spend a lot of time with her. I got an auctioneer to go down and sell it.

Apparently, some people in Columbia still had a plantation mentality. A white lawyer down there tried to pull a trick on me. He said, "I'm interested in buying your property, but business property in town isn't worth what it used to be because business has moved to the suburbs." Well, I knew that. Columbia is a lot bigger now than it was when I was a boy, but the growth has been outside town. But I was surprised and suspicious when the lawyer told me the property probably wouldn't bring more than one-fourth of what it was listed for. I did some checking and found out that he and some other white businessmen had agreed to bid only up to one-fourth of the value of each piece of property and not to bid against each other.

There was a young dentist who wanted a piece of property we owned in the Negro business block. So I made him a proposition. "All right, I'll see that you get that property for a song if you'll help me get fair value for some other property." He agreed, and that's what happened. On the day of the auction, the bidding went to one-fourth of the appraised value. Then the black dentist jumped in and raised the bid so that the white men wound up paying not one-fourth but the full worth of the property. I gave the dentist a check for $100 for his help and a nice break on the place he wanted. Then I divided the money among the heirs.

I have few relatives living in Columbia now. My brother Neill's widow lives there, but the Johnson blood is thinning out in that town and in that county. When the Johnson brothers and sisters got some size, we left. Our feeling was, "Hell, we're not going to put up with this damn place any longer." We left. New York and Chicago are loaded with Johnsons now.

On the Road to Higher Education

> Southern whites realized after the Civil War that Negroes had to have
> a certain kind of education. The key word is certain. They wanted the
> freedman to have only enough education to equip him to serve the
> white society better than he had before.

I GRADUATED from the "colored" high school in Columbia in 1924.
Since my high school was unaccredited, my diploma wouldn't get me into
college. So I stayed home a year and then went up to Knoxville Academy. I
stayed there two years—long enough to prepare for Virginia Union and
long enough to know I never wanted to be a Presbyterian. I wanted to be
good but not that good!

Our teachers set a standard for goodness I just couldn't reach. There
was Miss Wishert, my Latin teacher, who couldn't teach two lines of Latin
without bringing in a Sunday School lesson. One day she caught a kid
stealing in her class and sent him to hell—at least verbally. With all the
preaching and praying she directed at him, however, he probably would
have welcomed hell as a relief!

After I finished at Knoxville, I went up to Virginia Union in Richmond
in 1927. My folks put together what funds they could, and I put to good
use the carpentry and painting skills I had picked up working around
Columbia. With what I could make during the summer, I made it through
three years at Virginia Union, where I took Greek. I studied Greek because
it is the foundation of Western knowledge and because it was the subject
taught by my Uncle Will. If you squeeze Lyman Johnson even today,
Socrates will ooze out of him.

Both Knoxville Academy and Virginia Union, like most of the old
black schools in the South, were started by northern philanthropists after
the Civil War. And that's a story the white historian—damn his hide!—has
refused to write up. It is a malicious omission. Following the lead of that
infamous southern historian, Ulrich Bonnell Phillips, they've tried to
show that the only people who came down from the North were carpetbaggers. They've intentionally left out the people who started Fisk and
Morehouse and Virginia Union and Roger Williams—those northern
Baptists, Methodists, Presbyterians, and Congregationalists who were
descendants of the abolitionists. At one time in Nashville, there were
three colleges supported by northern philanthropists for blacks: Roger
Williams, run by the Baptists; Fisk, run by the Congregationalists; and
Walden, run by the Methodists.

In addition to Fisk, the Congregationalists had Atlanta University and
Talladega College, where a lot of the black elite went. There were, in fact,

private church-supported black academies and colleges scattered all over the South. Right after the Civil War, these northern church people picked out places where they thought Negro colleges were needed and started them. They were started to help the freedman get an education and become self-supporting. They were motivated by the same spirit that led to the Freedmen's Bureau, that much-maligned agency set up to aid the freed slaves. There were, of course, no black colleges in the South before the Civil War. In fact, in most places it was a crime even to teach a slave to read and write.

These northern philanthropists felt an obligation to continue the work their fathers had started. They said: "Our fathers fought in the battle for abolition. Now that battle is over, and we have four million black people turned loose, not knowing how to read or write or count. They never knew what it was to make their own money or how to go to the grocery and buy and make change at the counter. Now they've got to learn the same lessons as the people with whom they must compete." But these northern educators didn't stop with basic, practical education. They added, "And if we teach Latin and Greek and chemistry and mathematics at Yale and Harvard, we must also teach it at Morehouse and Fisk." Some southerners called them religious cranks. Perhaps they were. But they were not carpetbaggers. They came south not for their own good but for the good of the freed slave.

Indeed, southern whites realized after the Civil War that Negroes had to have a certain kind of education. The key word is *certain*. They wanted the freedman to have only enough education to equip him to serve the white society better than he had before.

The northern educators who came South believed that whites and blacks should have the same kind of education. In my day there were two kinds of Negro schools in the South, one run by the state legislatures that emphasized vocational education and one run by northern philanthropists that emphasized a broad intellectual education.

Like all the other northern-supported Negro colleges, the philosophy of Virginia Union was to give the black man the same type of education that the white man was getting. But southern legislators had their own philosophy of Negro education, and they began to establish their own Negro colleges. They were schools they wouldn't have dared send their own children to, even if they'd been all white. The state-owned black colleges were hardly equal to good high schools. Many of them weren't as good as first-rate high schools. And I don't need to waste time describing the squalid conditions in the public high schools and grade schools for blacks. I hate to have to use invectives, but the damn bastards in southern legislatures wouldn't provide Negroes with decent schools till they were forced to.

Why did the white legislators starve the Negro schools for money? It's obvious. They were the children and grandchildren of slaveowners. The Negro students were the grandchildren and great-grandchildren of slaves. And the pattern was one established back there in slavery. "To educate a person unfits him to be a slave. If he learns to read and write, he'll learn about Philadelphia and New York and Montreal, and he'll escape from slavery. So don't let him learn. All he needs to know is how to plow and work in the field." After slavery the pattern continued. "Keep the black man as ignorant as you can, and you'll keep cheap labor."

The president of Tuskegee Institute was smarter than most Negro college presidents. Booker T. Washington knew how to get the white man's money because he knew how to play to the white man's vanity. He'd tell the white industrialist: "I'm training the students at Tuskegee to be efficient, skillful craftsmen. A trained worker is an asset to you. He's better than an illiterate worker to whom you have to read and explain everything." A lot of white contributors to Tuskegee were very much surprised to learn that Tuskegee was also teaching tough courses in chemistry and physics and history. The white people thought Booker T.'s college was teaching Negroes simply how to be better servants. In the long run, he was teaching them how to be free. And he was using the white man's money to do it!

Tuskegee was a private college, but Booker T. took money from everybody, including the Alabama legislature. It was a far better college than the official state school for Negroes, Alabama A & M in Montgomery. When I was a student at Virginia Union, I wouldn't have wasted my time there or at Virginia State College or Kentucky State or North Carolina A & T or any other of the state black colleges in the South. The Georgia college for Negroes wasn't even as good as the one in Montgomery. I don't even remember its name. It wasn't enough of a college to get on my mind. The first job I was offered was at the Negro college in Alcorn, Mississippi. My salary would have been ninety dollars a month. No college could attract top-rate professors for that kind of salary.

The rascals in the legislatures were starving the black colleges. The Negro college president would go to them, hat in hand, and beg for his pittance. When he got back to his campus, he'd try to glorify his school with a pretentious catalog, listing a lot of high-sounding courses. The catalog said they taught algebra, but they'd be teaching simple arithmetic. For physics and chemistry, they'd be teaching agriculture. With the little bit of money they were doled out, they couldn't afford good laboratories or libraries or professors. And the white legislators were perfectly pleased that they were not permitting Negroes to get the same kind of education they were providing white students at the University of Alabama, Tennessee, Kentucky, or any other state-supported school for whites. The University of Kentucky had money for all sorts of programs in Lexington for white students. Just twenty-seven miles away in Frankfort, there was almost nothing for blacks at Kentucky State College.

The private schools for Negroes, of course, didn't have a lot of money, but at least they had an enlightened philosophy of education. And they had dedicated men and women with degrees from the best schools in the country as teachers. I carry a white man's name, and I'm proud of it. I was named after a young man from a rich family of Baptists in Providence, Rhode Island. He thought it was a disgrace that all the ex-slaves had been dumped out on the highway with nothing. So he came south to teach at Roger Williams, where my father graduated in 1884. That white man put in over twenty years down there, from about 1866 to about 1890. And he suffered for it. He was ostracized by the whites—the whites in Nashville who wouldn't even sell him a pair of shoes. He was a rich man and could have bought out the whole shoe store. But the whites said: "You're teaching niggers to read and write! You're a damn nigger-loving Yankee. If we catch you in town, we'll lynch you!" So this man—this unselfish man who was trying to practice what his Christian religion professed—had to call in a Negro student who had a foot about his size. He'd say: "Here's some money. I need a new pair of shoes. Those people downtown will sell you shoes. Go buy yourself a pair and get me one too."

This man graduated from Brown University and had all sorts of degrees. Yet he put up with all the indignity and embarrassment. "I don't work for pay," he'd say. "I work for the love of it." And when the poor little school would give him a paycheck, he'd endorse it and put it in the collection plate for the little campus church. When I came along, my father said: "There may not be any more children in this family. To show my respect for a man who gave up the riches that his family could afford and come down here and teach black people, I'll name my last son Lyman Beecher Tefft Johnson."

And so I fuss like hell with young blacks today who say that they don't like their "slave names." Hell, my name is a freedom name. No one is truly free till he is freed of ignorance. Lyman Beecher Tefft helped educate my father and so made it possible for me to get the education I have—and the freedom I enjoy. I'm proud of my name.

Lyman Tefft taught people who didn't have money to pay tuition, so there wasn't any tuition. The northern-supported colleges even paid some of the young men to come to school. And the money that made this possible was coming from the North—from contributions taken up in churches and missionary societies. Young black people knew it was a privilege to go to such schools. They worked hard and seldom caused discipline problems. Those were the attitudes as late as the 1920s when I was at Knoxville Academy and Virginia Union. We were told: "We know you can't afford to pay all the costs of your education. Pay as much as you can. But if you can't pay anything and you have the right positive attitude, come right on. We know where we can get the money for your education." When you get that combination of religious zeal and money, the result is a high-quality education. That's what most of us blacks got in those private, church colleges. And that's why we welcomed white teachers to teach us. That's why I'm proud to carry the name of one of them.

In the late 1800s and early 1900s, black professors began taking over most of the teaching jobs in southern black colleges. My Uncle Will was one of that early generation of black professors. Many times they were better educated than their counterparts in the white colleges. Graduate schools in the South were closed to them, so they were forced to go to better ones in the North. They weren't paid much, but they could live a good life as long as they stayed on campus. As soon as a black professor moved out into the larger community, he was nothing but a damn nigger regardless of how many degrees he had or how many books he'd written.

In the early 1920s, shortly before Uncle Will retired from teaching Greek and Latin at Morehouse, he and a young black Ph.D. from Chicago became good friends. Dr. E. Franklin Frazier taught sociology. He was about twenty-nine, erudite and scholarly but spunky and spirited. They were both bachelors and would often eat together, talking and bridging the gap between age and youth. When they went into downtown Atlanta to shop, they'd usually go together. My uncle said: "Franklin, don't go downtown unless I go with you. You're from the North and don't know these people. They'll kill you!"

One day they walked into a store to buy my uncle a hat. He picked up a hat and was looking it over when one of the clerks came up and said, "Well, boys, what can I do for you today?" The young professor looked at my uncle and said, "Professor Johnson, do you see any *boys* around here?" My uncle didn't answer him directly but said: "Franklin, let's look at these hats over here. Here's one I like." The clerk said, "Now, look, boys, pick out what you want and hurry up and get out." The young professor said: "Professor Johnson, who in the hell is he talking to? Who is he calling *boys*?" The clerk said: "Niggers, hurry up if you want to buy anything. Then get out. You're stinking up the store." Dr. Frazier glared at him and said: "That's an insult. What do you mean calling us boys and niggers? We came in here with money in our hands to pay for whatever we touched. And now you're insulting us." And he began to get angry and loud. By this time four other white clerks had gathered around to watch. One of them said: "Let's take these niggers downstairs and work 'em over. We'll teach 'em some manners. We'll teach 'em they may have book learning but they ain't learned how to behave in town around white people. We'll teach 'em they're niggers like all the rest of 'em." My uncle said, "Come on, Dr. Frazier, let's leave." That's all he said as they left. One of the clerks called out, "Don't you ever come to this store again unless you want the hell beat out of you!"

Dr. Frazier was indignant. "Professor Johnson," he said, "now I know what it's like to live in prison. On campus we have a cultured life. We have dinners, banquets, socials, dances, picnics, and we enjoy everything that white college professors have anywhere in this country. We have all these advantages as long as we stay on campus. But once we step off the grounds, we're damned niggers. Our campus is our prison." What could Uncle Will say? He'd lived in that prison all his life.

Uncle Will told me that story, I believe, to caution me. He was afraid I'd be just as fiery as Dr. Frazier. He recited that story—and others—over and over. Another story he told me also happened when he was still teaching at Morehouse. One of his students lived on a big farm about ninety miles south of Atlanta. It was pretty good farmland, but because it was so far off the main roads, nobody else wanted it. When the Negro farmer could get his produce to market, he could make a pretty decent living and even support his son at Morehouse.

One spring break the farmer's son invited my uncle to spend a weekend on the farm. The boy's father sent a car to pick them up in Atlanta. They drove down the main highways about forty miles, then turned off on some side roads for about forty miles. Then they came to a very narrow dirt road—almost like a pig path—and were driving along this dusty trail for about five miles when they overtook a two-mule wagon driven by two white boys dressed in overalls and jumpers. My uncle and his student were wearing their coats and ties. The wagon was in the middle of the road. The car tagged behind at about five miles an hour for a couple of miles, but the white boys made no move to pull off to the side to let the car pass. So the driver started to tap his horn, thinking maybe the boys didn't know a car was behind them.

Suddenly, the boys stopped the wagon, and one of them jumped off and ran back to the car. "Listen, niggers," he yelled in their faces, "blow that horn one more time, and we'll teach you something you won't forget. We're gonna drive right straight down the middle of this road for another two miles until we get to a creek. There we're gonna drive off to the side to let the mules get some water. Then you can go by. But if you blow that goddamned horn again before we get there, there'll be three dead niggers out here on this road. I don't give a damn who you are or how many cars you got."

The white boy got back on the wagon, and it pulled off dead center up the road. Uncle Will said to the driver: "Let's just park here and wait till they've had time to go the two miles to the creek. I don't want to take any chances out here." That's what they did. My uncle knew that was the only way black people could survive. "If you blow that horn, again, you're a dead nigger," they'd warned. They knew that no jury in that rural Georgia county would convict them for killing "niggers."

Black people back then who were educated or affluent had to be especially careful. White people didn't like Negroes who knew more or had more than they did. Those white boys were jealous. "This damn nigger boy," they must have said to each other. "He's riding around in a car. And we don't have nothing but these old mules and this old wagon that's about to fall to pieces. That nigger's daddy has got fat mules and horses that could pull this wagon a little faster. And look at him. That nigger is decked out in the latest fashion. And that old nigger. He must be a professor of some kind. But that's all right. We're still better than they are with all their money and cars and fat mules and book learning. We're white."

Those white boys may have secretly envied that black college boy. They may have thought he had advantages over them. Sometimes that was true. There were black families who could afford to send their children to college and get them started on a professional career. But not many. Most Negro families, especially rural Negroes, were dirt poor. They couldn't have paid a one-way bus ticket to a Negro campus. Most of us Negro students, therefore, had to work like the devil. We worked on campus waiting on tables, cleaning, gardening, and carpentering. We provided most of the college's maintenance services. And during summer vacations we worked full–time jobs wherever we could get them.

For two summers I worked as headwaiter at a Virginia Beach resort cottage. In June 1929 people were taking a last fling of prosperity and spent a lot of money. It was between my junior and senior years at Virginia Union, and I made enough that summer to last me all year and even to do a little showing off. The resort owners paid me $1.50 a day, plus a place to stay, my meals, and all the tips I could pick up. When I got to Richmond that fall, I rode out to the Virginia Union campus in a big Yellow Cab limousine. I walked into the business office, paid my tuition for the year, paid my room and board, and paid for all my books. Then I bought me some new clothes. My first three years I had skimped along on two pairs of pants, one coat, and one sweater. But now I got me a couple of real nice suits, not overly expensive but good-looking, two pairs of shoes, and a few other articles of clothing. And then I was broke. That was all right. I didn't need much. I was paid through the year. And I knew I could pick up some spending change with odd jobs on campus and around town.

It was Depression time. But it didn't bother me. I was paid up. Somebody lost his job, and his kid had to drop out of school. So what? I was paid up. Was I a cocky little cuss! During that year I had several electives to fill out my schedule. The dean said: "Mr. Johnson, you'll very likely end up as a schoolteacher. So why don't you take a couple of education classes?" I said: "No, Dean, education courses are for intellectual weaklings. Don't give me that soft stuff. I don't want any baby courses my last year." So he loaded me up with tough courses. I soon found out my mistake. I'd send applications out for a teaching job, but everyone wrote back: "We like your credits. But you don't have a teaching certificate. We'll put you on our emergency waiting list and call you if we can't get a teaching major."

I could see that I wasn't going to get any kind of professional position. So I called up the people down at the resort hotel at Virginia Beach. At least, I thought, I can make a little money this summer. "Lyman," they said, "we don't know what this Depression is going to mean for our business, but we liked what you did for us last summer, so come on down." The place was owned by three sisters. Two of them were married, and one was an old maid. They were all in their forties. I had more formal education than any of them. Not one had ever been to college. They didn't have much more education than their black servants, but they owned the business and were in control. And they were white, and this was an all-white resort in the days of strict segregation. Virginia Beach was so segregated that Negroes didn't dare go into the ocean to swim except at night.

Many a night after I had done all my work, I'd go down to the ocean for a swim. From about seven to nine o'clock every night, the Negro servants from all the resorts took over the beach. It was an unwritten law that whites stayed off the beach at night and let the Negroes take it over. But after seven o'clock the next morning, no Negro would do himself any good to be caught there on the beach in a swimming suit.

Given those restrictions, it was not a bad place to work. And the money was good. When they told me I could come back under the same working arrangements I had the summer before, I accepted. A place to sleep, $1.50 a day, tips, and all the food I could eat didn't sound bad at all in the summer of 1930. I already knew that a waiter who knows his way around eats what the white folks eat. They eat lobster; he eats lobster. A starving waiter is a damn fool! I was no damn fool.

It was a small resort, a two-story lodging house with sixteen guest rooms. It was sort of a forerunner of a motel. On the first floor, there was a kitchen, a big dining room, a lobby area, and living facilities for the three women who owned it. Each had a separate room.

So I worked there another summer. And to my surprise—though the Depression was getting worse and worse—I did as well that summer as the year before. We were open from May till Labor Day. Labor Day was the last fling. We used to say that the only occupation after Labor Day was to hang crepe on all the telephone poles because the town was dead. It would stay dead till warm weather came again the next spring. During the chilly days, it was an absolute cemetery. The one attraction was swimming, and when it was too cold to swim, you might as well be somewhere else. But from May to September, the place was jumping.

I was well respected by the three owners, and I carried myself fairly well with the staff of Negro servants. I knew how to get along with them because I was one of them. But as headwaiter I had jurisdiction over them. What I mean is that I was over all of them except for the cook. Nobody was over her! What a character! Sometimes she'd take one of her big pots and lay down the law. She wasn't terribly fat, but she was hefty, strong, mean, and efficient. The white owners liked her because she could fix up some tasty food and get it ready on time. But if one of them went back and started fussing about something, she'd get down a pot and shake it with a warning. "Listen here, white folks. Get out of my kitchen or I'll bust your brains out!" So the white woman would come running out, not knowing whether the cook was crazy or just mad. But the white woman wouldn't take any chance. She knew that the next time the cook got mad she might reach for a meat cleaver. The white women knew that if they left her alone to do as she pleased she'd come up with good food every time. That was one of the place's main attractions. We black people respected her too. We knew not to cross the cook.

The white sisters liked me because I was such an asset to them. In addition to being a waiter, I was a pretty good handyman. I was a plumber, carpenter, painter, and electrician for them. When they'd have trouble around the place, one of them would say: "Oh, Johnson can do this. Johnson can fix that." The black servants were also amazed that I could do so many things because I was a college boy.

Each of the sisters had her area of responsibility. One was a kind of hostess for the rooming part. One was the manager of the dining room part. And the third one was the bookkeeper, the finance manager. Sometimes the bookkeeping sister would ask me to help her with the business books. She would say: "Johnson, check over our books, will you? You're so good at this kind of thing." I'd taken a lot of mathematics and economics in school and knew how to do elementary auditing. I could balance their books and put everything in its proper category and ledger. They got a lot of work out of me for $1.50 a day. It would have cost a lot more to hire an auditor. They tried to pay me off with a lot of soft soap and sweet talk. But I knew to be careful around white women. In those days of "iron curtain" segregation, I knew if I got the least bit out of line I was in deep trouble. As long as I used discretion, I was all right. When black men and white women got too close, there was bound to be an explosion.

But my first brush with danger came from an unexpected source. One night about nine o'clock all the other servants had either gone home, to town, or out to the beach. I had finished up my work and didn't feel much like going down to the beach. There wasn't much for a black man to do in town. He couldn't go to any of the casinos or nightclubs. He served all day, and the only recreation he could get was on the beach at night. But this particular night I decided to go back to my room, which was at the back end of the place on the second floor, and do some reading. I was sitting back there with the door open but with a screen to keep mosquitoes out. It was long before any kind of air conditioning. It'd get up to 95 or 100 degrees in the daytime and didn't cool off much at night. But I was fairly comfortable, with a slight breeze blowing through my screen door.

Suddenly, I thought I heard something, perhaps a little child whimpering or whining. I put my book down and opened the screen door onto the back steps. I listened. The sobbing sounds seemed to be coming from under the steps. I walked down and sure enough there curled up under the steps was a little white girl about three years old. Then I did what I thought was the humane thing. I pulled the little child out, held her in my arms, and tried to console her. "I don't know where my mama is," she cried. "Now, don't cry," I said. "We'll go find your mother." That little kid took to me as if I were her father, and I held her till she stopped crying.

Then I carried her in my arms around to where the three white women lived. I gave her to the first one I saw and said: "Here's a little girl who I found crying under the back steps. She's lost from her parents." The white lady took the little girl and called the police. When they arrived, they said she was the kid they'd been looking for since about seven o'clock that evening.

I felt good and went back to my room thinking I'd done the right thing. After all, I'd found a little lost girl and restored her to her parents. I wasn't prepared for the reaction of the black servants. As soon as they learned what happened, they lit into me. "Lyman, you're a crazy man," they said. "Do you know how much danger you were in? Do you know that if the police had found that girl in your arms with you wiping tears off her face you'd have been in big trouble? Do you know they'd have accused you of kidnapping the girl and molesting her, and they'd have said that was the reason she was crying. That little girl was too little to explain, and the police would never have taken your word for it. Lyman, you did the damnedest thing you could! You knew that wasn't a black baby out there crying. You knew black servants weren't allowed to have their children around there. So if you even suspected it was a white child, you should have gone and gotten some white person to pull that kid out and pacify her. You had some nerve picking her up in your arms and having her hold you around the neck like you were her father. You better not ever do that again! Next time don't touch that child. Next time you may not be so lucky!" Then I realized how lucky I had indeed been. It suddenly chilled me to think what might have happened if I had picked that little girl up, she had started screaming, and the police had come up about that time. Even now I tremble to think of what could have happened. . . .

Those were hard times for black men. We just didn't know how to conduct ourselves around white women. I didn't want to take undue liberties with the three sisters who owned the resort, but neither did I want to be stepped on. One day one of the sisters got mad as hell about something. She came back to the kitchen and started raising cain with the servants. Finally, I couldn't take it any longer and decided to cash in on some of my standing with the lady. I said: "Now, look here. These people are doing the best they can. Why don't you just lay off? If you want this place run right, you've got to have everybody's cooperation, including ours." She shot back, "Johnson, who are you to be telling me how to treat my servants?" But I wouldn't back down from my defense, and finally she said: "Oh, Johnson, sometimes I feel like I can't get along without you, and sometimes I just can't stand you! Sometimes I'd like to take you out in the yard and thrash you!"

Then I really got my dander up. "Why don't you just try it sometime?" I said. "Try it!" She backed off and said: "Oh, Johnson, you know I don't mean any harm. But you do make me mad sometimes with your attitude." I said: "Well, if I do maybe this is the wrong place for me. But maybe a thrashing would be kinder than what they do to my people out in Texas. I know you read in the paper this morning about the Negro man who was supposed to be tormenting some white schoolteacher. A mob tied a rope aound his neck, dragged him to the schoolhouse, tied him to the top of it, and then set it on fire. They burn black people alive out there. So I guess in Virginia a whipping would be a kindness. . . ." All she said to me after that was: "Johnson, you hush. You know I don't mean you any harm. You take over the servants now. They're in your hands." And she left.

About three weeks later, something else happened. It was something that I was afraid to tell anybody about till years later. Finally, I told my wife. It happened at night when I was off work and alone in my room reading. One of the servants tapped on my door and said: "Lyman, Miss So-and-So said if you were in your room she wants to speak to you. She has some questions about her books." So I straightened myself up, buckled up a bit, and slipped on some shoes. About fifteen minutes later, I knocked on her door. It was about half past nine. Everything was quiet. All the whites had gone out on the town, and the blacks were down on the beach. The other two sisters had gone out for the evening. She said, "Oh, who is it?" I said, "It's Johnson." She said: "Come on in, Johnson. The door's unlocked." I walked in. It was her living quarters, her bedroom. She said, "Close the door." I pushed the door to but didn't completely close it. She said: "Uh, uh. Close it and lock it." I said, "All right."

I saw a bunch of books over on a table. At first I thought she'd gotten into some kind of tangle where the figures didn't balance and she wanted me to find out what needed to be done. So I sort of meandered over toward the table. As I did, I got a chance to get a good look at her. There she was sitting on the edge of her bed, dressed in something thin like a kimono. She didn't have on any underclothes. The kimono thing was supposed to button all the way from top to bottom but it wasn't fastened at all. Her breasts just popped out, and her private parts were as exposed as if she'd been completely naked. She was just sitting there and made no mention of the pile of books on the table. At first I may have been a little slow, but I was beginning to get the picture. I thought, "Now, what in the hell am I supposed to do in a case like this?" I thought of what the servants would say, the ones who'd attacked me for standing out there in the backyard holding that baby in my hands. They'd say: "Lyman, you big black fool! Up there in a locked room with a white woman who's practically nude! We don't care if she did send for you. We don't care if she did tell you to close the door and lock it. The noose is around your neck!" It was one of the most exasperating experiences I've ever had. I first thought: "It's a test. People say whites have blacks under such control that if a black man sees a white woman stripped naked, it won't affect him sexually. He's been disciplined to control himself. And this woman's just checking to see if I can pass the test." Then I thought: "Well, everybody's gone. I'm a fairly attractive young man. She's older but still somewhat attractive. Maybe she thinks this is a good night to have some fun and relaxation. And maybe it is!"

Of course, I wasn't about to make any advances. If any advances were to be made, she would make them. She had called me up there to work on some books, and there were the books. About that time I noticed that she was moving around on the bed, wiggling a little here and there, and wasn't making any attempt to pull her clothes up. I began to get nervous. This could be a trap. I said, "Miss So-and-So, could I take these books down to my room and work on them?" She said: "Now, Johnson, don't worry about those old books right now. You can do them tomorrow." I wanted to shout: "Well, what in the hell am I up here for? What *do* you want?" I knew I wasn't going to go over to the bed and put my hands on her. I wasn't going to make the first move. It took all my self-discipline to keep me on my side of the room. But the uncertainty of the situation held me back. I never knew when the door might burst open and a mob of white men might be all over me.

For a long while, I stood frozen. I didn't know how to get out of that predicament. I was afraid to leave suddenly. She might scream out that I had tried to rape her. Finally, when she apparently decided that I wasn't going to make a move, she said: "Oh, Johnson, you can come back tomorrow morning after breakfast and work on these books. It's getting late. I've got a toothache and don't want to fool with them tonight." So I kind of eased out—relieved and frustrated at the same time. In retrospect, it's pretty obvious what that white woman had in mind. Why should she have called me up there on a pretense with nobody around, almost naked, and then not have me work on her books? I suspected what she wanted. The evidence was plain. But I didn't know how far she wanted to go. Maybe she was having a little flash of sex in her mind, and she thought she'd get a kick out of tormenting me. Some women like to get a man all excited and then laugh at him. Or maybe she really wanted me to do it to her. Or maybe she didn't even know at the time what she wanted. In a situation like that, whoever breaks down first sets the pattern. I didn't break down—though I confess to being all man and being tempted by her—and she kind of pulled back.

Women have told me I'm naive—and I guess I am—when it comes to sex. A woman once said: "Oh, Lyman, I just love you so much you can have anything I have—anything!—even when I charge other men thirty and forty dollars for it. You can have it free. But you're so naive you don't seem to want it." So I say: "When it comes to that kind of sex, just put me down as naive. In the long run, it's safer."

I decided after that experience I'd better try to find summer work next year somewhere else. I still had the problem of what to do for a full-time job and what career to pursue. When I realized I couldn't get a teaching job for the fall, I decided to go to graduate school. I was accepted at Yale, Michigan, and Iowa. At Yale I would have studied theology, history at Michigan, and sociology at Iowa. I couldn't afford Yale. They required $1,000 deposit, and I didn't have that kind of money to tie up. So I chose Michigan because I had just about decided I'd be a teacher of history rather than a social worker. When the three schools accepted me, they said: "We're not putting our stamp of approval on your little college at Virginia Union, but we've had students from there before and believe you can do our work. If you can't, you'll have to take remedial courses. Then, if you can't measure up to our standards, we'll have to let you go." That was all I was asking for, a chance to prove myself in competition with the best students from around the country.

For my first year at Michigan, I had enough money from my summer work at Virginia Beach to pay my tuition and buy some clothes. For my room I got a job in the Negro fraternity I was a member of, Alpha Phi Alpha. The house accommodated sixteen students, and I took care of the house. I was custodian or housekeeper. I kept the place clean and neat. For my meals I waited on tables in a white fraternity house. The second year at Michigan I got my room and board the same way. For my tuition and spending change, I scrounged around my family.

When I arrived at Michigan, I was twenty-five but felt terribly inadequate as a graduate student. I had been taught in southern tradition that by being black I was *ipso facto* intellectually inferior to white people. It was with a great deal of trepidation that I went in for my first class at eight o'clock that first morning. I tried my best to hold my head up and walk in and take my seat like everybody else. When I looked around, I saw that I was the only Negro in the class. It was a new experience for me. Up to then, I'd been used to all-Negro classes. The professor—it was a history class—began rattling stuff off like a machine gun. I saw all the white boys copying down what he was saying. I decided that whatever they did I was going to do, so I copied down all I could.

We had lecture on Monday and Wednesday and discussion on Friday. I was afraid to speak up in class during discussion period. I was afraid I might ask a "Negro question" or give a "Negro answer." Even if I did the best I could, I feared that my Negro statement might be inferior. So I had decided that I wouldn't say anything in class so that the professor and my classmates wouldn't know if I was dumb. One day the professor said to me after class: "Mr. Johnson, I notice you don't speak up in class. Come by my office. I want to speak to you." In his office he said: "Johnson, you're just as smart as any of those white boys in class, but you've got to start talking out. Else you're going to fail. If I pass you, the other students will say it was because of sympathy for a Negro. So get on out there and start talking. Don't wait for me to call on you." After I started mixing with the white students in class and talking out, I never had any more trouble.

I soon got to the point that I was pretty self-assured. I found out quickly that white people can give some dumb answers. I saw that white professors chewed out white students for bad work. In one history seminar of about twenty students, each of us had to present a paper to the class. The professor barked rough. Sometimes he'd cut a student to pieces. One time he cut up a white woman so badly she went outside and cried. He said: "Hell, go on and cry. Either you get this classwork right or you get out of my class." So I decided that if he treated me rough it wouldn't be because I was black but because it was the nature of the old cuss.

I even got to the point of being spunky. When I gave my first paper, I paraphrased something that Gen. Ben Butler had said when he was occupying New Orleans during the Civil War. The professor stopped me and said, "Mr. Johnson, I don't believe Butler said that." I promptly reached down on the floor by my desk, picked up a volume of the *Records of the Rebellion* that I had cited, and said, "Professor, I can read from the official record." By that time all the class was pulling for me. We'd all gotten to the place when he started chewing up a poor devil, we'd sympathize with him. So I read the direct quotation that I had paraphrased. The professor looked at me and then around the class kind of sheepishly and said: "Well, if old Butler said that, he was either crazy or he was a damn fool. But you can keep it in your paper." I got in the last word. "Professor," I crowed, "he may have been both crazy *and* a damn fool, but that's what he said." After class everybody came to me to congratulate me. "Lyman," one of them said, "I wish I knew how to talk to him the way you did." I said: "Wait. Don't congratulate me yet. Wait till I pass this course and get my degree."

I was beginning to get back the self-assurance I had had at Virginia Union, where I'd question my professors and make them defend their statements. Some of my fellow students even got concerned about my cockiness. "Lyman," they'd say, "how in the world do you expect to pass your courses when you talk to your professors the way you do?" I'd say: "I believe a university should develop my intellect. Our professors should encourage us to think for ourselves, not just to repeat what they say. We didn't come to the university to learn how to be parrots."

I picked up my attitude toward teaching and my teaching philosophy mostly from my father and my uncle—both of them master teachers. And all the years I taught high school and did relief teaching in college and before all the groups I've spoken to over the years, I've tried to stimulate people. I'd say: "I'm not here to make converts of you. I'm here to stimulate you to think for yourselves. The quality of your own brain will be the measure of what you think. So don't worry about what *I* think. Put together all the stuff I've said with what you've picked up from books and from other people, and then think for yourselves."

I know that some of my professors at Michigan assumed that my preparation was second rate because I had attended a southern black college. In those days not all the prejudice was in the South. One time a professor at Michigan gave me a "C" on a paper and explained, "Why, Mr. Johnson, that's a good grade for a Negro." He assumed I was second rate because I was black. He assumed my college was second rate because it was black. Hell, I don't want anybody to say, "Your college is good for a Negro college," or "Your bank is a good bank for a Negro bank." That's why I don't want any institution or business to get a reputation as "black." In Louisville we have a fine bank that is under the general supervision and control of blacks. But it must never be thought of as a black bank! If it gains such a reputation, some people, blacks included, will think: "Oh, I don't think I'll put my money there. It won't be as safe as it would be in a white bank." A good bank is a good bank, regardless of who its directors are. A good school is a good school, regardless of its racial mix. I hope I never hear anyone again say: "Dr. So-and-So is a good physician, even though he graduated from Meharry Medical School. Professor So-and-So is a good teacher, but he didn't graduate from the University of Michigan." If something is good, it's good. There should be no racial qualification.

I think my own experience and that of thousands of other graduates of private black colleges in the South have validated the quality education they provided several generations of black people. But what about now? What role do predominantly black colleges serve this side of integration? Many of the more than 100 mostly black colleges are in financial trouble today. They've lost many of their best black students to what were once segregated white schools. They compete with other institutions for the best black professors.

Do these schools with a black tradition have a future? Do they have a purpose, a mission, as we approach the end of the twentieth century? It's a question I'm still wrestling with. There's absolutely no question about their worth in the past. They were absolutely necessary. They helped to raise the Negro from serfdom. They provided an education—an intellectual education—for southern Negroes when the South would not educate them adequately in public institutions. There was nowhere else for southern Negroes to go to find quality. Even the white church colleges were closed to them. In Richmond, for instance, there were two Baptist colleges, the University of Richmond for whites and Virginia Union for blacks, both good schools. But we blacks were not allowed to use the white campus, the library or gym or anything. Black Baptists couldn't go to that white Baptist school, but white Catholics could. It's all changed now, of course. Black students can go to any college they choose. So why keep Virginia Union? Should I try to make it and Fisk and Morehouse and Talladega and all the other traditionally black schools better? If I make these schools as good as the traditionally white schools, then why should a black student go to the white school? So the better I make a black college, the more I justify segregation. It's a dilemma.

I do think, however, there is justification for keeping open these old black mission schools. I see more and more whites going to them because of the quality of their education and because of convenience. Traditionally white private schools continue to justify themselves. They emphasize their intimacy, their personal care, their freedom to experiment. So if Kentucky needs private schools like Spalding and Bellarmine and Georgetown and Centre and Pikeville, why does not Virginia need a Virginia Union? Why does not Tennessee need a Fisk? Why does not Georgia need a Morehouse? With some academic redesigning and more public support, I think we can even justify retaining most of the old state-supported black colleges.

I was twenty-seven years old when I took my master's degree in history at Michigan. I had a good education. But I didn't have a job. After my first year at Michigan, I scattered all over the country looking for a job. I had no luck. So I went back to Michigan for another year. The next year I looked again for a job, again with no luck. I went half into my third year at Michigan, and finally, I ran out of money, patience, and endurance.

I was living hand to mouth. I didn't steal, and I didn't rob. But for a while I was a fit subject for communism. It didn't make sense to me for a country as rich as ours to be in such a deplorable condition—with wheat farmers in Iowa freezing for lack of coal and people in Appalachia sitting on a coal mine hungry for bread. I took on odd jobs, anything I could find. I would do anything for something to eat or a place to stay. I was too embarrassed to go back to my father's house. I was a college graduate, with two and one-half years of graduate work, and I was broke, jobless, and depressed. I couldn't go back to my father's table and live off him. He had only one biscuit. Why should I go home and eat half of that?

I was scrounging around the country doing odd jobs and living in flophouses for twenty-five or fifty cents a night. On March 3, the day before Roosevelt was inaugurated president, I passed through Washington, D.C. But I didn't have enough interest to stay over. I didn't believe anyone could save us from the Depression. I went on down to my old school in Richmond. When I got on campus at Virginia Union, I went to the maintenance supervisor who I had worked for when I was a student. He said, "All we can do is give you a little work in exchange for a place to sleep and a little food in the dining hall." That was better than I had, so I started doing a little carpentry, plumbing, and electrical work around the campus. That's where I was when my sister Cornelia in Louisville wrote me: "Come on over. We can't promise much, but we'll give you a place to stay and enough food to eat." She sent me bus fare, and I headed for Louisville.

Way up North in Louisville

Louisville Negroes would boast, "We're up North." We who were from down south used to say: "Hell, so you're from up North? You didn't even get as far as Indianapolis!"

NEGROES used to think it was such a blessing to get out of Alabama and Mississippi. If they couldn't make it all the way North, they'd try to get to Memphis or Nashville or Knoxville. To them even Tennessee was glory land! But I was from Tennessee, and I used to think, "If I could only get to Kentucky, it would be heaven." When I was a boy, I didn't know much about Kentucky, but I knew it was north of Tennessee and that was a good direction.

When my sister invited me to come to Louisville, I had already decided that I didn't want to settle in a northern city. It was too expensive and too cold to live up there. I had eliminated Detroit. People just dropped in there from everywhere to work in the factories, and they never meshed into one people. It looked like a scrap pile to me. I had a brother living in New York. He said: "Lyman, it's a fast life here. If you can keep up with the pace, it's the best place in the world to live. But you've got to run to keep up." Hell, I didn't intend to get in a rat race! I had even given up on Chicago, which had always been a kind of dream place for me.

And I certainly didn't intend to settle in the lower South. My Uncle Will didn't even want me to go to college down there. When he was teaching at Morehouse in Atlanta, he had advised me not to come there. "Son, Morehouse is a fine school. But I don't want you living in Atlanta. When you're on campus, it's a good life, but when you step foot off campus and get out in town, the white people will be mean and vicious to you. Negroes have no rights in town. Go to college in Tennessee or Virginia or Kentucky, but for God's sake stay out of Georgia!"

Neither did I want to go back to my hometown. Conditions for Negroes were horrible—racially, economically, and culturally. Negroes in Columbia didn't have any opportunities at all.

So in the spring of 1930, I came to Louisville to live with my sister and her husband, who was librarian at the Western Colored Branch of the Louisville Free Public Library. They gave me two rooms and my meals in exchange for my work as a handyman. In my spare time, I began to find out about Louisville and Kentucky. Blacks up here enjoyed a few advantages over their cousins farther south, but as a whole Kentucky was a hell of a place when I came here. It seemed to me that even Tennessee was a better location. I thought Tennessee had a better brand of people. Friends used to ask me, "Lyman, how can you stand to live in Kentucky?" I would say: "Because I break Kentucky into two parts, Louisville and the rest of the state. Louisville is oriented to the North, culturally and commercially. The rest of Kentucky looks to the South."

When I moved to Kentucky, one of the most hellish places I ever experienced was a little town called Shelbyville. It bothered me to have to drive through that damn place just to get to Frankfort, where the state Negro college was located. In those days Kentucky State was an important cultural adjunct for black people in Louisville. But in order to go to the cultural affairs on their campus, we had to drive through that damn Shelbyville. It was as bad as any town in Mississippi or Alabama. White people had black people who lived there under the most rigid discipline. If a bunch of white people walked down the street, Negroes got off the sidewalk to let them by or they got their heads beat in. One time some of the Negroes in Shelbyville tried to hold their heads up and invited some church people to a two-day conference. White men in town tried to proposition some of the Negro women attending the meeting. They'd call out to them on the street: "Woman, come over here. This is your day today!" After some of the women from Louisville were insulted, they asked their hosts, "How do you stand it here?" The Shelbyville blacks shrugged and said: "Oh, we're used to it. We know how to get along with these white folks. We just pass it off."

At first, Louisville blacks thought I would accept such treatment. They thought I would have an Uncle Tom mentality because I was from Tennessee. Louisville blacks were rather impressed with themselves because they thought they were northern people. They looked down their noses at Negroes from the South. They considered themselves culturally superior.

I soon concluded, however, that it was probably harder to crash into black society in cities like Memphis or Birmingham or Atlanta or Charleston than it was in Louisville. Black society in those cities was classier. What did Louisville have to offer Negroes when I came here? It had no college worthy of the name, only struggling little Simmons University, which no black would go to unless he had to, and Louisville Municipal College, the starving little public school. By contrast, Nashville was a lot smaller than Louisville, but it was known as the Athens of the South. For Negroes there was Fisk University, a well-established Negro center of education and culture, and Tennessee State, which didn't have much prestige but had a respected football and basketball team. There was also Meharry Medical School for Negroes and Hubbard Hospital attached to it. Nashville had Vanderbilt and Peabody for whites. Louisville had a poor city university and a couple of seminaries. By comparison with southern cities, Louisville had little in terms of culture to offer Negroes.

Louisville Negroes would boast, "We're up North." We who were from down South used to say: "Hell, so you're from up North? You didn't even get as far as Indianapolis!" In those days Indianapolis was no paradise for Negroes. We caught hell when we tried to sleep in their hotels and eat in their restaurants. So we'd say, "If you really want to claim you're from up North, you'd better move on up to Detroit or Chicago."

I don't mean to put Louisville down too much. When I moved here in the early 1930s, there were a lot of places blacks could go and things to do. When the black community wanted to have a big party, we'd use the Pythian Temple, which had a big ballroom on the top floor of the black YMCA at Tenth and Chestnut. It may have been small compared to the ballrooms white people had in the big clubs and hotels downtown, but it was big to us. It had a nice hardwood floor, big windows, and when it was decorated for a fancy dance, man, it was a sight to behold! When the orchestra tooted their horns and we started tripping the light fantastic, we didn't think the white folks had any better. If you wanted to keep in the swing of things, you made sure you got an invitation to the big balls there.

The bands and orchestras would play whatever music the people wanted, jazz to jitterbug. My wife liked more elegant music, but most of us wanted something livelier. A little later, during the zoot-suit days, it was *the* place to go. I had a zoot suit with one pocket so high I had to get on a stepladder to reach it and another pocket so low I had to get down on my knees. Man, I was a sport in those days!

Right around the corner from the Pythian Temple was the Allen Hotel. It had a dance floor, but it was so small two couples made it crowded. A lot of the more socially elite belonged to fraternities and sororities they had joined in college. Then there were organizations that took care of socially minded people who didn't go to college, though many college people joined them. They were the Masons, the Elks, and the Czars. At their meetings and parties, you'd expect to bump into people who didn't speak correct English and whose manners didn't always observe the fine points of high culture. Their music might get a little rowdy, and after a while the people might drop all their cultural pretensions and get down to basics and enjoy themselves. There were also small clubs of ten or fifteen members that met in homes—a bridge club or a dinner group. There were a lot of these small private clubs that would last maybe ten years and then disband. At least once a year, each club would throw a big ball either at the Pythian or at a skating rink at Ninth and Magazine, which they could rent for the night.

I know now what pitiful places the Pythian and the skating rink were for social gatherings. But the worst was an old abandoned tobacco barn on Hill Street. It was drafty, and the floors were warped. They buckled from one end to the other. Dancers tried to skip the places where splinters stuck up from the floor. It was a hell of a place to hold a dance. One time three of us schoolteachers rented the barn for a party. A reporter for the Negro newspaper wrote it up and said: "What kind of culture do these school-teachers think they have? To get to this party, you had to take your lady friend—dressed in her high-heeled shoes, long flowing gown, furs, and jewelry—out Hill Street, walk at least a block through mud to get to their social event of the year." Well, he was right. It was a sorry place for a dance. But we had to have some social outlet, and it was the only place we could afford. We tried to hide the shabbiness with fancy decorations, but that didn't take the mud off your feet or the buckles and splinters out of the floor.

There were also public places around Sixth and Walnut where Negroes could go for entertainment. There were liquor joints, beer taverns, and little dance halls. There were also little restaurants—actually hot dog stands where you could get a sandwich and beer and maybe hard liquor. If, however, you moved on behind the food concession, you might find a gambling den and, farther back, rooms where you could get women. Just about every place was a joint where you could get almost anything you wanted and could pay for, depending upon how far back in the joint you wanted to go. Sometimes there would be a juke box. You could put in a nickel, and if you were about half drunk, you could get one of those backroom girls to jump around and carry on with you. There was loud music and loud talk and everybody was having a ball.

These little joints didn't usually have live bands. But sometimes there'd be an old piano in the place and somebody would pound it for a while. Sometimes somebody would be picking on a banjo or a guitar. Or sometimes a fellow with a saxophone or a trombone or a cornet would drop in and play. Sometimes there would be a singer.

Our high-class entertainments were the formal dances at the Pythian. There the men would dress in tuxedos or tails and women in their long evening dresses, and the music would be by a real band. But the same people who would go to these formal dances might also go to the public joints on Saturday nights. At least my wife and I did. We would go down to see what it was all about and to show other black people that we were regular—that we were not high-hatting them. I'd tell my wife that this kind of fun was the only kind that a lot of Negroes had. I'd say, "Come on, honey, let's drop in on them and get us a bottle of beer." She'd say, "Lyman, I don't want any beer." I'd say, "Well, you can get a bottle of ginger ale, but don't tell anyone you're not drinking anything stronger."

The two big public places were the Top Hat and Rivers' Place. The rest were little joints. At the Top Hat and Rivers' Place, you could get drinks at a front bar and sandwiches and short orders like hot dogs, hamburgers or sometimes ribs. You could drink your beer at the counter, or you could sit at the tables. There was also plenty of room to dance. Behind the dance floor was the gambling den. If you didn't want to get raided, you paid the police off. It was cheaper to pay than to get raided. In the last compartment, there were the women. I never got that far! I wasn't a gambler, and I didn't go in for prostitutes.

A man named Charley Moore ran the Top Hat. Maybe he didn't get rich, but he was well-off. Nobody knew the real name of the man who owned Rivers' Place. Rivers was his nickname. His place had a reputation as a big-time gambling den. All the gambling bunch would assemble there anytime after six o'clock in the evening, any night of the week, and gamble to one or two o'clock in the morning. Anytime you had ten dollars, you could go in, and Rivers would find somebody to gamble with you. Everybody understood that the gambling regulars were supported by Rivers. One night they gambled till about three o'clock in the morning. Then Rivers showed up: "Well, fellows, we have got to close up now. You have got it all. This is one time you cleaned me out."

The men all went out on the street and celebrated. "We broke Rivers," they shouted. It was a cause for celebration because usually the cards or dice were so rigged the house couldn't lose. But this particular night they cleaned his safe. They waited on the street outside till he closed up, turned the lights off, and locked up. He always had a pretty, highly polished Cadillac parked in front of his place where everybody knew not to park because it was his space. Go down there and take his place, and he'd cuss the hell out of you! Park anywhere else, everybody knew, but don't park in front of Rivers' Place. So here was his nice, pretty Cadillac parked out front. The men were waiting for him and began to taunt: "Hey, Rivers, you want to borrow some gas to get home on? You know that big old car takes a tank to go one block, and you don't have enough money to get you a refill. You want to borrow some gas? Want us to lend you some gas, Rivers? Want us to lend you some money so you can buy some gas?" They just went on and on, rubbing it in, saying all sorts of things like that. Without saying a word, Rivers got in his car, cranked it up, and eased on down the street.

The next day at four o'clock there was a sparkling Cadillac parked in front of Rivers' Place. The word kind of sprinkled around in the gambling circles that Rivers was open. And all the gamblers said, "Well, let's go down and see." When they got there, they saw his Cadillac in its usual spot, and directly across the street they saw another Cadillac, pretty as it could be and brand new! After the gambling bunch had gathered inside, Rivers said, "All right, fellows, put your money on the table." But everybody was curious about the new Cadillac across the street. They thought maybe it belonged to some celebrity from out of town who had dropped in to play some games at Rivers' Place. But Rivers wouldn't say a thing about that car. Finally, one of his staff told them: "That's Rivers's lady's car. You rascals thought you broke Rivers last night. You went to work this morning, and you made five or six dollars, and you bring it down here, thinking you're gonna break Rivers again. Well, Rivers, he just went downtown this morning and bought him a new Cadillac and parked it over there, just to let you guys know that if you break him on this side, he's got a car on that side to put up. Yes, sir, Rivers is in business tonight!" That was the big-time way Rivers operated. He made a lot of money and was almost a legend in the black community.

Rivers made his money on two things poor Negroes liked to do, drink and gamble. Some people would add a third, fighting. But I don't think poor blacks like to fight or drink or gamble any more than other people on their level. But fights were commonplace in the black nightclub district. When you mix whiskey, gambling, and women, you've got an explosive combination. A lot of people got cut up, and some people got killed, especially on Saturday nights when the streets and joints were crammed full. Sometimes a fight would start over no more than a nickel. Fortunately, I was never in one of those places when a fight started. My wife was always afraid I'd be caught in one. I'd say, "Don't worry, honey, I'll thin out if I ever see any trouble coming." She'd say: "They're too sudden. You won't have time to get out." She was right. But I was lucky never to be there when tempers flared on hot nights and ended in a cutting or a killing.

Maybe one reason Negroes were fond of drinking and gambling and fighting was that they were cut off from so many other forms of entertainment that white people had. Black people couldn't spend a lot of money drinking and gambling because they didn't have much to spend. In poker and crap games, the stakes were very low. Usually, the whole pot was worth no more than a couple of dollars. But I will admit that I've seen gambling among Negroes everywhere I've lived. Down in Columbia a piece of my family's rental property in the Negro business district was rented to a barber. I often wondered how he kept up his place so fine with such little trade. One time I found out when I put on my overalls, got my carpenter tools, and went over to fix the guttering on the back side of the shop. When I climbed up the ladder, I could look down into the back room. I saw fifteen or twenty fellows around a table gambling. It's amazing how long a game can last when there are twenty people playing even if each one only has fifteen dollars to lose. Gradually, the gamblers would go broke and drop out, until there would be two or three left. By that time, there'd be a pretty-good-sized pot.

Another time, I had to do some repair work inside that back room. They didn't pay me any attention but went on gambling. I came back several times, but I made sure I always had some tools in my hands in case the damn sheriff or police decided to raid the place. I'd say: "I'm the carpenter. I was sawing this board when you came in. I don't know what those fellows over there are doing. I'm not with them." Of course, the gamblers weren't fools. They had an alert system. They had somebody stationed in the front room of the barbershop. If a policeman came in the front door, a signal was given—maybe a certain way of grunting or a certain greeting—that would be passed on to the back room. By the time the police could get back there, the place would be so clean you couldn't find a card or dice anywhere. All the money would be off the table, and the gamblers would be reading joke books and telling comic tales. The police would burst through the door, stop and listen to the off-color jokes, and then laugh and say, "Hell, we messed up again." I think the police knew they had simply been outfoxed. I'm sure there were some police payoffs in Columbia just as there were in Louisville, but occasionally the politicians had to stage a raid to keep the church people happy.

Drinking and gambling were practiced by middle-class Negroes but in a much more discreet fashion. Most of the Louisville Negroes who wanted to be in society wanted to be like upper-class white society. Where did Negroes learn about upper-class white society? They learned it from the Negroes who worked as servants in the homes of wealthy white people. There the servants learned the fine points of etiquette: what foods to serve, how to serve them, which silver to use, how to place the napkins, how to dress and be well groomed, even how to walk. Everything had to be just right. In the upper-class white homes, they heard the best English. They were surrounded by the best of everything. When these servants came back to their black communities, they brought all that training with them. Other blacks looked to them as social leaders and trendsetters.

Black society, therefore, could be quite elaborate. It was based on higher standards than poor whites could manage or imagine. It was even above middle-class whites.

What kinds of people and which professions made up black society? Professional people like doctors, lawyers, and teachers were in black society. But so were waiters and just about anybody else who had the money to afford it. The main requirement was money. Waiters were among the best-paid Negroes in Louisville when I arrived in 1930. A headwaiter at a first-class white hotel could make more money than a lawyer.

There wasn't much of a class system among blacks when I came to Louisville. Negro doctors, however, enjoyed a special place in the black community. There were more of them then than now. In those days white doctors didn't like to treat Negro patients unless there was no Negro doctor available because his white patients wouldn't approve. Now, of course, Negroes go to the doctor of their choice. The Negro public is finally being emancipated from the idea that they have to be served only by other blacks. Negroes can walk into stores without bothering to look up to see who's waiting on them. Blacks don't have to ask, "Who is the best Negro doctor in town?" Hell, I never wanted the best Negro anything. I wanted the best.

There were very few Negro lawyers when I came to town. That's a profession that has opened to us since World War II. Before then Negroes needing lawyers would go to whites. A Negro lawyer would have been a disadvantage, since the judge, the jury, and the opposing lawyer would most probably have been white.

Doctors and lawyers were highly thought of in the black community. But there weren't enough of them to have a decent society. Even if you added the teachers, preachers, and other professionally trained people, there still wouldn't have been enough. In order to have any kind of cultural activity, we had to rake across all the groups and let anyone in who could afford the cost.

When I was in school up in Michigan, there was a fancy place called

Idlewild where the big-shot blacks would throw big weekend parties. The main requirement was money. If you were a doctor or lawyer or dentist and couldn't afford to blow $2,000 or $3,000 to set up everybody, you weren't qualified. But if you were a waiter or gambler or nightclub owner and could spend that kind of money, you were in. It didn't matter where you got your money. You just had to have it.

One year when my fraternity had its national meeting in Chicago, I went to a party given by John Johnson, the man who publishes *Ebony* magazine. He invited us two months ahead of time. "I'm having an open house at my place. Drop by if you have time for food and refreshments." I heard that the man spent $14,000 on that party. It was high class, with all kinds of expensive hors d'oeuvres and drinks and dressed-up waiters and a big orchestra. And who came? Anybody who could get him a full dress suit and a bow tie. Johnson didn't stand at the door and say, "Who's your pappy?" In high white society, you've got to have credentials to get in a party like that. The party was supposed to be a come-and-go affair, but most of us came and ate and drank and stayed.

In Louisville my fraternity used to hold meetings in each member's home. In those days we couldn't use the club rooms at the hotels or at any nice restaurant, and we had outgrown the little Negro hash joints. One of our members was J.O. Blanton, who used to teach mathematics at Central High School before I came to town. In 1927 he had quit his job and helped open up a Negro bank, but it was one of the first to fold when the Depression hit. From 1930 to 1940, Blanton was on the rocks. He couldn't get his job back at Central. He picked up some piddling jobs but had a hard time feeding his family. We didn't ostracize the man because he was on hard times. We didn't run away from him. When we'd have our meetings at his house, we'd know ahead of time that his wife would serve us baked beans with strips of bacon across the top. That was all right. He was still one of us.

Maybe the next month we'd have our fraternity meeting at Dr. J.A.C. Lattimore's. He'd practiced medicine around Louisville for fifty years and had a mansion for his home. That man's family and house were the epitome of culture and refinement. About thirty of us would gather in his upstairs meeting room. When dinner was ready, a maid would come to the door and announce, "Gentlemen, dinner is served." We'd follow him into a big dining area where the table would be set with linen tablecloths and linen napkins and four or five pieces of silver and crystal glasses. The same bunch that ate baked beans last month would now be served a seven-course dinner. There weren't any white folks in Louisville who had any better than what we had at Dr. Lattimore's.

Maybe the next month we'd meet at Dr. P.O. Sweeney's. He was a dentist. Several years before he died in the 1950s, he said: "Lyman, I've deprived myself long enough. I'm getting old and don't have much longer to live. I'm going to buy myself a nice place. I'm going to have a clean linen napkin placed by my plate three times a day. I think I'm entitled to it. I've seen how white people live, and I want to live like that a few years before I die." That's what he did. He bought a big farm on the highway between Louisville and Frankfort. He paid $13,000 for one bull. He showed me the $25,000 check that he paid to have his house remodeled. It was a fancy place.

In our fraternity when it came your time to entertain, you entertained at your level—whether you could serve baked beans or filet mignon. All of us blacks started from scratch at the end of the Civil War. We don't have much social background to brag about.

If you go back far enough, you'll find that we're all descended from slaves. "Yes," I could say, "my grandfathers were slaves. Now, what are you going to do about it? What can I do about it?" In fact, there was nothing I could do about it. There wasn't anything my grandfathers could have done about it. That's why we learned to accept all our brothers and sisters. Most of the members of my fraternity had, of course, gone to college. But that was no prediction that a man would get his degree or that in ten or fifteen or thirty years he would be a successful doctor or dentist or banker. We didn't disown a brother if he didn't succeed as well as others.

We also had a way for noncollege men to join our fraternity. To use a basketball expression: If he could come in the back door and get the ball in the basket, we'd put him on our team. It was like giving him a GED membership in the fraternity. If a man was successful and hadn't been to college, why should we try to keep him out? He might be able to write a $1,000 check to the NAACP or the Urban League. We'd say, "Hell, college might even have ruined the man!"

The point I'm making is this: Black society didn't have a large enough group to select from to be very exclusive. You didn't have to be a doctor or a lawyer or a school principal. You didn't have to be a college graduate. You didn't have to have light skin. All you had to have was money to get into society. To stay in, you had to behave yourself. When I came to this town, the man who set the pace for black society was a Dr. White, who owned a pharmacy at Sixth and Walnut. I bring up Dr. White because he was deep black. He was dark as they come, and he could chew you up if you told him he didn't belong to Louisville's top black society. He'd say, "Show me a yellow nigger who doesn't own his own home, who doesn't have a car, who doesn't have enough money to send his children to college, and I'll show you a yellow nigger who is not in society—I don't care how light his color is." I never knew of any clubs or groups in Louisville that a Negro couldn't get into because he was dark skinned.

I know all about skin lighteners, hair straighteners, and other products designed to make Negroes look more Caucasian. I know there have been some light-skinned, blond-haired, blue-eyed Negroes who have tried to establish their own circles. Like everyone else, Negroes—especially before the 1950s—have had a kind of social stratification. But by and large, it hasn't been based on ancestry or skin tone. If you were light skinned and held yourself above other blacks and didn't try to go on and pass for white, you were likely to be ostracized by both races. So in self-defense light-skinned blacks quickly came to the conclusion that it was better to be a good fellow with dark- and brown-skinned Negroes than to become outcast from both groups. It was always a great risk to try to pass for white. If you managed to pass for a while, and then someone discovered your black secret, white society would throw you right back to your own race. And the Negroes wouldn't take you in. They'd say: "All right, Mr. Big Shot. You tried to get away from us. You disowned us. Now we disown you. You're an untouchable." Indeed, it was always better for a Negro—regardless of his skin shade—to claim his race.

"But," you say, "why do I see so many light-skinned, almost-white faces looking out from black college photographs made in 1900, 1910, 1920, and so on? Doesn't that prove that light blacks had certain advantages?" Yes, sometimes light Negroes got breaks. But the break didn't come from the black race. Let me explain with an illustration. Three of my wife's best friends came from Birmingham, where their mother worked for a rich man five or six blocks away from their home. He was their papa and was as white as any man in Alabama. Their mother was very dark, ginger colored. These three girls were light-skinned and knew who was responsible for it. They knew who their daddy was. In fact, he admitted it to them. "I'm your papa," he said. "I love your mama. I have loved her since I met her, and I have loved no other woman but her. But state law and society won't let me marry and live with her and with you. So she comes to my home every day, cleans and cooks and takes care of me, and then goes back to live with you. I'm not disowning you, but since your mama is a Negro, you've got to go to the Negro school. That's the law. Later, if you want to go to college, I'll pay all your expenses. I'm supporting your mother and you. I always have and I always will."

A man like that would send his sons and daughters to Fisk or Howard or Virginia Union or a state college for Negroes. I suspect that a lot of the southern white support for black colleges after the Civil War came from the fathers of illegitimate slave children who wanted to pay a debt of conscience. Whether or not that's true, I imagine that many southern white men with offspring by slave women decided to take advantage of the new black schools—the state ones and the ones founded by northern missionaries. "Well, now that the damn Yankee carpetbaggers have begun these schools," the white papas said, "I'll make sure my child gets in one of them."

All three Birmingham girls chose to go to Tennessee State College in Nashville, where my wife became a friend of one of them. That girl had more money to spend than anybody else on campus. She wore the best clothes. She had very light skin but cultivated friendships with black girls, yellow girls, and girls with her own complexion. She knew she could never go to live with her father's people. And she knew she couldn't use her color for special favors within the black race or she'd be cut down. So her friends were a rainbow of colors. She finished her degree, became a teacher, and eventually got a master's degree. One of her sisters dropped out of college, but the other one got a Ph.D. and became a college professor in Ohio. Yes, the girls got a break. They got it from their white father, who gave them advantages as well as their light skin. And their story is not uncommon. It was repeated thousands of times, from slavery days right up to now.

I'm not suggesting that it was an ideal situation. It was not. But given the circumstances, it worked out pretty well for some of the children of mixed parents. However, in most instances the white fathers rejected and disowned their children by black women. They gave them no support. And if there was a black husband, think of what it did to him. It castrated him! In such a family, you might have two sets of children who were half-brothers and sisters—children with the same mother but different fathers. In the first generation, there would be light-skinned and dark–skinned children. In the second generation, since the light-skinned children would likely have to find mates in the black community, you might have a gamut of colors, ranging from very light to very dark—even if a light-skinned Negro married another light-skinned Negro. That's why black people couldn't afford to base social position on skin shade. That's why it was dangerous for light skins to try to pass for white. You never knew when two very light blacks would have a very dark child. The genes begin to get realigned in the second and third generation, and babies pop out in a rainbow of colors.

Today no black person would dare try to take advantage of his light skin. A young black who tries to get a job in a black-owned company on the basis of his color would be laughed out of the employment office. "I don't care how white you look," he'd be told. "I can't use your color. If you can type sixty words a minute, I can use you. If you can sell insurance, you've got a job. If you can work a computer, we'll put you on our payroll." It would be an insult for any black to try to capitalize on his light skin. Hell, with four-fifths of the people in the world not white, it would be stupid for him to try to get preference for his white blood.

Negro society has been a hell of a lot more democratic than white society. We've always known that prejudice against any Negro was preju-dice against all Negroes, regardless of our skin shade or profession or income. We've always known that no matter how high a Negro could get, outside our society he was still a damn nigger. For more than three hundred years, we've known that two commands have applied to all of us—slave or free, rich or poor, doctor or ditch digger: "Get back where you belong" and "Stay in your place." It's never mattered how much education, culture, or refinement we've had; we were still niggers. It didn't matter how much money we had; we still couldn't get admitted to white-only restaurants.

White prejudice has, in fact, tended to make us more democratic and helpful to each other. It has kept the upper classes of Negroes from getting too far from the bottom class. Both classes knew they needed each other. The lower class knew they had to count on the black intelligentsia for leadership. The upper class knew that their real base of support was the poor, uneducated black masses yet to be raised up. Both extremes knew that even though there was always upward movement, it was just as easy to slip back down.

Let me illustrate with my own family. One of my brothers down in Tennessee never went beyond high school. The rest of us rose above him academically, but we tried our best never to let any distinction show. When we visited him, we'd have a big family dinner and socialize just like brothers and sisters ought to. We didn't let a little bit of education separate us. We tried to maintain close contact with all our relatives and growing-up friends, despite our differences in education and jobs.

Take Congressman William Dawson from Chicago. He was elected to Congress so many times he became chairman of some very important committees in Washington. Yet when he went back to his South Side district in Chicago, he showed himself as one of the masses of poor blacks who had elected him. He'd visit chili parlors, bars, hash joints, and churches, backslapping the people to show that he was one of them. Those people were not impressed by his learning as a lawyer or by his important position in Congress. Like every Negro minister, every Negro doctor, every Negro real estate man, he knew his base of operations and where his support came from. All these successful Negroes knew that if they got too high and cut the connecting link between themselves and the masses of the black race they were dead ducks. Without this black support from lower down, they were nothing. They could not count on support and patronage from whites. Black leaders had no white clientele.

There's always been a kind of camaraderie among Negroes—a closeness developed from the awareness that black people are their own best friends. That awareness has kept the successful Negro from looking down on other Negroes. That awareness has made Negro society democratic. That's why, when I was in my heyday, I could go to fancy dances and see a schoolteacher with a master's degree dancing with a janitor or the headwaiter from the Seelbach Hotel. Black society has changed in recent years. But blacks still know who their best friends are. As long as unemployment for blacks is three or four times the rate for whites and as long as black professionals make thousands of dollars a year less than their white counterparts, we know we have not yet reached the Promised Land. It's still not Paradise, but it's a hell of a lot better than it was when I got off the Greyhound in 1930.

An Iconoclast in the Classroom

I've always tried to teach my students straight history—not colored white or black or brown or yellow.

WHEN I CAME ALONG, there weren't many professions open to Negroes. Teaching and preaching were about the only ones I could choose from. Since my father and uncle were teachers, that's the profession I finally chose. But I got out of school during the depths of the Depression, when there were no teaching jobs open. Then in September of 1933, I got lucky. I was living in Louisville with my sister and brother-in-law, doing odd jobs for my room and board, when a fellow who was supposed to teach at Central Colored High School unexpectedly resigned. It was two weeks before school opened. The Depression was getting worse and worse. Jobs were so scarce that within two days thirty-one people had applied for that job. I was one of them. When the principal looked down the list of applicants, he said, "Well, if everything else checks out, I'm going to give the job to that fellow who has two and a half years of study beyond the college degree, and he has it in the field we're looking for." I was that fellow. My last year at Michigan I had taken a special program in education to get a teacher's certificate. Then I had done my six weeks of practice teaching in Louisville at Madison Junior High School. So I was fully qualified. I got the job, and that first year I taught two classes in history and three in math.

Nobody seemed to care about what I said in the math classes. But I got into trouble when I taught history, especially American history. I always taught my students more than was in the textbook. Sometimes I debunked the book because sometimes the book was wrong. Not only did I try to teach the facts of history, but I wanted to give my students a point of view. What I mean is that I wanted to help them develop their own point of view. That sometimes got me into hot water with the school board and the superintendent—all white, of course. Many of my kids' parents worked as servants for affluent white families. The kids would go home all wrapped up in "what Mr. Johnson said" and tell their mamas. The next day at the white folks' house, the mama would say to "Miss Ann," without intending any harm, "My little girl said Mr. Johnson said. . . ." Then Miss Ann would call the superintendent and complain: "What's that nigger teacher teaching these nigger kids? Do you know what Alice said he said? No wonder our Negro servants are getting so uppity!"

The superintendent would call me in and tell me to stick to the book. "What if the book is wrong?" I'd ask. "Furthermore, education isn't a matter of taking one person's word. It's a process of examining and analyzing a lot of words and coming to your own conclusions." I don't think he would appreciate my lecture. He would simply repeat his warning. "For your own good, Johnson, stick to the book."

I didn't intend to stick to the book when the book was incomplete or slanted. I used to chide the other teachers at Central. "Why don't you stand up and tell them like it is?" They would say, "They may let you get away with it, but they won't let us get started." Perhaps they were right. That's why I didn't criticize my colleagues too much. Maybe the white establishment in Louisville allowed me to be a token mouthpiece for the more militant blacks. Maybe the white powers were afraid that if they put the finger on me all the silent blacks would rally to protect me. "If we whip Johnson," I think they reasoned, "we'll stir up the whole mess of Negroes. So we'll have to tolerate his big mouth and let the damn fool speak out." I think they saw me as a safety valve to let out a little pressure, a little black frustration. But they didn't know how much a *little* was, and I didn't know how much a *lot* was! For forty years I tried to use my position to great benefit.

Sometimes I let out a lot of pressure. In a letter I wrote to the *Courier-Journal* in 1954, I called the superintendent a cheap peanut politician. I attacked him for his tongue-in-cheek idea for integrating the Louisville public schools following the Supreme Court integration decision. The man was making liberal remarks and using conservative actions. He said he would integrate the Negro kids into the white schools, but he wouldn't take any of the black teachers because they were not capable of teaching white children. I said that if black teachers aren't able to teach white children, then they're not able to teach black children and ought to be fired. But, I said, you can't fire a black teacher without a hearing. Otherwise, you're condemning him without a fair trial. And, I concluded, that is beneath the dignity of a first-rate superintendent.

What the superintendent was trying to do was "integrate" black teachers out of their jobs. He sent 3,600 Negro pupils into all-white schools but not one single Negro teacher. He had a teacher shortage but refused to use any of the 100 black teachers put out of work by the transfers. It was a waste of taxpayers' money. This was the man who Mr. Eisenhower so highly honored. I knew what a humbug he was. His integration plan was based on an assumption of inequality. It was a dried-out system. If no black teacher is qualified to teach any white children, then all blacks must be inferior to all whites. That was the logic of his plan. It sounded to me more like 1854 than 1954. Eventually, he was forced to back down and to integrate the faculties as well as the students.

But I'm getting ahead of myself. When I started teaching at Central Colored High School, the schools were rigidly segregated. The word *colored* told the story. Every Negro school in the city had "colored" inscribed over its entrance. That was a part of its official name. It was not only a racist tradition but a thoroughly ridiculous one. Why should a school be named Frederick Douglass Colored School or the Booker T. Washington Colored School? Before 1954 no white student in Louisville would have darkened the doorway of either school. There would have been no Booker T. Washington School for whites! Nevertheless, we were required to have "colored" on our buildings and in the names of our professional organizations. I was a member of the Louisville Association of Teachers in Colored Schools. The white group was called the Louisville Education Association, not the Louisville *White* Education Association. If the name didn't have "colored" or "Negro" in it, you knew it was for whites only.

Central was the one black high school in the whole county. Students were bused downtown to Central from everywhere in the county, from as far east as Harrod's Creek and as far south as Okolona. That's why I laugh at the reaction of white parents who complain about busing today and react as if it's something new under the sun. At first, little black children had to walk long miles—often past white schools—to school. Finally, they were given buses and rode long miles past the same white schools. "Busing is not so bad," I say to white parents. "Blacks have been doing it for years."

Central didn't serve as large a territory as the Lincoln Institute over near Shelbyville. Lincoln was a boarding school for Negroes from all over the state. A lot of little Kentucky towns had so few Negroes it wasn't practical to set up a whole school for them, so they would pay their room, board, and tuition at Lincoln Institute. Lincoln was established by Berea College in 1907 after the state legislature passed the infamous Day Law in 1904. That law was the climax of efforts in Kentucky to reenslave the Negro—efforts that had been going on in Kentucky and throughout the South since the last federal occupation troops were withdrawn in 1876. Quickly, the aristocracy got back in the saddle and began to strip their former slaves of any semblance of first-class citizenship.

Kentucky's Day Law mandated separate facilities for blacks and whites from kindergarten through graduate school. It was the most vicious segregation law of any southern state. The law was named for a legislator who found out that Berea College had Negroes in some of its classes. Day said, "Get those niggers out." Berea said: "We're a private school. We're here to help all the poor students from Appalachia. Our students have to have a good moral character, a reasonable mental ability, and a desire for an education. They've also got to be willing to work for their tuition and board. Other than that, we don't care whether they are male or female, black or white." Berea's motto was "God hath made one people of all nations," and they tried to practice what they preached. But that wasn't enough for Carl Day. He prevailed on the legislature in 1904 to pass a law that said that *any* student who goes into a classroom obviously intended for another race is in violation of state law. The bill imposed a fine on the student, the teacher, and the institution. The law was aimed at Berea. No other private school was admitting Negroes. And the state already required separate public schools for white and colored.

The Day Law was passed during what I call the Dark Decades of American race relations, the period from about 1895 to 1915. It was a dismal time for Negroes, worse than the first days out of slavery. In some ways Negroes were more helpless, vulnerable, and threatened than they were as slaves. Berea fought the case all the way to the Supreme Court, but in 1907 the court sided with the state of Kentucky. That was when Berea started the Lincoln Institute to educate the Negroes they wanted to educate—at much less expense—at Berea. Even now when you travel the highway between Louisville and Frankfort, you can see that handsome administration building up on a hill, a reminder of the times when the state forced Berea to drive its Negroes off its main campus. Lincoln was operated by Berea till about 1950, when it was turned over to the state. Ironically, most of the Negro students got a better education at Lincoln Institute than the white children were getting back in the county schools that the Negroes were not allowed to attend!

Most black schools in Kentucky, however, were grossly inferior to the white schools. They were separate but certainly not equal. On the other hand, Central had better facilities than most other southern schools for Negroes. I know what I'm saying because I was business manager for Central's ball teams, and I traveled with them to such schools as Pearl High in Nashville, Austin High in Knoxville, and Parker High in Birmingham. We also played schools like Dunbar High in Dayton and Wendell Phillips in Chicago, which were better schools, even though they were practically all black.

Their teachers and coaches were often white. One time the Phillips basketball team came to Louisville to play Central. As usual, I arranged for the players and coaches to stay at the Negro YMCA—the players on cots in the ballroom and the coaches in private guest rooms. When the Phillips outfit arrived, I found that the coaches had made reservations to stay at the Kentucky Hotel, a white-only hotel. The student body was almost all black—the school was named for the great abolitionist—but the faculty, including the coaches, were almost all white. So the three coaches stayed at the Kentucky Hotel with the other white people. When they got back to Chicago, they sent me the bill, which I refused to pay. I said, "Hell, you stay where I provide for you, or you pay your own bill. I don't put visitors in a tent or a barn. I put you up in as nice a place as we could find. Black coaches from other schools stay at our Y. I don't give a damn about your being white! If you white fellows can't stay with your team, you ought to have black coaches up there!"

Of course, when we played in northern cities, we'd be given pretty good accommodations. But on our southern trips, we'd usually have to stay at the black YMCA. That's what we offered visiting teams in Louisville. It would cost us a dollar for each player we put up. We also had to pay the transportation and food expenses for the visiting team. Sometimes we didn't sell enough tickets to cover expenses. Then I'd get raked over the coals by the school administrators. "Johnson," they'd ask, "how is it that you've got a powerful team—you can beat anybody—but you can't make enough money to pay your bills?" I said: "That's easy to explain. Even when we fill our little cracker-box gym, we still only have 300 people. The white gyms at Male and Manual hold three or four times as many. Another reason is that the only nearby teams we can play are scrawny little fellows from places like Elizabethtown or Horse Cave. The Negro school at Bowling Green is so small it takes all the boys from the eighth and the twelfth grade to make one good team. People don't want to come see us clobber hell out of teams like that. We can put fifty-five boys in uniform, and we scare hell out of those little teams. They're no competition. Our real competition comes from the big Negro schools in other states, and they cost a lot of money to bring here."

I used to tell our coach that it was morally wrong to be playing those backwater schools. We had no business mauling some little team from out in the sticks. That's what we usually did, and the little players would go back home all bloody and bruised. Except for one time. One year we played a little black school from Lynch, Kentucky, and we got a big surprise. They only had eighteen players, and some of them had to play the entire sixty minutes. Only a handful of people came to the game because they didn't think it would be a contest. They were sure Central would slaughter the Lynch kids.

Before the game started, I was so bothered by the mismatch that I said to the Central coach: "For God's sake—and for the sake of public relations—don't run up the score too high on this pitiful team. Take over the game with your first team, then send in the fifth team to give them a little practice and to keep the score from getting too one-sided. But please don't humiliate these poor people from Lynch. Beat them, but don't crush them." He said: "Lyman, go on back and sell some tickets. Don't worry. You take care of the business end, and I'll take care of the playing end." I said, "All right, but I warn you: if you beat these little boys up too much, it'll be hard for me to get money to buy new equipment for you next year." When the game ended and we'd lost 13–7, the coach ran over to me and said: "Damn it, Lyman, don't you *ever* try to tell me how to run a game. You stick to selling tickets, and I'll stick to coaching." News that Central had lost to a puny eighteen-boy outfit from Lynch spread over town like wildfire. It was an embarrassment to us for years.

Central usually came out winning, but how could we know that we were champions? We were only allowed to play other black teams. On the other hand, how could the white teams call themselves Kentucky champions? They could only play other white teams. I've always told my students: "Don't brag about being the best *black* players in town. Be the best. Then you can brag." No one can know who is best till he's taken on all comers.

Before the schools were integrated, however, we got a chance to prove which teams were best. One year a white team from the eastern end of the state won the "state championship" in basketball. Prompted by the Central team's business manager, one Lyman T. Johnson, our students began writing letters to the paper, saying: "How can this white team gloat about being the state champions? They haven't played all comers." Before long I heard from that "championship" school. "Dear Mr. Johnson," they wrote, "we've read the letters from your students saying we can't be sure we're state champions till we've played all challengers. Put us on your schedule next year. We'd like to see how we rank." So we played them the next year and tore them to pieces! After that I told my students they could brag. But till you've taken on all comers, you can't brag. You can't brag that you're the best *black* anything! You can't brag that you're the best *white* anything! You can brag only when you're the best of all!

I've tried to apply that principle at all times inside the classroom as well as outside. One semester the son of the editor of the *Louisville Defender*, our black paper, wrote a paper in one of my classes about his professional ambitions. He thought he'd done a good job. He was smiling with pride when he came up to my desk to pick up his paper. I handed him the paper and said: "Son, just tear it up. Throw it in the trash can." He said: "But Mr. Johnson, I thought I wrote a good paper. I put in a lot of time on it. What's wrong with my paper?" I said, "Read your first sentence." He read, "This paper will show why I plan to be the best Negro journalist in the United States." I said: "Now stop. That's what's wrong! Son, I don't want you to be the best *Negro* journalist in the United States. I want you to be the best journalist. I've just had my appendix taken out by a Negro surgeon, not because he's one of the best Negro surgeons in town, but because he's one of the best surgeons. I certainly didn't choose him to put me to sleep and start chopping inside me because he was black!" I've always taught my students that one-race standards—whether black or white—are not good enough.

I have always objected to segregated education, but there wasn't much I could do about it as long as the Supreme Court approved. Occasionally, I would protest when my students had to sit in segregated sections at cultural events. I would tell them not to go. One time a school board member said, "Johnson, how can you expect those children to become cultured and refined if you keep them away from plays and concerts?" I said, "Mr. Board Member, you're not picking up much culture and refinement when you have to degrade yourself in the process."

Finally, in 1954 the Supreme Court gave its decision outlawing segregation in public schools. I was teaching at Central. Everybody was buzzing about it. To many of us it seemed like a second Emancipation Proclamation. For the first time, there was at least hope for equality in education. I went to the first school board meeting after the decision, and one of the board members looked at me and said: "Well, Mr. Johnson, we're going to have problems now, aren't we? There'll be headache after headache." I said: "We'll have no problems if people like you do what's right—and what's legal now. If you develop a headache, it'll be of your own making. Just remember that what I've been saying for years is now the law of the land. You and your people have been sitting in easy chairs a long time, and we've been sitting on the hard benches. So move over. We're all going to sit in the same chairs from now on."

The decision should have come sooner. Back in 1896 in the *Plessy* v. *Ferguson* decision, the court could have struck down segregation. Instead, it sanctioned an unequal society for another sixty years. Maybe the just decision would have caused another civil war. So what? We'd had one war and could have justified another one to finish the work. I'm a pacifist. I would rather not fight. But if I have to fight to get my natural rights, I'll do it. Negroes didn't rebel against legal second-class citizenship as they should have! And they had to put up with separate and unequal treatment for two more generations. Finally, the federal government came through, first the Supreme Court and then the Congress. That's why I love the federal government so much. It makes us all see that though we may live in a little province somewhere in south Mississippi, we're all citizens of one great big whole country.

I've always tried to teach my students straight history—not colored white or black or brown or yellow. And I've tried to teach about the bad as well as the good. I've tried to teach it all. Consequently, I've had to debunk much of what has been passed off as history. Historians have been too prone to embellish what they fantasize as the good life. Historians who pick out the glorious parts and gloss over the shaded parts are humbugs.

Take the so-called centennial history of Maury County, Tennessee, published back in 1876. I see very few references to black people. The statistics for 1850 show how many slaves and how many free people of color lived in the county. The book shows in detail the good life of people who lived on the backs of the slaves but almost nothing about how the slaves lived. It gives almost no credit to those people on whose backs the slaveowners rode to the good life. The slaves are treated just like the old mule hitched in the backyard. He got you to town, but you never told anybody that you rode him. I don't find any place in this purported history where black people are even given credit for washing Miss Ann's dirty drawers. Miss Ann certainly was too nice to wash them herself! Is there any mention of the long hours of unpaid service the slaves put in? Is there any mention of the house servant who was always on call and worked before daylight till way after dark? Is there any mention of the field hands who worked in the hot sun from the time the dew was still on the cotton till it got too dark to see? I don't see any mention of these people. Does it mention the good, God-fearing plantation owners who went to church and recited the Golden Rule and then did not do unto their slaves as they would have wanted to be done unto? There is here no mention of Mt. Lebanon Baptist Church, founded by slaves in 1843 and still going. My grandfather, Dyer Johnson, gave $100 to help start that church. That's history too. It's just as important as the Presbyterian church the book does mention—the one that would allow Negroes only if they sat up in the balcony. There is no mention of any black church or any black school. Aren't they a part of Maury County's history too?

The slaves and later the freedmen were treated like the foundation of a house. It's there. It's necessary because it holds up the house. But you don't show it. In this centennial history, the Negroes are hidden like the black people in the movie balcony in my boyhood. My father used to say: "They intend for you to go up there out of sight and sound in a dark place. Since you're black, you won't be seen in the darkness. And since you must keep quiet, you won't be heard. If you keep still in the dark, the white people won't even know you're watching the same movie."

Here is the last paragraph of this "history."

In view of all we have said; in view of the richness of her soil and the salubrity of her climate; in view of the water-power and other resources at her command; in view of the great progress made in agricultural and mechanic arts; in view of the intelligence and refinement of her people, their elevated moral and religious tone, and their unswerving patriotism and chivalry, Maury County cannot, consistently with her past history, fall back from her proud position among her sister counties. By every consideration of duty, interest, and honor, she is impelled to lead in the future, as she has done in the past. Let the memory of our sires, who found this a wilderness, but left it to their sons, ready to blossom as the rose, stimulate us to carry on the world of improvement begun by them, until, at no distant day, Maury County shall be what Nature designed her to be—a terrestrial Paradise.

Now what kind of history is that? It's Confederate rhetoric! It's hogwash!

For the first twenty years of my life, I lived under the influence of that kind of sloppy sentimentality that evaded reality. Don't misunderstand. For some white people, it was a glorious life. If you benefited from this way of life, you were bound to defend it. I understand why those Vanderbilt professors published their little book called *I'll Take My Stand* in 1930, extolling the gracious life of the southern aristocracy. When I was a kid, even the Negroes halfway believed the myth! They would say, "Tennessee is a nice place to live in, but Maury County is the dimple of the universe." Oh, Negroes could be just as chesty as white people in talking about this dimple of the universe, this garden spot of creation. My, we are proud of Maury County.

And it wasn't any better when I got to Virginia. Negroes up there had been fooled too. There was so much prejudice and crudeness between the races in Richmond. Segregation was everywhere. All the black people were "niggers." But at some high-class Negro affair, I would hear someone say, "I belong to the FFV." I'd say, "What in the hell is the FFV?" He'd say, "First Families of Virginia." And I'd say, "Hell, you mean the First Damn Niggers of Virginia." Yes, a lot of Negroes in my time were hoodwinked.

As a student I spent a lot of time trying to unhoodwink myself. In graduate school I specialized in southern history and did a pretty good job of digging up the truth. It meant I had to debunk a lot of the crap that had been written as history. All through the 1930s—even at schools like Princeton, Harvard, Yale, and Columbia—brilliant young "scholars," so-called, from the South came up and wrote their Ph.D. dissertations glorifying the slavocracy and the Southern Way of Life. I'm glad I've lived to see all that southern embellishment and "darkies are gay" and Gone-with-the-Wind crap debunked, just as I was trying to do at the University of Michigan.

One of my Michigan professors said, "Mr. Johnson, you are as right as can be, but no university is going to accept your ideas." I didn't expect them to then. They were all under the spell of that accepted authority on southern history—the biggest devil of them all—Ulrich Bonnell Phillips. Oh, he was the last word on southern history, and if you contradicted him, you simply didn't get your Ph.D. in southern history. That old devil is one reason I didn't get my Ph.D. The more I think about him, the more I hate him and all he stood for! He was a professor of history at the University of Georgia. He was a brilliant man, make no mistake about it. He was so prolific he rolled off material for book after book. But it was all fantasy passed off as history. It was a romantic dream, the myth of the glorious Old South.

Even the University of Michigan offered him a chair in its History Department. But Phillips said: "Oh, I'm doing all right down here. I'm not getting paid much, compared to what you fellows pay up there at Michigan, but I'm respected down here. And I take part of my pay in knowing that I'm doing something good for my fatherland." But Michigan kept on sending him offers. Finally, when he saw that his salary would be doubled, he agreed to move. "I'll come," he said, "and I'll attract a lot of students, and I'll write a lot of books, but there's one thing I won't do. I won't change my philosophy." The Michigan people said: "Oh, don't worry about your philosophy. We want just what you stand for." That was in the 1920s, but when I went there, his spirit was still walking around the campus. In my classes when I tried to refute his ideas, his spirit was there, saying: "Lyman, keep on saying that and you won't get a passing mark. You're refuting the accepted authority, Ulrich Bonnell Phillips!"

As incredible as it may seem, here was a prestigious northern university putting its stamp of approval on all the crap that old Phillips had been dishing out at the University of Georgia. But Phillips didn't stay there long. He went on to even better things—Yale. Yale said: "Professor Phillips, we want the best southern historian there is in the country. Forget what Michigan is paying you. We'll double it." So Phillips heeded the call of the dollar and went to Yale. From there he put his stamp on all historical scholarship about the South. If your research and approach didn't conform with Ulrich Bonnell Phillips, you didn't get a Ph.D. That's when all those brilliant young southern boys who had been thoroughly baptized in southern fantasy went up North and got themselves Ph.D.'s from the best schools. They ground out southern tripe in the name of history. Princeton was the worst offender of them all. It was called the southern man's northern university.

I hope I will not see my life go out before he is thoroughly and finally discredited for the way he embellished the Old South in his venomous books. One of them, *The Old South*, was dedicated to his three daughters who he hoped would grow up to love the South, although they were born in the North. Then he goes on for 400 or 500 pages of baloney about how happy the slaves were to be working out on the plantation for ol' master and ol' mistiss, how they all loved each other, and how reports of dissatisfaction from the slaves were just ballyhoo. Well, Phillips's book is ballyhoo. So how could Phillips be right? Happy, contented slaves don't threaten revolt.

As a graduate student and later as a teacher of history, I had to debunk much of what is called American history. A historian named Frederick Jackson Turner, who taught at the University of Wisconsin, came up with a thesis about how the West came to be settled. He said it was all a part of this country's manifest destiny. What is manifest destiny? It is just one polite excuse for white, Anglo-Saxon, Protestant arrogance. There were the mountains, rivers, deserts, Indians, Mexicans, Chinese, and Japanese—whatever and whoever—and then came the white man saying: "Get out of my way. It's God's will! Don't blame me if I have to push you around. God knows what He's doing through me." It was nothing more than another occasion for the white man to do as he damn well pleased.

I'm not saying the Spanish and French were much better. They were white Europeans too. When Africa was being chopped up in the late 1800s by Europeans, the Africans didn't know the difference between the English, the Germans, the French, and the Belgians. They were all devils. They were all Europeans.

But I see a difference in this hemisphere. And I believe it helps explain a lot of American racism. The Spanish, the Portuguese, and the French got to the New World first and took what they wanted. The English came last and took what was left. They also came for different reasons. The Spanish, the French, and the Portuguese admitted they came over here to get rich and to take their riches back home to enjoy with their wives and families in their homeland, but the English came with all they had, including their wives and children. The first Europeans didn't intend to make the new land their home. The English did. Since the Englishman had a different motive for coming over here, he set up a different pattern of life. He said: "I have a wife and children over here. So when I go out on the frontier and run into a black woman or an Indian woman, she and I can pull the shade down and have a little ping-pong party together. Women are all alike in the dark. But that's just for one night. When the sun comes up, it's a new day. So I have to leave and go back to my wife and children at home." Home for the English might be only a few yards or a few miles or a few hundred miles. But for the Frenchman or the Spaniard, home was several thousand miles away. So the Frenchman said: "Hell, I won't see my wife for five or six years. I might as well stay here tomorrow and tomorrow night too." The next day the chief said: "Now, look here, paleface, you have violated my daughter. What are your intentions?" And the white man said: "Oh, I love your daughter. I want to marry her. I want to play ping-pong with her every night." So the white man and the Indian woman would live together openly on the frontier as man and wife. When the little half-breed children started coming, he claimed them as his own. That made the Indians respect the French and caused them to side with them in wartime.

On the other hand, the Indians despised the Englishman because he would violate the Indian girl and then scrap her and go home to his family in the settlements. He knew he had to sit with his wife and children in their regular pew in church on Sunday morning. But come Monday night he'd be back down in the wigwam with the Indian girl. Of course, the Frenchman might also desert his Indian wife after he got his riches, but the Englishman never made any pretense about living as man and wife with a colored woman. The self-righteous, puritanical, hypocritical Englishman never treated his colored sex mates with anything but condescension. Much of the racism, therefore, in American culture can be laid at the feet of the Anglo-Saxon Protestant.

Catholic Europeans were generally more gracious to dark-skinned people, whether Negro or Indian. Maybe it was partly because they were more olive complexioned themselves. Maybe it was partly because their church told them that God would punish them if they mistreated inferior people. So when the priests and the bishops, backed up by the pope, breathed down the necks of the ordinary Catholics, there was a better relationship between master and servant.

The English Protestants were not much in awe of authority. They had told the pope to go to hell and had chopped off a king's head. The Englishman was left with no absolute authority—except himself. He had become a god unto himself. That's why the Englishman felt that everyone should bow to him—king, pope, and God! And the Englishman in America felt he was the only authority he needed. "Here I come," he said. "Get out of the way." There is still a lot of resentment by Latin Americans of mixed blood against Anglo-Saxon Protestant Americans. Remember what happened when Richard and Pat Nixon went to South America with their haughty, white, superior attitudes. Those Spanish and Portuguese people spat in Pat Nixon's face. Oh, they'll play Uncle Tom when they have to, grinning and smiling in the white man's face. But after they get the money and the technical know-how to build their industries and sky-scrapers, watch out. They're getting bolder.

The time of Northern European and North American Anglo-Saxon, Germanic domination is almost at an end. Hitler's blatant Aryan racism was the beginning of the end. Soon we people in the United States will no longer be able to call ourselves Americans. It's always been a haughty concoction that ignores people in Argentina, Brazil, Chile, and all the other countries of this hemisphere. When a man from Argentina goes to Europe, he never says, "I'm an American." He says, "I'm an Argentine." Canadians are just as blond and blue-eyed as people from the United

States, but they don't rear back and say, "We're Americans." They say, "We're Canadians." But here comes a cocky son of a gun from the United States who says, "I'm an American." If we don't have a word for an inhabitant of the United States *of* America, we ought to make one up. But, no, we're so haughty that we take over all of North and South America and say, "We're Americans."

Another romantic fable I've done my best to expose concerns why Europeans came to the New World. By and large, they didn't come here to spread the Christian religion. They came here to get rich. The Spanish and the Portuguese came to get gold from the Indians. When they didn't find enough, they'd make the Indians go down in the mines and dig up more. English and French privateers waited on the high seas to rob their gold-laden ships. They were robbing the robbers! There was nothing honorable or Christian to any of it!

The Puritans and Pilgrims were a bit more sincere about religion, but they were interested only in freedom of worship for themselves. They couldn't get along with the English church because they thought it hadn't gone far enough in purifying itself of Rome. About all it had done, they said, was remove the pope and replace him with the king. Not long after they arrived in the New World—their New Jerusalem—they started building ships and plying the seas with their slave trade. Whatever religious principles and intentions they had soon gave way to greed.

Some of these people were good people, truly God-fearing. But in the story of mankind, good people are always so scarce. Why? Why? Why? So many of the early white Americans went to church and prayer meeting and read their Bibles. But see how they treated the black people, the Indians—even the poor whites. There is no way to square their treatment of these people with their Christian principles.

So many history books on Western civilization cover only the good things. In my classes I tried to balance the record. I'd tell my students: "I hope old Leopold, that devil Belgium king, is still roasting in hell for the way he forced black people in the Congo to bring rubber sap into the villages. He paid them nothing and beat them if they didn't do it." I got a lot of my first-hand information on African colonialism from a Negro Presbyterian missionary named Shepherd, who used to live in Louisville. He said if women claimed they couldn't carry a five-gallon bucket of rubber sap on their heads, the Belgians would take a pronged, hooked, metal instrument and pull out their breasts and with a sharp knife chop them off and then say: "Anyone else want to claim you're too weak to carry these buckets? Now, get on back there and bring in the rubber!" When a black man would complain, the Belgians would pull his tongue out, chop it off, and say, "Now, go ahead and say what you want to." To get the natives to bring in the rubber sap, they'd mutilate other parts of the body in public.

Cecil Rhodes was just as bad. He'd send recruiters to Angola to find laborers to work in his Johannesburg gold mines. The blacks would have to walk for three months over 1,500 miles and then work for almost nothing. If that's Christianity at work, I want no part of it. This kind of Western civilization flowered out into its naked meanness under Hitler.

Our economic system is rotten to the core. It's responsible for so many of the problems black people face today, from racism to the breakup of the family. Negroes have so many economic problems these days it's a marvel that any of them stay married ten minutes! The father can't get a job. He's no good to the woman and the kids. They can do better under our welfare system if he leaves. So get rid of him! Our capitalist system has never provided a solution to that problem. It goes back to the days of slavery. Any children my grandmother had down in Tennessee before she was bought by my grandfather belonged to her master. They were his property. They were a part of his profits under that capitalist system. They were slaves, and all slaves were assets—to be used any way the owner wanted. If the master got into economic difficulty and needed money, he'd not hesitate to sell the mother one way, the father a second way, and a child a third way. The Negro family has been a permanent victim of the American economic system.

This country is based on ruthless, cutthroat capitalist competition. Profit is the only principle. There is no true Christianity within 10,000 miles of our economics. I've always been torn between all those beautiful religious concepts that my father and mother planted in me and the vulture practices of our "Christian" economic system.

I know I'm out of step with most Americans. I plead guilty to being a leftist. But I don't care. I'm in good company. Jesus Christ himself in whose name capitalism has been promoted was not a capitalist. He was a Communist if there ever was one! To call myself a Christian, then, I've got to follow in his footsteps. It's redundant to refer to Christian socialism. Socialism to me is Christian. Jesus said to the capitalist, the rich, young ruler, "Give all you've got to feed the poor, and then come back and I'll tell you what else to do." The young capitalist said: "Go to hell, Jesus. I can't do that." And he never came back.

We make a big to-do about the Christian principles on which the country was founded. Why don't we tell the truth? Most of the people who came here didn't come for "Christian principles." England unloaded her jails and sent the jailbirds over here to Georgia. The Spanish came over here and took all the gold they could get from the Indians. When they got halfway home with their loot, Queen Elizabeth would send her seadogs to rob the robbers. She told Sir Walter Raleigh and all the rest of her bastards: "If you rob the Spanish and bring your treasures home, I'll take half and

give you half. If you don't, I'll have you killed for piracy on the high seas."
Was that Christianity at work? Hell, no, that's highway thuggery. It was
piracy of the first order, and to gloss over it with any idea of "Christian
principles" is to pervert the name Christian. What about those God-
fearing Puritans up there in Massachusetts, Rhode Island, and Connecticut? Most of their big shots got rich off the slave trade. Church deacons
paid their dues off profits they made selling slaves. And you call that
Christianity? If Jesus Christ had come through about that time, he would
have taken a whip and run 'em all out, saying: "I did it once. I did it 2,000
years ago, and I'll do it again. Give me the whip! You have made a den of
thieves out of my house!"

I know that Christianity sets a very high standard. I know that greed is
a characteristic of human nature—of all nature. When I was a kid, I'd take
half a biscuit, throw it out in the backyard, and watch the chickens'
reactions. One chicken would look all around, then rush over, get the
biscuit and run off in a corner, spin it around, and peck it to pieces. He
knew if he stayed where the other chickens could see him, they'd run over
and take some. So he hid with his treasure till he could eat it all. That's
nature and that's human nature. We have to acknowledge it. On the other
hand, society is possible because of people's ability to discipline themselves. If we do not work constantly at overcoming the greed of nature,
then we become as selfish as any beast of the woods. There are always a
few people who try to control themselves. These are the people who help
to condition other people to become socialist in nature—to work for the
common good.

What is the role of government? Government should do for people
what they cannot do for themselves as individuals or in small groups.
Here is a good example. The Tennessee River is too huge for one little
town along its banks to dam it up and make it work big hydroelectric
turbines. It's too big a project for all the towns on the river or for all of
Tennessee or for all of the South. The whole resources of the United States
are needed to control the Tennessee River. Then when the electricity is
ready, it ought to be sold cheaply to the people. After all, it was their taxes
that built it. It ought not to be sold to a bunch of vultures like Commonwealth Southern, which tried many years ago to buy TVA electricity
cheaply and sell it at a high price to the people. I used to complain loudly,
and people would say, "But that's in keeping with our capitalist system."
And I'd say, "Well, that's where our 'capitalist system' is dead wrong." It's
wrong for capitalists to pressure politicians to give them electricity, which
they are going to sell around Paducah on down to Memphis, at a price five
or six times what the people would have had to pay if they got it directly
from TVA. Those greedy capitalists had a good thing for themselves till a
bunch of us socialists exposed it. It was the people who built TVA, and it

ought to be the people who receive benefits from it. That's socialism of the first degree. You can call it communism if you want to!

I will toss capitalism one grudging compliment. The capitalist system got us on the road. But whatever benefits it got for us in developing this country, it has now outlived its usefulness. Sensible people ought to move on to higher ground and adopt a system that will wipe out poverty, ignorance, and disease. The New Deal that we started back in the 1930s was a great step forward, but those social changes made the capitalists cry like everything. And they were the very ones who had led us into the worst depression this country has known. They were the ones who took us to the bottom of the trough. The New Deal measures were stopgap and went only as far as tradition and mores would let us, which wasn't far enough. Since then we've only been refining those measures—like Social Security—and we've not gone the extra mile to get the job done the way it ought to be. Many of the people who benefit from this halfway socialism won't call it socialism, but that's what it is.

You can't blame our welfare system on socialism. It's not socialistic. It's been bad for the people. People at the bottom have come to rely too much on government. They've become too dependent. They ought not to be given free food stamps. They ought not to be given free housing. They ought to be made to work for it. That's socialism! Some people jump right straight on me and say, "Lyman, you want to give away all that the rich people have!" And I say, "Yes, I want to 'give' it away to people who will work for it." Why should I work every day and be taxed to pay the man who won't work to keep himself alive? If he contributes to the Gross National Product, I don't mind his sharing in it.

It's the capitalists who are responsible for our half-assed system. They won't let the government provide jobs that private enterprise cannot provide. If I run a shoe repair shop on the corner, I may need only three people to do the work. But the man across the street needs a job. I can't hire him if I don't need him. If I did, I'd go bankrupt. But what about that flood wall? We've built three-fourths of it. Why the hell don't we finish it? There are still a lot of people at the mercy of the Ohio River. Give that unemployed man I can't afford to hire a useful job working on the flood wall. In the long run, he'll benefit not only himself but all of us. There are farmers out in California who could raise more lettuce, carrots, and peas if their lands were irrigated. Why not put that unemployed man to work building an irrigation system to tap all the water from the Colorado River? We have to give him food and a place to live anyway. Make him work for it. There's still a lot of work to do. Put him to work.

It doesn't bother me how much of the economy the government would own and control. I don't care if the government takes it all. After all, we are the government. And government should be run for the benefit of all of the people. Unfortunately, we often have a bunch of bureaucrats in charge who run the government as if they own the 'corporation' and are working for themselves. I'd like to say to the governor right now: "Look, Mr. Governor, I call you the Honorable So-and-So, but I don't know why you should be called 'honorable.' You're just a hired hand, just the top hired hand of the state of Kentucky. Now damn it, get about *our* business and do *our* work! We're giving you a lot of honor, a mansion to live in, a helicopter to fly about in, and a lot of cash. You ought to earn it! You and the president and the janitor are all alike. You were all hired to perform services for us."

There need be no conflicts between democracy and socialism. I don't like to use the term *Christian Socialism* because 90 percent of the people who use the word *Christian* don't know what it means. They don't know it's a powerful, radical word. So I say I believe in Democratic Socialism, which means that the government is under the control of the people and exists for their benefit.

Government can be just as efficient as private enterprise and a lot more humane. Building flood walls is beyond the conscience of any local business concern. In addition, private business doesn't have the clout to operate in certain areas. If, for the common good, a private piece of property needs to be taken, only the government can exercise eminent domain. If the government needs private property to benefit society as a whole and agrees to pay fair compensation, a private individual should not be allowed to stand in the way. Private companies usually don't have the financial ability, the legal authority, or the conscience to do things for the common good that government can do.

Whatever government does best for the people, it should do. Whatever private enterprise does best for the people, it should do. The two branches of society can often work well together. For example, the Jefferson County School System has a maintenance staff for its schools and other property. Usually, they can keep the buildings in good shape, but when big jobs come along, it might be best to let out bids and hire a private contractor. It would be wasteful for the school system to keep a maintenance staff large enough to meet all emergencies. Most of the workers would sit around idle most of the time.

What happens when an industry—say, the railroads—gets into trouble and starts to lose money? Essential private industry should not be allowed to take such big chunks out in the name of profit and dividends that they don't have enough money to run on. We have to have a transportation system, and the railroads know it. So they dump the defunct, no-longer-profitable system on the government. The government reaches over into the common treasury and takes enough money to get the industry back on its feet. Then the capitalist vultures come back and say: "All right. It's running again. Turn the railroads back over to us." What they want to do is take over again and run them as before, which means taking out huge profits and giving them to private individuals. We shouldn't allow that. After the government has bailed out an industry, any profits should be used for the public good, such as building schools and hospitals. It's crazy to give an industry back to the damn fools who ran it into bankruptcy in their greed for profit.

I gave the students in my American history classes many examples of public abuse by private enterprise. Back when the New York Central Railroad was being built, members of the state legislature were *given* stock in the railroad corporation for nothing. They paid nothing! What they did was vote to give the rights-of-way for the railroad to pass through. But why pick on New York? The L & N did the same thing right here in Kentucky. Back in the 1890s the legislature took Kentucky for a ride, a railroad ride. The politicians were sent over to Frankfort to protect the interests of the people of Kentucky but sold out to the L & N Railroad. I don't know how much they got. There's no way to tell.

There are examples from all over the country. Up in Michigan, Wisconsin, Minnesota, and across to Washington State, the railroads were given a strip of land ten miles wide along their rail route. The companies cut the timber down and got rich. The money went into private pockets. Why didn't the government cut the trees down and use the money to support schools? Instead, the schools had to get by on handouts.

The capitalist system appeals to our love of gambling and our greed. I used to tell my students it was like a poker game or a game of marbles played for keeps. A poker player says to himself: "I know all the players can't win. But I believe I'll be the one who does." Used to, little boys about ten or twelve would draw a large ring in the dirt yard. Each one would put in three marbles. After about ten boys had put in their marbles, they'd take turns trying to thump them out. After fifteen minutes two boys would be on the fence, looking down at the other eight still shooting. After about two hours, there'd be eight boys on the fence, looking down at the two boys still playing. Finally, nine of the boys would be broke. They'd lost all their marbles. That's the capitalist society, playing for keeps. My mother and father wouldn't let me play for keeps. They said: "That's gambling, and you can't do that. It's trying to get more than is rightfully yours. It's stealing from the weak and the unlucky."

When the little marble players got a little bigger, they'd get two bones, little cubes with dots on them—dice. But the outcome was the same. Sooner or later, you'd have nine young men sitting on the fence broke. Older and more sophisticated men play the stock market up in New York. But it's all a gamble, whether playing marbles or playing the stock market, and it's based on the hope that *I* won't be the one to lose. And what is the loser's consolation? "Well, I've had a little recreation. And next time I'll win!" Every player knows that not everyone can win, but each one thinks he'll be the lucky one. It's like betting on the Kentucky Derby or playing bingo. Not long ago a man said to me: "Lyman, now I'm down and out. But I won't be down and out forever. I have faith I'm going to hit the jackpot. So I'll keep on gambling." I said, "Man, don't you know the slot machine is fixed to keep the sucker broke?" He said: "Yeah, I know that 90 percent will lose. But I'm going to be one of the lucky 10 percent."

Most poor suckers think they have an even chance, but they never do. The odds are always against them. There's always someone smarter or craftier than he is. I have a very brainy, well-read nephew who's a member of that egghead society called Mensa. When he was about fifteen, he was in my house one day playing solitaire. My three-year-old daughter came in the door, saw him so engrossed in his cards, and asked, "What's that you're playing, Tom?" He tried to explain the game to her, but of course she couldn't understand it. But I know she understood one statement he made. "I never play any game where the sucker has an even chance to win." Under a purely capitalist system, the odds are against most of us suckers.

I think morality—not profit—should be the cardinal principle of a good economic system. Honesty, truth, and fair play ought to attract customers to my store. They'll come, I believe, if they know I don't put my hands on the scale when I'm weighing a piece of meat and if they know I'll never try to sell them a bad piece of merchandise at regular price. I'll go back to the mechanic who does a good job and charges a reasonable price. One Sunday afternoon several years ago I had a fellow change a tire for me. He charged me $4.75, which was twice too much. But I had to have it done. He knew I had to have it done. I will never buy a thimbleful of gas from him! A good man would never take advantage of a situation like that.

Oh, yes, I've been called a Communist. But I've decided it's best to ignore such defamations. Not long ago a woman called me and said: "Mr. Johnson, did you know that So-and-So called you a Communist on the radio? Why don't you make them give you time to refute it?" I said: "Ma'am, I have the feeling that if I attempt to fight it, I will dignify the accusation. Regardless of how I defend myself, some people will believe it anyway. So I will ignore it."

Like a lot of Americans, I had a hard time during the Depression. That experience made me question our capitalist system and see values in socialism. I couldn't get a job. I was willing to work anywhere, do anything. Nobody wanted me to teach Greek. So I tried to teach history. But there were thirty or forty applicants for every job in the classroom. I even applied for a job as a redcap at the bus station and the train station. But they were turning out redcaps. I tried to be a waiter, but there were no openings. I couldn't get a job at any kind of plant. There I was, an able-bodied, intelligent, well-educated young man. What was I to do? Starve?

It was then that I decided the problem was not poor production but poor distribution of resources. We were burning wheat out in Iowa, wheat that could have kept people from going hungry. We were dumping milk on the ground in Wisconsin, milk that could have kept babies from starving. We were driving pigs into the Ohio River here in Kentucky, pigs that would have made some mighty nice pork chops for hungry families. And we did it all because of the fetish of dog-eat-dog capitalism and its almighty profit. If you can't sell wheat for a profit, burn it. If you can't sell pigs for a profit, drown them. If milk won't sell, pour it out. Then let the government pay for it. But what about hungry people? Food was being destroyed, and people were going hungry. You didn't have to go to college to see that there was no logic to that system.

I'll admit I was a fit candidate for wrecking this country! Instead, I spent more than two years in graduate school at Michigan. It kept me from turning Communist. But I did attend so-called labor schools over in Detroit. They were actually Communist outfits. They challenged anyone to refute what they were saying—that the capitalist system was not working. But no one challenged them. No one could explain the burned wheat, the dumped milk, the drowned pigs. These labor people helped us start a co-op bookstore on the Michigan campus in Ann Arbor. We took books on consignment and sold them for 10 percent over the cost. Private bookstores were making a 40 percent or 50 percent profit. We'd sell our books as fast as we got them in. We also opened up a co-op eating place. I was right in the middle of these socialist enterprises, promoting and proving that they would work. Capitalists went to the legislature and tried to put us out of business.

The Communists helped us. But we were not Communists. We were not anarchists. Most of us were conscientious socialists. We had nothing to do with that crazy bunch of people who were out to burn and destroy and kill just for the fun of it. We socialists had to keep our eyes wide open so we wouldn't be duped. We kept a distance between ourselves and the Communists. We never signed any cards or papers. They did their best to rope us and send us out as their missionaries. But we knew they wanted to start a violent revolution and wanted us blacks to help. Of course, a revolution would not have been successful in this country, not even during the darkest days of the Depression. If a revolution had started like the Russian Revolution of 1917, it would have been wiped out right straight by the capitalist establishment. They had—and have—control of the soldiers and the weapons, and a violent overthrow of the government was not possible then. And it's certainly not possible now.

In 1917 it was different in Russia. There over 90 percent of the people were down-and-out. They were living on dirt floors. They're better off now. But we can't measure their success by our standards. We have to measure them by Russian standards of 1917. The same is true in China and Cuba. Measure the success of the Chinese Revolution against the standard of living when Mao Tse-tung took over. Measure Castro's success by the living standards under Batista. It was Booker T. Washington who said: "Don't judge me by your standards. Measure me by how far I have come from where I was."

We blacks—almost to a man—have found it to our benefit to string along with the establishment. And in this country the establishment has always been capitalistic. We would have been slaughtered if we'd tried to overthrow the system. We have tried, therefore, to survive within the establishment rather than be butchered by it. Nevertheless, the hunger marches on Washington in the last months of the Hoover administration showed how desperate a lot of people had become. Just a little bit more suffering without any hope of relief, and I would have joined them.

Instead, I have stayed within the system and have preached my brand of socialism. Back in the 1930s we socialists insisted that the American economic structure needed a major overhaul. We wanted to put people to work, and we wanted to charge prices based on production costs. But the straight capitalists said, "Oh, no, that's no way to run a business." We said: "We're not interested in how business used to be run. We're interested in taking out-of-work people off the streets and giving them constructive work to do." To us, it seemed simple. People work. They produce. They are paid wages. They buy. More people work. Everybody benefits.

I have always preached the gospel of work. When I was teaching economics, I sometimes had trouble staying inside the ballpark. But I always did because I insisted that every able-bodied person should work. When Franklin Roosevelt and his bunch started their experiment with Social Security, I was opposed to *giving* anybody anything. I wanted everybody to earn what he received. I still do.

The American system was in real danger throughout the 1930s, but not from us blacks. It was in danger of destroying itself. I think Hitler saved the American capitalist system—or what was left of it. The Germans had a depression years before it got to us. When the little paperhanger came along, he said he'd put people to work. He did. But he had to cook up a war to do it. His wars put unemployed Germans to work, and World War II put a lot of Americans to work.

So I can't give Roosevelt much credit for saving the American capitalist system. His programs were not solid remedies for what was ailing the economy. Whenever you give people food, clothing, and shelter without having them work, you encourage a bad attitude toward work.

When a healthy person consumes without producing, he is a cheat and a fraud. In the 1930s, then, our government tried to buy the people off by giving them things they hadn't earned. It didn't work for the Romans. The Roman generals went out and extracted grain and stuff from the provinces and brought it into Rome and swapped it for the people's support. Finally, the Romans got to the place where they would not work. They were not worth a cuss. "Why should I work?" they would say. "I'll wait till General So-and-So comes. He'll bring us food. He always has." When Rome got to the place where the people thought they could live without working, the empire went to pieces. It also happened in Spain and Portugal in the 1400s and 1500s. The people began waiting for the ships to come back from the provinces loaded with supplies, and they stopped producing. As a man of history, I know there are many reasons why nations go on the decline. Trying to live without working is one of them.

And the United States—God bless her!—had better wake up and realize that capitalism has carried us just about as far as it can. It's like an old jalopy that needs to be abandoned and pushed off the side of the road. We need a new machine to carry us on to the next station. I don't know precisely the kind of vehicle we'll need to take us there. What I know is that the present machine is not working well. When an economy produces high unemployment and high inflation at the same time, something is wrong with that economy.

I believe the new machine, the new system, will be some form of socialism. We must have a planned society where every able-bodied person works. If a man is missing a hand or a leg, I suppose we can excuse him. Or maybe we'll let him simply use his mind and teach something—like Greek! But he'll have to do something. Everybody will do something.

I think it's wrong to give people in ghettos in Detroit and Philadelphia and Louisville food and supplies and to subsidize their rent. I used to be chairman of an apartment house for the elderly and handicapped, where renters were required to pay no more than one-fourth of their income for rent, up to about $190 a month. Some people paid only $25 a month. I don't think they should have been *given* that extra $165 each month. Somebody has to pay it. You don't just pull money out of thin air. Why couldn't such people be given something useful to do? Let them weave baskets, if nothing else.

Although I don't think the Roosevelt administration can be given much credit for patching up our economy, I can't criticize their make-work projects like the WPA and the PWA. Many of them were very worthwhile and needed doing. More important, the people worked for what they got. On the other hand, when the government starts handing out money to people for no work—such as the aid to dependent widows—you start a class of people who expect to be paid for not working. I'm simply opposed to handouts. If a man is destitute, I'll give him dinner tonight, a nice cot with clean linens to sleep on, and breakfast tomorrow. Then I'll tell him: "Now, buddy, don't come back for lunch with clean hands. Do some work between now and lunchtime and show me your dirty hands. Then you can come in to the lunch table."

Don't ever mistake my goodness for stupidity. Don't think I'm dumb enough to sweat out in the hot sun while Joe's resting in the cool shade and then share equally with him. If I go fishing and on my way back should pass Joe and say, "Hey, Joe, what you been doing?" and he should say, "Oh, I been sitting around playing marbles all day," then I would say: "Well, Joe, you can go home now and eat your marbles. You can't come home with me to eat my fish." I'll go home, put a deadbolt lock on my door, and fry my fish in a hot skillet. The pangs of hunger and the smell of my fried fish might entice Joe to my door, but I'll not let him in. I hope he'll see the error of his ways and tomorrow go fishing for himself and plant his own bean patch. I *know* he's not going to eat my fish and beans today. I'll share my last bean and last piece of fish with a helpless person. But if you're able, you get out in the field and sweat. I want to see that sweat roll down! I want to see that you've made some effort to help yourself. Then if you still need help, I'll do what I can.

In my ideal commonwealth, everybody works. I like to let each person choose what he will do, but damn it, he will have to do something constructive, something that other people say they want done. I would have everyone contribute something to what we call in good American English the Gross National Product, the GNP. Maybe I would have 1,000—or 6,000—job titles, and I'd say: "All right now, pick out what you want to do, then damn it, do it! I don't care if your name is John D. Rockefeller XX; you will have to contribute something to this society. If you want to be an artist, that's fine, provided people want your kind of art. Otherwise, you're going to have to do something else that is marketable to earn your bread. After you've made your bread, you can do any kind of art you want to. You can paint pictures nobody wants, and you can play music for your own enjoyment. You can even study Greek and read the New Testament for personal satisfaction. But first you've got to do something to earn your bread."

It's important for white people to study all of American history, not just white American history. It's important for white people to study all of Western civilization, not just white contributions to Western civilization. It's important for white people to study all of world history, not just the roles that whites have played in it. In this country our history books have romanticized and exaggerated the contributions of white people to the almost total neglect of nonwhite people in the world. If a white person learns only the white half of history, he becomes a half-baked scholar. It's false teaching to ignore the parts played by any group in history—whether black, Indian, Hispanic, or Asian.

As a historian I try to be objective and to take a long view of human civilization. Sometimes I get pessimistic, especially when I think about the horrors that darken our past. When I realize that almost everything that Western civilization has produced has been geared toward destruction, I want to close my eyes and stop my ears. But I must face facts. The concentration camps of World War II were, in many respects, the fatal flowering of Western civilization. We have been hell-bent on destruction. The good things we enjoy have been mainly side effects and by-products of the lust for destruction. Our civilization is based on the power to destroy. Atomic energy, hydrogen energy, nuclear research—all are basically for destruction. We may eventually use nuclear energy to heat our homes and propel our cars, but we developed it mainly to destroy the Japanese or the Russians—or whoever our enemy happens to be. Ironclad ships were not constructed originally for pleasure cruises. They were made to destroy Confederate ships. If we really wanted to do away with heart disease, cancer, and kidney disease, we could stop producing war implements and use the funds for peace and health. But we won't. Our energy and our wealth continue to go mainly to destroy.

I try not to despair. I try not to give up. If we give up, things will get even worse. We've got to keep running like hell to keep from falling behind. The most industrious fellow—to use a religious image—who walks the earth is the devil. He never sleeps. He's always ready to attack, to slay, to devour. He's awake when good people lie down to sleep. "Eternal vigilance is the price of liberty," Jefferson said. It's also the price of keeping together what little civilization we have. If we give up, we're lost.

I believe American blacks can contribute a lot to making this world more peaceful. They can help break down walls between people and nations. We must get to the point where no one gets any credits—or demerits—because of his color, his family's economic status, his religion, or his nation. We've got to learn to treat everybody right, regardless of who a fellow is or where he's from.

American blacks are in an unusual position. Immediately, they feel a kinship with other nonwhite people all over the world as soon as they come into contact with them. Those black boys who went over to Vietnam—and my son was one of them—were put in a terrible position. In the battle zone, a black soldier zeroed in on a colored Asian, and he had to pull the trigger—he had to pull it in the name of the white man. It was almost as if the brown enemy was saying to him: "Hey, colored man, what are you doing over here trying to kill me? You're no more white than I am." Long ago, black and brown and yellow Americans learned this: As long as they hold up the American flag, they're white—no matter what color they are. The American red, white, and blue flag means white. Colored people around the world still see the American flag as a symbol of white supremacy. But if you're black and are wearing the uniform of the United States, you have to shoot at the man who's shooting at that flag. If you don't, you're a traitor. What a strange predicament for an American black soldier to be in!

Black people have always been a minority in this country. Most of us never thought very much about the fact that we are actually a part of a worldwide majority of nonwhite people. Now we are aware! I get a kick out of going into a practically all-white audience and reminding them of it. Not long ago I was talking to a group of about 450 people at a Presbyterian church. The only blacks there were my wife, me, and the Negro custodian. I said: "Ladies and gentlemen, in this room and in this country, you white people can do just about anything you please because of majority rule. But please be careful how you treat us colored minorities because once you get outside the United States, *you* are the minority. When you leave these borders and go into most parts of the world, you no longer carry the protection of being white. In fact, your white face is a badge of dishonor to most people of the world. It represents exploitation, injustice, and prejudice. If you've got any sense, you'll learn to get along with the other four-fifths of the world. In the long run, you know you can't whip them."

The fact that he is a part of a world majority is the black man's best protection in this country. I know I'm a minority in Louisville, Kentucky, but when I go up to the United Nations building in New York and look out at the people representing the nations of the world, I see few white faces. The white man is mighty scarce in the world.

In the future the white man is going to be drinking from the same cup as the black man. And he'd better not wipe the rim or go wash his mouth out and gargle with an antiseptic to get rid of nasty "nigger germs." Even a politician like George Wallace knows now that we're all going to drink from the same cup. When he last ran for governor of Alabama, he even reached down and picked up a little black baby and kissed him! He couldn't have done that ten years ago. The white people of Alabama would have killed him. Now the black man says: "Look, man, I got to vote for George. He done kissed my baby." George Wallace hasn't really been converted to anything. He just knows good politics. George Wallace knows he has to survive in a new world. The Vietnam War was a turning point. For the first time, the white United States was defeated by a colored race.

A young black intellectual stopped by to visit me recently, and we talked from half past ten till half past two in the morning. He listened to my philosophy of history and my ideas about the world of tomorrow. Then he looked at his watch and said: "It's late. Get my hat and let me go. If you were twenty or thirty years younger, you would be a hell of a threat to this society." I never intended to undermine this society, only the parts that needed undermining. In my classes I tried to teach my students the truth as I understood it. I tried to give them a perspective on history that would help them face the future as informed, proud, and confident human beings who happened to be born black.

Black & White Niggers

Everybody in the South was a victim of slavery. . . . The American economic system has worked to the disadvantage of all colors of poor people.

WHEN I WAS a little boy in Columbia, Tennessee, I heard people talk about the masondixieline. I thought it was one word. It wasn't till I saw the word in a history book that I realized it was Mason-Dixon Line. But I always knew it meant one thing to black people—freedom. Before the Civil War, for slaves in Tennessee, Mississippi, and Alabama, it meant the Ohio River. To escape slavery, they knew they had to make it to that river. "Keep on running," they were told. "You better be prepared to keep on running. You may get away from your master's plantation, but it won't do you any good if you wake up on another master's plantation. He'll just put you to work as his slave till somebody comes and identifies you, puts you in chains, and takes you back. So you better run on. And don't stop once you cross that river. The southern parts of freedom land are rough. Run on till you reach northern Ohio or Michigan. And if you want to clinch your freedom, you better keep on to Canada."

Some blacks today don't like to talk about slavery. They try to pretend it never existed. But I'm a history man, and I have to know the past and tell the truth about it. We blacks must look at slavery and what it meant to our fathers and how it affects us today. We even have to admit the complicity of Africans in the enslavement of their brothers. African tribes fought each other for two things: cattle and women. So one tribe would beat another tribe and take its cattle and women. A white man would come by and say, "What you going to do with these men over there in the corral?" The African would say: "Oh, we gonna kill them. If we turn them loose, they might come back and kill us and take all our cattle and women." So then the white man would say: "Oh, what a shame. Don't kill them. I'll give you ten dollars a piece for them." He'd chain them up, take them down to his slave ship, bring them to the New World, and sell them for a nice profit.

The slave dealer also bought Africans in jail. The authorities didn't have bars and stone walls to hold in the criminals, and it was a mess to hold a bunch of men in a yard and dare them to leave. So the white trader would offer five dollars apiece. The authorities took it because they picked up a little money and got the jailbirds off their hands. They also felt good because they didn't have to kill anyone who might have tried to escape.

This is my point: Black people sold black people to white people. I'm not saying that white slavers didn't also capture and steal Africans. Of course they did. But we cannot put all the blame for the slave trade on whites. Some of it rests on blacks. I'm not lifting the burden of guilt for slavery from white shoulders. White people must bear the lion's share of responsibility. They were the ones who benefited most from it. They had the benefit of slaves who did all their dirty work in the house and in the cotton, rice, and tobacco fields. They made the profits. But one of the ironies of American slavery is that if black Africans hadn't cooperated, slaves would not have been brought here in such great numbers. And the South might not have become so dependent on slave labor. The South could surely have developed without the help of the slave. But I'm a historian and have to deal not with what-might-have-been but with what was. The fact is, then, the South developed on the backs of the black slaves.

I try not to be too hard on the South. The kind of slavery that developed in the Western Hemisphere was profitable only in a plantation economy. The slave was not profitable in an industrial society. If slavery had been profitable in the northern states and in Canada, it would never have been outlawed. All capitalism is based on profits. If a thing pays, you keep it. If it's profitable, it's good. Morality has nothing to do with it.

When you get to the far North, the winters last too long for slavery to pay. The slaves were used to warmer climates. Many slaves who escaped from the lower South to Canada found the weather there rough sledding and moved back as far as they could with safety. Last March here in Louisville I heard a man from Canada say: "It's good to see your forsythia already blooming. It'll be five weeks before ours begins. We still have six inches of snow on the ground." That's the reason slavery didn't work in those cold climates. In winter weather you've got $1,000 or more wrapped up in a slave, and it's too cold for him to go out and work. But you've still got to feed, shelter, clothe, and protect him. He's a deadweight expense. You can't make him work hard enough in four or five months to make up for the seven or eight months you've carried him. A free labor system is the only one that is profitable in that kind of climate—and in the industrial societies, it was soon able to develop.

Kentucky's winters are longer and more severe than those in the plantation country down south. That's one reason there were so many slave breeders here. It was a way of making slavery profitable in a marginal climate. But slave breeding took a long time and was a long-term investment. A slave wasn't really valuable till he got to be about eighteen or twenty. The younger ones were worth something, but till a child passed thirteen or so, he likely cost his owner more than he was producing.

There were compensations, I suppose, for being a slave. It was in the best interests of the owner to make sure slaves got adequate food and medical care. After all, they represented the bulk of the plantation master's wealth. Even the discipline forced on the slave was mostly to his own good. The master would say: "It's Saturday night, and you've worked hard all week. So I want you all to have a good time. But don't get drunk. Don't get into fights. Don't carouse too much. Get your sleep. I don't want any noise in the quarters after ten o'clock." It was a discipline that benefited the slave. Naturally, the owner was looking after his investment. He had to take care of his property. That's why—and blacks don't like to hear me say this—I don't believe owners beat their slaves very much. They would have been damaging their own property.

Since so much of the master's wealth was in slaves, when he got into a financial bind, he knew he could sell a slave or two to tide him over—provided the slave was healthy. He knew he couldn't sell a slave who had scars all over his body from whip lashes. So I imagine the owners made sure the overseers—they were the ones who might use the whip to get the slaves to toe the line or work harder—didn't use the whip often. Of course, a slave was sometimes singled out as an example and was sacrificed as a warning to the other slaves.

There are times when I almost feel sorry for the poor slaveowner! Look at his predicament. When he got to the end of the year with a little cash profit left over, he'd have to use it to buy either more land or more slaves. He couldn't use it to take a vacation to England or France. He was always trying to make his land and his slaves even out. He was always gambling on how many slaves and how much land he'd need for the next crop year. A lot of plantation owners were land-poor and slave-poor. Everybody in the South was a victim of slavery!

Free labor is necessary in a civilized, democratic society. But I have apprehensions about what Lincoln would have done with the freed slaves had he lived. Until recently there have been huge wage differentials between whites and blacks doing the same work in this country. Lincoln was a man from the poor, laboring class of whites. Was his intention to rid the country of cheap black labor so that white labor would have no competition and would thus be worth more? Would he have tried to send all the freed slaves back to Africa? I'm not sure what he had in mind.

I do know, however, that it would have been cruel to send all those freed slaves to Africa. Where would they have gone? What did they have in common with native Africans? The slaves had been forced to give up their heritage. They could not have been repatriated to a certain tribe. Many of them no longer had the blood of a single tribe. Their blood had been messed up with white blood. They were brown, yellow, and olive shades. Anyway, it would have been impossible to determine where a slave of "pure" African blood came from. The procuring of slaves had been a continental affair. As slave caravans passed through, they would pick up slaves all along the route till they arrived at the slave pens on the Atlantic shore. When the slaves got to the Caribbean or to the English colonies, they had to give up their tribal languages and customs. They had long ago lost all connections and memories of their African roots.

To send the blacks to Africa would have been worse than trying to send all American whites to Europe. Where would you send a white person? To France, to Italy, to Germany, to England? Where? You certainly can't look at a person's face or name and tell his bloodline or his national origin. So American blacks are foreign in Africa, and American whites are foreign in Europe. Today Africans say to American blacks: "Come on over and visit us. But remember you're a foreigner. You're not a Nigerian or a Ugandan. You are an American."

That little experiment with Liberia didn't work. In the first place, it got started wrong. It began like Israel. In Israel the English went in and scraped away all the Arabs and brought in Jews from all over Europe. That's what we did in Liberia. We pushed all the natives out. We set up a fine little harbor and named it Monrovia for the nice president who was helping with the project. And we named the country Liberia to show our goodness in making a free place for the freed slave. But, damn it, when the American blacks got to Liberia, what did they do? They began to enslave black natives! And they kept slaves till the League of Nations made them break it up.

So this back-to-Africa movement is futile and always has been. It's hogwash to think American blacks would be more at home in Africa than in America. Like American whites, they are so mixed in blood they don't know where their roots are. You can't look at an American black's size or physical features and say what his African origins are. Of course, there are tribes of pygmies and tribes of giants over there. But you can't measure an American Negro today and say: "Oh, yeah, you're *so* tall and your nose is *so* big. That means you come from *this* tribe or *this* place." There has been so much migration and so much mixing—in Africa and in America—that there's no such thing as tribal or racial purity anywhere. I used to tell my students, "Young people, when the sun goes down, men and women are going to play ping-pong without any bother about color or size or tribe." Men have left their seed all over the world.

It's hard for a black person to trace his family back very far. I think Alex Haley did a good job telling about what *was*, considering that he didn't know what *was*! Because of the way slaves were brought to this country, the way they were bought and sold and mixed and moved after they got here, it's impossible to tell for certain where anybody came from or who their ancestors were. Haley didn't know where in the hell his people came from. You can also look at him and see that he's not altogether a black man, so he must recognize that part of him came from Europe. All his "roots" don't go back to Africa and Kunta Kinte.

When I look back at my own family, I don't throw in any fantasy. I know that at least half of me didn't come from Africa. Hell, I'd be stupid if I tried to pretend that all of me came from Africa. So if I go back to my roots—all my roots—I've got to go down this limb to Africa and down this limb to Wales. Otherwise, I'd be cutting off limbs or pretending they're not there. And I'd not be true to history. I can go back to about 1850, maybe a little earlier. Before that it's just too hazy. One time the editor of the *Columbia Herald* went out to our cemetery and nosed around and found out that one of my grandfathers was born in Tennessee in 1810. But I have no idea where they came from before that.

One night I was speaking at a public forum when a couple of young blacks interrupted me to say that we must create a sense of our "identity." I said, "Young men, what do you mean by your identity?" They said, "Our people." I said: "Who *are* your people? You don't know who your people are!" Most of us can trace our ancestors back a ways, but when we get to a drunk or a jailbird, we kind of lose interest. All of us, black and white, had reprobates, scoundrels, and cuthroats as ancestors. They weren't all Presbyterian ministers! White people, in fact, have to be very careful because a lot of their people were brought here from jail. The turnkey would unlock the jail and say: "All right, if you fellows go to America, we'll turn you loose. Stay here and you canker where you are."

No black person, then, can know exactly who they're kin to. You just can't trace your black ancestry. It would be easier for me to trace my white line if I had access to family records. But when I came up, whites kept those records to themselves. A Negro was not allowed to go probing into the family trees of prominent white families to whom they were related. The grandchildren of a woman named Nancy White, who used to own my grandmother, would have my two older sisters over to their house for dinner. They would eat together, sit down in the front room, and play the piano. My sisters and these white girls were second cousins, and that was all right as long as no one *said* it. My sisters couldn't be invited when the white folks were there because then they would have been treated like Negroes. They were treated like kinfolks when they came by themselves. We knew we were kin. They knew we were kin. But no one *said* it. If they had admitted our relationship, they would have lost standing with other white people.

Now, I don't care whether my white kin admit our relationship. I've just about lived out my day, and I'm on my way out. It's too late to dig much into the bitterness of the past. Anyway, it's irrelevant. The attitude of my children toward their white relatives is this. "Hell, you didn't *respect* us then. We don't *need* you now. We can make it on our own. So now we mark you off from our family the way you marked us off in the past. Then you were ashamed of us. Now we're ashamed of you."

Like my children, I don't see any good that can come of blacks and whites claiming kinship this late. Two or three generations ago it could have benefited blacks, but I don't see it now. Anyway, it would remind blacks that if they go back a few generations, their white relatives—their white ancestors—could (and did!) buy and sell their own children. It's still nauseating to blacks that a white man could have a white wife up there in the big house but go down to a cabin, have sex with a black slave, and have a daughter by her. Then when the daughter got to be, say, fifteen, her daddy could screw her and have a bunch of babies by her too! And he could sell all of them if he got mad or needed money—even the children of his own children! Who in his right mind would want to claim kin to a man like that? So most young blacks today say, "To hell with our white 'relatives.' "

Yes, I'm bitter about those crimes of the past. But I don't hold white people today accountable for what their ancestors did. I don't think you should ever hold the present generation responsible for the mistakes of past generations. Down in Columbia there are some black people who don't like some things my daddy did. When they have tried to make me feel guilty about it, I've looked them square in the face and said: "Hey, wait a minute. You may be right about not liking my papa, but don't try to get even on me just because he's dead. *I* didn't do it." So how can I blame white people today for the sins of their dead? I judge them only by what they do to me today.

Not long ago I was on a car trip to Washington, D.C., with two prominent local Negroes, a successful attorney and the president of a building and loan association. At one point we passed a family of poor whites sputtering along the highway in an old, beat-up truck. In a few minutes, we stopped at a drive-in and got us some sandwiches, which we were eating when those whites drove by in their battered pickup. It was coughing and smoking, and the family looked hungry and worried. I said: "I feel sorry for those poor white people. Nobody gives a damn about them." The lawyer looked at me. "What in the hell do you mean, Lyman?" I said: "I feel sorry for them. White people don't care about them. And black people have no reason to like them. I imagine it's a miserable existence to be a poor white. Not only do upper-class white people look with scorn upon them but so do black people."

The lawyer said: "Listen, damn it, if you have all that much sympathy for these poor whites, why don't you get out of this car and ride with them? You don't belong with us." I said, "Don't you have sympathy for them?" He said, "No sympathy at all. None!"

Both of my companions were dark of complexion. If you saw them a block away, you would know they were black people. If I had my hat on and my coat all buttoned up, it might take you a few more paces till you would know that I'm black. The lawyer was making a valid point. He had a degree from a good college, a law degree from one of our better law schools, and a good practice. But he was still black. He said: "That white man who just passed—all he has to do is wash his face, shave, comb his hair, put on a clean white shirt and pressed pants, and walk down the street—and nobody a block away is going to stigmatize him as a second-class citizen until he proves he is no good. He has an avenue of escape I don't have. No, I'm sorry, but I don't have any sympathy for him at all. If he's down in the gutter, chances are he's there because that's where he belongs. But if you see me there in the gutter, you'll have to check up to find out whether it's because I'm black or because that's all I can measure up to. I don't believe that damn bastard wants to do any better."

Of course, I understood what the lawyer was talking about. Poor whites have opportunities blacks don't have. Take President Andrew Johnson. He wasn't anything till he married a woman who said to him: "You are ignorant. I've got to teach you something." Lincoln is another man who was nothing till the times gave him a chance. The times haven't given many chances to black people. Nevertheless, I have always felt sorry for the poor whites of the South. Back when the South was being settled, the best land was taken up by the wealthy whites. They had the money to buy the rich bottomlands near the rivers. They had the money to buy the slaves to work their plantations. The poor whites couldn't buy the good land and couldn't compete with slave labor. So they were pushed back into the piedmont and farther and farther into the hills. The whites who got stuck with the rocky hill soil were eventually degraded by it.

The slave had a number of advantages over poor whites. His master gave him medical treatment. After all, it benefited the master to make sure his slaves were healthy. Slaves lived in cabins, but they were often better built than the hovels that poor whites lived in on the hillsides. The slave ate better food. Down in the valley the slaves got the same kinds of food the upper-class whites ate. The poor whites up on the hill were victims of poor nutrition. Some of them even ate dirt! Their poor diets made them weak and disease-prone. Poor white children stricken with hookworm and pellagra never had a chance. Like ghetto blacks today, poor whites have suffered from generation to generation.

And sometimes when the slave wanted a special treat he knew how to go about getting it. He knew how to exploit his master's fondness for indulging his slaves. This is how I illustrate it. A slave takes a sledgehammer to the pigpen, cracks one of the fat shoats on the head, and lays him out. He goes in innocently to his owner. "Massa John, you know that mean old mule of yours? You know he ain't got no sense at all. You know what he just done? He done kicked one of them pretty hogs in the head, and that hog out there now dead." Massa John says: "Sam, you sure it was the mule that kicked him? You sure he's dead?" "Oh, yassuh," Sam replies. "I just saw him kick that pore hog to death. He laying out there now dead. What you want done with that fresh meat? It's too hot to salt it down. It'll spoil." Massa John is no fool, but he plays along. "All right, Sam, before he begins to spoil, do you suppose you could dress him and fix him up to be barbecued? Then you can call the rest of the slaves." John can already taste that barbecued meat. "Oh, yassuh, I can fix up that hog real quick." And Sam goes out to where the other slaves have already dressed the hog and are waiting to put him over the barbecue pit. Of course, Sam hasn't fooled Massa John. The master knows it wasn't a mule that kicked and killed the hog, but he thinks: "Well, the damage is already done, so I'll let them have their fun and barbecue tonight. Come Monday morning I'll work them a little harder."

But there was nobody like Massa John around to indulge the poor white. When he got hungry, there was no fat hog that a mule could accidentally kick in the head. Even if he had a hog, it was probably so skinny that it deserved the name it got—razorback. If this little hill farm produced any corn, it would likely be little nubbins with a few grains of corn. Meanwhile, down in the rich soil of the valley plantations, the corn grew long and plentiful. The black man had roasting ears whenever he wanted them. He didn't have his freedom, but he was nonetheless fat and greasy!

The condition of the poor white didn't improve after the slaves were freed. The freedmen mostly stayed on the plantations and continued to work for the landowners, who changed their tactics in order to continue getting cheap labor. They promoted hostility between the blacks and poor whites. The poor white began to see the Negro as his enemy, when it was the wealthy white man all the time. Racial antagonism between poor whites and blacks has been aided and abetted by rich whites for their own greed. Rich whites have used poor whites to do their devilment. Even the Ku Kluxers were mostly a bunch of poor hellions doing the bidding of rich white people who didn't want to get their hands bloody doing the dirty work.

American history textbooks have glossed over such unpleasant facts as the bargain struck between the northern capitalists and southern bigshots in 1876. Since the days of slavery, the plantation owners had wanted cheap labor—at any cost. In those times slavery was the cheapest. Following emancipation, freedmen and poor whites were pitted against each other to keep down the price of labor. As a part of the so-called Compromise of 1876, the northern capitalist said to the southern overlord, "You can run the poor whites and the niggers any way you please as long as we can run you." That was a Gentlemen's Agreement that lasted till after World War II. It made an economic system that kept blacks and poor whites down.

Sometimes I don't know whether it's worse to be a slave and have a master feed, clothe, and own you or to be a day laborer for the same man at a dollar a day. When the black man says to the white boss: "I'm hungry. The dollar didn't go around," the white boss says: "Sorry, that's not my fault. You're not my responsibility. Scram!" The black man began to find out what the poor whites had been suffering all along. It's a pity that the poor blacks and the poor whites didn't realize immediately that they had a common cause.

I blame the capitalist system for the antagonism between these two sets of poor people. The system is rotten to the core. It drove a wedge between the two peoples by telling the white man that he was automatically better than any black, and it made the black man believe it. It kept both sides at war—and poor. It's a reason black people even today don't have much sympathy for poor white people. They say: "Oh, no. They don't need any help from us. They've got a means of escape we don't have. No matter how much money we get, how much education, if we show up at the front door, the white people in the big house see our black faces and say, 'Nigger, go 'round to the back.' But if a poor white man gets his hands on a little money or gets a little education or bathes, brushes his hair, shines his shoes, cleans his fingernails, puts on a collar and tie, he can get in at the front door. He's got the one thing that gets him in. He's got a white face."

White people know they can't all win. But they say, "With this white face I might succeed, and if I ever get to the top, they'll never crush me down again." Abraham Lincoln, Jefferson Davis, Andrew Johnson—they all came from the poor whites. When they began to ease on up the line, nobody could point to them and say, "Yeah, but he's a nigger." Somebody

just the other day said to me, "Damn it, Johnson, you're a spunky nigger."
He meant it as a compliment. But I'm on the Board of Education. I'm a
graduate of the University of Michigan. I've done forty years of teaching.
I've been a leader in this community for almost as long. But I'm still a
nigger! I still haven't made the grade. I've got a cousin in Chicago who
hasn't been to college, who has received no plaques of commendation or
appreciation, but he's going over big. He's going as far as he wants to go
because he's passing for white. That's still the difference. And it bugs the
hell out of me. I've worked hard all my life, and I've accomplished more.
But I'm still a nigger.

There are almost no places in this country where a black person can be
treated fairly without reference to his color. Senator Edward Brooke up in
Massachusetts was going over big till he began to have certain domestic
troubles, but I think his family problems were blown up because he's
black. When Adam Clayton Powell rose high, he got a little too cocky.
Some of us blacks warned him: "Adam, don't forget that you're black.
When they close in on you, they'll grind you to death." And they did. He
admitted that he was guilty of this and that but added, "So are a lot of other
men." That didn't matter. The difference was they were white.

So the American economic system has worked to the disadvantage of
all colors of poor people. It has kept great numbers of people poor and has
fomented racism. And upper-class white people are to blame for this
economic and racial system that works only to their advantage. They set
the pattern and then smugly have that policy implemented by the next
rung of white people. That next rung does the dirty work. I don't mean the
poor whites. I'm not that far down yet. By the upper class, I mean the
owning class, the man who owns the farm, owns the bank, owns the
plant. So the owning class makes the policy to be carried out by those
lower down. The owners know that the black man wants to work, and
they use that as leverage to get cheap, docile labor from the white laboring
class. If a white man working for five dollars a day causes trouble by
wanting more pay, better working conditions, or what not, the owner
says, "Hell, there's a black man out there at the door who can do what
you're doing, and he'll do it for one dollar less." So the black man has been
used as a threat to the laboring white—a hammer held over his head.
While the hammer was there, the white man couldn't ask for six dollars
because outside was an unemployed black man who'd work for four.

Upper-class whites only wanted the races to compete at the blue-
collar level. They didn't want competition in the professions and have
tried to keep blacks out of professional schools like law and medicine. I've
heard white men say: "You niggers don't need a law school. What in the
hell do you need with a law school? Law's for white folks."

It appears that poor whites are more racist than upper-class whites. However, this isn't true. White people are racist all up and down the class line. Racism just shows up and breaks out at the lowest level. The street clashes, the lynchings, the harassments are carried out by low-level whites who are simply doing the dirty work of their bosses. The upper class initiates the action and then, like Pontius Pilate, washes its hands and goes out and acts innocent. Here's an example of how this culture pattern works. One night down in my hometown when I was a boy, the chamber of commerce was giving a banquet. Between seven and eleven o'clock, the big-shot farmers and businessmen were on the second floor of the Maury National Bank building about a block from the courthouse. That same night a bunch of their underlings went out and rounded up a Negro on some trumped-up charge—I believe they said he'd been spying on some white woman—and they took him to the courthouse and dropped him out of a window on the second floor. He had a rope around his neck, and before he hit the ground, his neck was broken.

That lynching went on while the chamber of commerce was having its meeting. And don't tell me they didn't know it! They were bound to see and hear all that cheering, yelling, hooting, and hollering. They were up there standing and looking out the window. They had to know about it. You can't carry on a meeting with that much noise going on. They're a bunch of silly cats if they think I'm going to believe they didn't know that lynching was going on. Sure they knew it. And this is my point: They could have stopped it! They wouldn't have tolerated that kind of lawless behavior on their farms or in their factories and banks. But they allowed it. They encouraged it by their silence. They knew it worked to their benefit. As long as the downtrodden, frustrated, poor whites had a convenient, weak scapegoat, they knew the owning class couldn't become a target.

Industry has frequently set blacks against whites to keep wages low for both races. When white union workers at Ford in Detroit went on strike in the mid-1940s for about two dollars a day more, the Ford managers went to the black neighborhoods and offered unemployed blacks jobs. Ford had a union shop, but when the union called the strike, the company said the contract was broken and they could hire nonunion workers. Those unemployed Negroes were hungry, so they took the jobs at less than what the whites had been paid and made good cars. People who bought Fords couldn't tell whether a hubcap had been put on by white hands or black hands.

Then the white strikers got hungry, and they began to gather outside the gates as the Negro workers left the factory. "Damn you scabs," they said. "You've taken our jobs. How can we feed and clothe our families if you take our jobs?" They got angry and violent and took pipes and beat the Negroes over the head. The blacks had to retreat back inside the plants for safety. Finally, the president of the United States, the governor of

Michigan, and the heads of several Negro groups got together and said, "We've got to stop this thing before we have a race riot in Detroit." The long and short of it was that Ford agreed to take the whites back into the plant; the union agreed to take in Negroes; they all got a pay raise; and black and white workers made the same wages. It benefited everybody, except maybe Ford, whose profits may have been cut a bit. At last, working men of both races saw their common interest, and they refused to let owners use one race against the other.

I didn't mean to defend those Negro scabs. I don't like scabs of any color. But when I am unemployed, I can't accept the philosophy that a scab is bad. When I don't have work, I'll work for whatever I can get and for whoever will give me a job. I'll do that rather than starve or see my family starve. And as long as I will do that, I am a threat to the white man. This is a basic truth that working whites, southern and northern, have had to recognize. The black man will take the white man's job if it's offered to him, even at a lower wage. The white man will not get a raise in pay—he won't even be able to keep his job—as long as the black man is out of work.

The economic philosophy of the South has always been based on keeping poor whites and poor blacks at each other's throats. It's a reason they've never wanted unions in the South, where both races could join in a common front. The mill owners in North Carolina are wild over union-busting. But they've learned one thing: They must keep the poor whites one step above the blacks economically, socially, and culturally. Then when the white workers threaten to get out of line, the owners use the blacks as a warning. "If you don't want to work for what you're getting, damn it, get out of my factory. There are a lot of niggers just waiting to take your place—and for less."

In the beginning the New England states had a colonial system operating within this country. They had the South raise the cotton and other raw materials and sell it to them cheap. Then they would manufacture finished goods from it, have their manufactured goods protected from overseas competition by a high tariff, and sell them throughout the country at a high profit. But in the late 1800s, the northern workers began to unionize. That's when northern factory owners said, "We think we'll move our textile factories down south to cut our transportation costs." What they intended to do—and did—was to take advantage of nonunion white labor in the South. They paid white factory workers about half what union workers were making in the North and pacified them by keeping Negroes out. That's why very few blacks have ever worked in the cotton mills. "Let the Negroes do the field work, and let the whites do the factory work," the industrialists said. The only people who really benefited from this racial division were the capitalists.

Back in the early 1930s, my daddy bought stock in a cotton mill being built in Columbia. It struggled along for a while but finally failed just before Papa died. We settled for about fifteen cents on the dollar. While it was in operation, however, I couldn't have gotten a job inside that factory. Blacks and whites were not allowed to work together under the same roof doing the same jobs. Whites worked inside, and blacks worked outside. I think the managers were afraid that black males and white females would get too close. They might have bumped into each other or brushed against each other. You just couldn't have any mingling of the races in the daylight.

What went on after the sun went down was another matter. There were always white boys coming down to the black neighborhoods trying to see which black gals they could rape. And there was nothing anybody could do about it. A black girl's father could get lynched if he made a complaint. This was part of a system that the northern industrialists helped to support and perpetuate. It was a system that the industrialists made work to their advantage. The managers who ran these mills were usually southerners who were simply strawbosses for the northern capitalists whose profits got bigger and bigger. The black man was paid maybe twenty five cents an hour as a common laborer. The white man was paid about twice as much for skilled work. Together they didn't make as much as a union worker up north.

It wasn't till white and black workers realized that they had common cause that this vicious exploitation was stopped, and that was a long time in coming. I used to ask my brother who worked for Monsanto: "Why don't you all start a union? You've got six children, and you can't raise and educate them on what you make. Why don't you blacks get together with the white workers and tell the boss man that you want to make as much as the company's workers up north where the headquarters are?" He said: "Hush, Lyman. Don't bring that union talk down here. People will say the Communists are behind it, and we'll all be fired, black and white. We don't want a union. Go on back to Louisville and leave us alone."

Sometimes, even in cities like Louisville, the poor whites are worse off than the poor blacks—even when it comes to government services. Most people think the West End of Louisville is all black, but it's not. The Portland neighborhood is almost all white—poor whites who are surrounded by a bigger bunch of blacks. They often complain that being white doesn't help them at all. The city fathers don't take their problems seriously. But every time a West End black makes a complaint, the people in City Hall say: "We've got to hurry and do something. We've got to keep those blacks from raising hell. We've got to pacify them." They usually forget that whites living nearby may have legitimate complaints that also need to be "pacified."

The poor whites who left the backcountry and bettered themselves were saved by two inventions—the automobile and the radio. The automobile built roads right by their shacks, and they could see civilization passing by. Soon they managed to hitchhike their way out of their backwoods and hollows. Sometimes they were even able to buy used jalopies and drive themselves out of little settlements that some of them had never left before. The radio helped too. For ten or fifteen dollars, they could buy a little battery-operated radio box and hear music and news from the outside. They began to know how ignorant and deprived they were. They began to know what civilization was. Their eyes were opened, but they didn't all succeed. The poor whites are still with us, especially in the inner cities, and they still use the Negro as the scapegoat for their failures. The white power structure sits back, as always, manipulating and enjoying the racial conflict—and the economic and political benefits.

No wonder I feel so sympathetic to poor whites. It irks the hell out of my black friends. They say: "Lyman, for God's sake, worry about your own people. The damn white people can take care of themselves." Yet I see their plight and predicament. And I feel sorry for these poor white people—these "white niggers"—who have been used and abused for as long as the black man—and by the same white overlords.

Lifting Bales & Other Vocations

Blacks were selling their dignity and self-respect for a little pocket change.

FOR MOST of American history, black people have been the hewers of wood and carriers of water and pickers of cotton. We've done the backbreaking menial work. Much of the progress this country has made has been on our backs. In our own time, for example, black convict labor has helped build some of the finest highways in the South.

Back in the 1930s when I was doing a lot of driving in Kentucky, Tennessee, and Alabama, I was always impressed with how good Alabama's roads were. By comparison, Kentucky's and Tennessee's roads were mudholes. One Christmas my family and I were driving back to Louisville from Tennessee on Route 31-W. The road got worse and worse. Finally, I thought I had lost my way and pulled into a little filling station in southern Kentucky. "Where is the main road from here to Louisville?" I asked. The attendant said: "Buddy, you're on it. It may look bad, but if you get off it, you won't get to Louisville for another two days."

The Kentucky and Tennessee roads were holey, muddy, and rough, not just in winter but in all seasons. In the summer of 1935, I drove down to Montgomery to visit my sister. After I arrived, I told some people at a party how relieved I was when I got to the Alabama line and found much better roads. Most of the people accepted the compliment, except for a doctor who said: "Young man, if you'll come to my office at ten o'clock tomorrow morning, I'd like to take you with me when I go out to see some of my patients. I want to show you some things. In fact, what I want to show you is so important, I'll even pick you up."

The next day we drove all over the city and county seeing his patients, some of them so poor they couldn't pay him anything. They gave him a chicken or eggs or a piece of meat as payment. At one stop a young woman gave him a couple of choice watermelons. He put them in the trunk of his car with the other payments, turned to the woman, and said: "That's fine. Here. Tell your mother to take this medicine." This happened time after time. Finally, we stopped out on a highway where a Negro convict crew was working. The doctor looked at me and said, "Have you gotten the point yet?" I said: "Yes. You want me to see how these fine highways are built and maintained." He said: "Correct! This is how Alabama got her nice roads. The sheriff goes into a Negro district. He sees a bunch of men playing craps on the street, and that's against the law. All the money these poor fellows have is in the crap game, and it won't total fifty dollars. He arrests them all, maybe even the bystanders, and takes them to jail. They're found guilty, and each one is fined fifty dollars. 'What?' says the judge. 'You don't have enough money to pay the fine? Well, you can work it out at twenty five cents a day.' When a Negro man is put in jail, he leaves a family behind without any support. You've seen how I'm often paid—with the only money they have, the pitiful rations from their own table."

"Now," said the doctor, "you're a bright young fellow. How long do you figure it will take a man to work out that fine? Now look over there." He pointed to a white man sitting up on a little hill by the road where the convicts were working. "Now look," he said. "That white man has a rifle in his hand. And see that white man with a whip in his hand? Now look at our pretty, smooth highways! Now when you go back to Tennessee and Kentucky, learn to appreciate your poor, rough roads. At least they were constructed by free labor!" He turned from the black convicts sweating in the hot Alabama sun to face me. "I just wanted you to see how we got our highways."

At that time Alabama and Georgia were getting beautiful highways built for twenty-five cents a day, plus keep and barrel slop. As we started to leave, we heard a whistle blow for lunch. "Now watch them," the doctor said. I looked as the poor, hungry fellows scuffled up to a barrel, and each dipped out his own slop with a tin cup. I remember thinking that I fed the pigs on my daddy's farm better than they were feeding this highway construction gang. I'm sure the white convict was treated about the same way, but at least he had one advantage that was his eventual passport to freedom—a white face. But a black man—no matter how far he escapes, no matter when he is released from prison—is still black. Just like in slavery days, it was a badge he couldn't shake off. The work pattern developed during slavery wasn't wiped out by the Civil War. It was still there in the 1930s. The pattern had just been adapted to a new system called freedom. So when the whites wanted highways built or cheap farm labor, they'd send the sheriff down to a Negro neighborhood to arrest everybody at a crap game. And if an onlooker said, "But, sir, I wasn't doing nothing; I was just looking," the sheriff would say, "Don't tell me, boy; tell the judge." That's why my daddy told us boys: "Sons, when you see other boys gambling—even with nickels and dimes—don't stand around. I don't want any of you taken to jail."

Down to the present, most blacks have worked as unskilled or common laborers. A world of Negroes worked for the old L & N Railroad, but they were laborers or servants. They were never given any jurisdiction over white workers. A man who lived next door to me worked at L & N for twenty–five years. Just before he retired, because of new government regulations, he got upgraded and was made a supervisor. But he wasn't allowed to supervise. His job remained the same. I knew a black musician who for ten years went around to all the Negro schools as a helping teacher in music. In the white schools, a white woman who did the same work was called a music supervisor. One day the superintendent told the school board: "I want to recommend a change in the position of music helper for the Negro schools. I want her to be called a supervisor of music. Her work won't change. But she deserves the title for what she's been doing." Of course, it was all right for blacks to supervise blacks under the watchful eye of white administrators, but it was not all right for blacks to supervise whites. That attitude is hard to change—even now.

There have always been a few exceptions—I should say partial exceptions. One of my brothers who had some college work but didn't complete his degrees went to work for Monsanto down in Tennessee. Eventually, he was put in a supervisory position over some white workers. Many of them got wages for skilled work, but he was never paid more than the scale for unskilled labor. When I asked him why he didn't protest, he said: "If I did, I'd only get fired. It's better for me to make the top wage as an unskilled worker than to have no job at all."

It was hard for Negroes to earn their fair wages in industry because they usually weren't allowed to join the skilled trade unions. Skilled trades like the painters, carpenters, the electricians, and the bricklayers had no apprenticeship program for Negroes, and therefore, Negroes could not become members of these unions. Negro workers would go out on a job as "helpers," even though they often did the same work as the white workers. Many times construction companies would hire nonunion Negroes and pay them low wages in order to make a larger profit. That was the name of the game: profit.

Just a notch up from laborers were the black waiters, porters, and others who served whites. When I was a young man in the 1930s, waiters could make good money, not in wages but in tips. When I was a student at Virginia Union in Richmond, I worked as a waiter at the Jefferson Hotel. It was a ritzy place—for whites only, of course. The headwaiter at the Jefferson would call a fellow named Toben on campus and say, "I need seventy-five waiters for a big affair on Saturday night." Toben would get a commission for each waiter he recruited. We'd be guaranteed one dollar and a meal. We'd get there at half past five to start setting up tables and to get everything straightened up for dinner that would begin at half past seven. About a quarter after six, we'd serve our own plates in the kitchen and go off to a certain section and eat. We had to be finished and dressed in our white jackets and bow ties, looking spic and span, by seven o'clock, when we had to stand inspection—our hands and faces scrubbed and clean, our shoes shining like a mirror. The headwaiter would say, "Boys, this is a first-rate hotel you're working in now, and we give first-rate service." We'd go to our assigned tables, ice up the glasses, pour the water, make last-minute checks, and be ready to stand at attention when the people started filing in.

After they finished eating, we'd clean off as much as we could, but when the headwaiter gave us the sign, we had to clear out. Once the speaking started, we'd go back to the room where we ate and wait till the speeches were over. We were stuck in that room from about half past eight till eleven o'clock. We'd brought our books, so we'd study as much as we could. I tried to read ancient history or study Greek. When the white people had finished their meeting, the headwaiter gave us the sign, and we'd rush back in the banquet room, clear off the tables, and push them to the side so the dancing could begin. Many nights we stayed till one or two o'clock because we had to wash all the china, silver, and glasses and then dry them. For all that work and time, we got one dollar and dinner. If we got a table of cheapskates—we called them "snakes" but not to their faces—we might not get much of a tip—say $1.50. But if you pulled a lot of monkeyshines, grinning and humiliating yourself, you might be left ten dollars or more. When I found out what I had to do to get people who had money to pay off, I knew I could never live as a waiter. I could not play that game, and it was a game you had to play if you wanted a good tip. If you were quick and properly humble, you could make good money as a waiter.

Some people call that kind of behavior the "coon act." It means shuffling around, acting like you approve of the servant's role you're playing. It means grinning and saying "Yassuh, yassuh" all the time. You're catering to the vanity of someone who assumes he's superior but has to be reassured by your behavior. If you play the role convincingly, the white man will feel sympathetic to the poor Negro and extend him favors—a tip, a handout, a cast-off piece of clothing.

Sometimes I caught a little hell from my wife about how little money I made. "Can't you do something that pays more than teaching school?" she'd say. "With all your education, you should be able to make more." What she meant was that she wanted me to make as much as a white man. But we got along and kept our dignity. Somebody once said to me, "Lyman, I'm amazed at how far you've gotten in this world with so little money." I said: "I don't want or need a lot of money. I'd like to have a little more to pay my bills and provide better for my family, but I don't need all the things I see my friends selling their souls for."

When I was a young schoolteacher with a growing family, however, I sometimes had to swallow my dignity and pride and do temporary work as a waiter at Colonial Gardens on New Cut Road near Iroquois Park. I was never able to get big tips. When a white man would say to me, "Waiter, I need a glass," I'd say, "Yes, sir, I'll bring you one immediately." It was a mistake. I was speaking the white man's language, and they wanted me to talk "nigger" talk. So I'd run all the way to the kitchen and get a clean sparkling glass—the kind of glass I'd want, not a germ within ten miles of that glass. When I'd get back to the table, the man would say: "Nigger, where in the hell did you go? I needed that glass in a hurry. I don't need it now. You're one slow nigger." At that point I could still have saved my tip if I had said: "Yassuh, you sho' right, Mistah. Ah am one bad nigger." But I didn't. I never made any more than about two dollars in regular pay and $2.50 in tips for work that lasted half past five Friday evening till sometimes two o'clock on Saturday morning.

One time I was in the waiters' dressing room changing clothes and getting ready to go home when one of the regular waiters asked me how much I made in tips. When I told him, he said: "Mr. Johnson, you ought not try to wait tables. You better stick to teaching school. And I'm going to tell you why. You know when that man asked you to get him a glass and you were gone so long? Well, he was cussing you out all the time you were gone. Then he asked me for a glass. I said, 'Yassuh,' and what did I do? I turned my back, got a used glass off another table, wiped it out with a soiled napkin, and put it in front of him—and he handed me five dollars. You see, Mr. Johnson? You waited on him, but I got five dollars' tip off your table. Hell, the germs won't kill him."

About that time the white couples were leaving the dance to go home. My waiter friend said: "Now watch me. I'm going to show you how to get some money. Follow me and stay close enough to see." So I followed him out of that little, dingy dugout to the door, where he sat down on a broken-down crate. As the white people passed by, he'd mumble in "darky" dialect: "You white folks sho' are mean. You the cheapest ol' no-good white people I ever see. You ain't got no sense at all!" About then a white man said, "Nigger, what you mumbling about?" And he said: "Mr. Charley, you all right. But you got some mighty cheap white folks out here. We got to work here all day. We got to work like slaves, and the old lady back home waiting for us to bring some money back. But this place don't give us nothing. And you folks—you got everything. Mr. Charley, I ain't got no money, and I got to get home." The white man growled, "Oh, quit your griping." He reached into his pocket and handed him a ten-dollar bill. A ten-dollar bill! And the waiter had done nothing for him. The white man said: "Now, take this money on home. Don't drink it up. Don't gamble it up. Take it home and give it to your woman." And the waiter said: "Yassuh, I will, Mr. Charley. Some of you sho' got good sense. You are right, yassuh. I'm gonna give every penny ob dis money to my ol' woman. Yassuh, every cent!" The white man said, "Just be sure you do," reached into his pocket, handed him another five dollars, and said, "All right, this is for *you*." And as the white man left, fifteen dollars lighter, the waiter was still muttering, "Yassuh, yassuh. . . ." When the white man was out of sight, he turned to me and said, "Now, see if you can make fifteen dollars that fast." I expect he took all that fifteen dollars, went back where the other waiters were, and had him some fun in a crap game.

That's your monkeyshine, your coon act. I couldn't do it. I kept remembering what my daddy had said to my brother who worked as a chauffeur. "Son, I didn't bring you into this world to be a slave." I'm afraid if I'd been a waiter, I'd have taken my family to the poorhouse. I'd have been too conscientious, too professional. If you had wanted a clean glass, I'd have germ-proofed it myself. If necessary, I'd have taken a .44 pistol and shot every germ on your glass to make it clean. But I'd never have gotten good tips because I'd never have done monkeyshine for you. That man who picked up an easy fifteen dollars did it because he had to. It was his technique of survival. He survived. But he survived at the cost of his dignity, his worth as a human being. And he didn't help the cause of black people. Rosa Parks did that.

Some waiters around Louisville made a lot of money bowing, scraping, and waiting on tables at hotels and white clubs. To them it was simply an act they performed in front of white people, and they were handsomely rewarded. One fellow was Captain Dan, whose son was a graduate of Fisk University and a high school principal. When he sent his son to Fisk, he said: "Son, I don't want you to be a waiter. I want you to be something that carries more self-respect." Captain Dan was headwaiter at the Brown Hotel, and I'm sure he made more money than his son. All the white customers, including J. Graham Brown himself, thought the life of Cap'n Dan. Everybody called him Cap'n Dan and tipped him liberally. He could put on his coon act and rake in the money. He lived in a very comfortable home on Twenty-second Street near Magazine before that section began to deteriorate. He lived in a cultural environment at home with his wife and children, but when he got down to the hotel, he never made any ado about what he had at home. He was a smart man. You can make excuses for a man like that because he did what he had to do to survive and so that his children could have advantages and not have to demean themselves the way he did. I can excuse the father, but I cannot excuse the children who pick the same row of cotton.

All the way back to slavery days, blacks have been playing Bre'r Rabbit for their own benefit. When I was in graduate school at the University of Michigan, I knew a young black fellow who had graduated from a black college in South Carolina. He came from a very humble family. His father made a decent living running a barbershop for waiters. The young man wanted to go to medical school, and that was expensive. How did he manage it? He played the system for all it was worth. "Yeah," he admitted to me. "I kowtowed to Senator So-and-So. I'd say: 'Senator, suh, my people always fussin' 'bout you white folks, but they don't understand. Now, I understand y'all. I know you got our best interests at heart. You do the best you can for us.' And the senator would say: 'Thomas, you're a smart man. How can I get the other Nigras to think like you do and stop criticizing me? I know what I'll do. I'm gonna get you the best education money can buy, so you can come back here and tell your people what you've just told me.' "

Here was a young black man with all his expenses paid to medical school by a white senator from South Carolina! Every summer he'd go back home and butter up his benefactor. You know what happened to him? When he graduated from medical school, he kissed South Carolina good-bye and moved to California! He said: "Hell, I wanted to get through school and not have to worry about my bills. All I had to do was *tell* that white man what he wanted to hear. Now I've got my medical degree, and he can't take it away from me. He can't make me pay his money back because we didn't sign any contract. I made the system pay off!"

The white man has always assumed that he's the smart one. Is he? The wise man knows the first law of nature is survival. When I talk to young black people today, I say: "My God, if a bunch of slaves in chains could figure out a technique of survival, why in the hell can't you, in freedom, at least do as much? In fact, you have an obligation to your struggling ancestors not only to survive but to climb higher. Don't let yourself be pushed down. Wake up. Start from where you are. My grandfather was a slave, and he worked and saved his money and bought himself out. He wanted his children to go farther than he did. Don't go back to where my grandfather was. Don't go back to slavery." To my own children I say: "I didn't have it as bad as my father, but I had it rougher than you. Don't you go all the way back down to the foot of the hill. Each generation should climb a little higher."

Blacks have made remarkable progress since my grandfather's days. More blacks are now going into business and the professions, and they are competing successfully with whites. There are black lawyers, doctors, dentists, professors, and others who serve both white and black clients. Until this generation most black professionals served only other blacks. In fact, many Negroes preferred to patronize white professionals because they thought they would get better service. Although there were a few black lawyers, most southern blacks hired white lawyers when they got into trouble. Few white people would patronize a black storekeeper or doctor or dentist. In most places black teachers taught only black students. Black ministers served only black congregations.

The ministry has always been an important black profession. If a man went into the ministry and pastored a sizable congregation with members who had regular, steady jobs, he could have a good income and a leadership position. Preachers still wield a lot of power in the black community. They are often the spokesmen on black issues.

When I came to Louisville during the Depression, there were a number of black businessmen who catered to black customers. The two main Negro business and professional centers were at Sixth and Walnut and Tenth and Chestnut. The Pythian Building at Tenth and Chestnut housed a Negro lodge and a good pharmacy on the first floor. The second and third floors had rooms for rent, meeting rooms, and several doctors' and dentists' offices. On the top floor was a ballroom. About 1935 the Pythian Lodge was just about defunct and sold the building to the YMCA. It was located at a busy intersection, with the black public library across the street and a black tavern called the Brown Derby nearby.

In Louisville the two mainstay professions were in education and the post office. There were a few blacks in other professions such as real estate and accounting, and many, many Negroes worked as maids, cooks, laundresses, gardeners, and handymen for affluent white families; but teachers and postal employees supported the Negro community finan-cially and culturally. We used to say that nobody in the Negro community could pay his bills—doctors or lawyers or ministers—till the school-teachers and the postal employees got paid. They had regular paychecks coming in year-around. As a rule postal workers made more than teachers. A Negro really thought he was something when he was taken off a mail delivery route and made a clerk. I remember when the first Negro was put at the window of the main Louisville post office selling stamps. The black community buzzed: "Did you know that Mr. So-and-So is a stamp clerk? You can go up and buy stamps from him at the main window!" A lot of us went in to buy stamps just to see the sight. Why was that important? He was the first visible Negro at the main post office. There were others working in the back rooms, but his was the first black face we saw in the window. I think the postmaster wanted the Negro community to *see* how liberal he had become.

Louisville also had a few black policemen and firemen. The black fire unit was called Engine Company Number 8 and was located on Thirteenth Street. The white authorities must have thought they were making real progress when they gave Negroes their own unit. "We have a bunch of Negroes in our fire department," they could boast, "even if we do make them work under another roof." I don't think there was any law against putting whites and blacks together in the fire department, but local mores are sometimes more powerful than the law. "Since everything else is separate," they reasoned, "why mix up the firemen?"

The black policemen in Louisville were never promoted to positions that gave them authority over white policemen or white people in general. I'm sure there were a few occasions, like a downtown parade, when a black policeman might have had a theoretical authority over whites, but he was very wise if he chose not to exercise it. What I'm saying is that black policemen had real authority over other black people only. The black policeman was *schooled*—I'm using that word to keep from using *told*—in how to be discreet, for example, in making arrests. "Don't you *ever* let a Negro violator of the law escape," he was told. "Now, if possible, don't let a white man escape." He knew he had to use his head when handling white citizens.

When Negro firemen or policemen absolutely had to use their authority over whites, there were problems. When people who gathered to watch a fire got in the way of the fire department, a black officer could bark like hell at some black guy, "Get the hell out of the way or I'm gonna run you in!" But if a white fellow was standing in the way, he would say, "Mister, please, sir, will you please move to let the equipment get by?" Or if a black policeman came upon a gang of black boys shooting craps in an alley, he might say, "All right boys, cut it out and scram or I'll take you to jail." If he caught a group of white boys doing the same thing, he'd have to be more careful. "Now, young men, you know this is against the law. So move along, please." He knew he couldn't use any kind of force with whites. If he did, it would be hell to pay when his white superiors heard of it.

All Negroes, of course, lived under these unwritten restraints when dealing with white people. A black woman could say to a black man who'd made some ugly proposition to her, "Ah, go to hell!" If a white man made the same proposition to her, she knew to be careful what she said. On and off the job, Negroes were conditioned to "behave" properly toward white people. Negroes learned to adjust to living between a rock and a hard place. Even when the law was on your side, you knew you might lose. In the long run, you might win a legal victory, but in the short run, you might get your head bashed in. Or you might lose your job.

I remember a man named William Hughes, one of the first black policemen in Louisville. He finally got to be a major, but he started out as a patrol officer back about 1936. He had the job of directing traffic around Jackson Junior High School when school took in and when it let out. His station was at a busy intersection where thousands of black and white drivers whizzed by every day. He had absolute authority over blacks, but he was told not to arrest white people. One day a white fellow came by exceeding the speed limit for a school district. Hughes had already held up his hand for the children to cross the street, and he held out his other hand for the white man to stop. The white man pulled up, rolled his window down, and shouted at the black policeman: "Get out of my way, nigger. I don't have time to stop. Nigger, you got a lot of nerve. Get out of my way or I'll run over you."

The black man forgot his orders and pulled out his pistol. "You come any closer," he said, "and you'll be dead." The white man stopped, and the little black children crossed the street. But that isn't the end of the story. The white man went straight to the chief of police and the mayor and said, "Who is that nigger over there telling me what to do and pulling a gun on me, a white man?" Mr. Hughes was called in by the chief. "You've violated regulations," he said. "You've got all the authority you need to arrest, handcuff, or physically restrain a Negro, but you have no authority over a white man. I thought you understood these restrictions. You're not supposed to talk the way you did to a white person. Now you've got to apologize!" Hughes not only had to apologize, but he almost lost his job. I went with a committee to the chief's office to plead on his behalf. "This is ridiculous," we said. "Here's a man driving at excessive speed through a school zone with children already crossing the street. This policeman was trying to do his duty and protect their lives. He deserves to be commended, not demoted or fired!" Our pressure worked, and he wasn't fired, but he had a blot on his record that he had violated regulations.

Whether they're waiters, lawyers, teachers, or policemen, it has always been hard for blacks in this country to earn a decent living and to keep their dignity as human beings. The attitude that blacks are inferior and are therefore not fit for equal status with whites is one that I have lived with all my life. It is an attitude that my daddy insisted his children resist. When I was a boy in Columbia, we had a big downtown hotel called The Bethel about one block from the courthouse. It was the hub of high-class white society. All the management and guests were, of course, white. All the waiters, cooks, bellhops, and other servants were, of course, black. The black servants had to go down the back alley to get in to work. They couldn't use the front door. However, once they got inside and put on their white coats and uniforms, they had the run of the place. They were in their servant's dress.

My daddy didn't like the way the hotel management treated Negroes. "I don't want to catch you going near that hotel," he warned. "If you try to get a job there, you can just change your boardinghouse. I don't want you back here." I can remember passing by the hotel and seeing upper-class white people sitting in the big rockers on the front porch. On hot summer days, they were immaculately dressed. I could hear snatches of their talk. A man in a clean white suit might say: "Nigger, bring me a bourbon and water," or "Nigger, bring me a scotch and soda. Goddamnit, get it here quick!" A woman in an expensive silk dress might say, "Nigger boy, get me a glass of lemonade." The Negro servants knew what they had to do. The more the waiters and busboys bowed and scraped and pranced about, the bigger the kick the white people got out of them. Papa wouldn't let any of his children work there, but when I got to be about sixteen or seventeen, a number of my classmates took jobs at the hotel. They had to take a terrible amount of humiliation. They took abuse and insult. They had to put on the monkeyshine to get tips. No monkeyshine, no tip. Blacks were selling their dignity and self-respect for a little pocket change.

Maybe my classmates felt it was a soft way of earning a living—better than doing hard manual labor in the yards and fields of Maury County. There was nothing wrong with being a janitor or a yardman or a waiter. It was honest work. But there was—and is—something wrong with being made to play the role of the master's servant. That's the role blacks were expected to play, especially if they were waiters and a white man wanted to show off in front of his lady friend. The black waiter had to play the game and humble himself to the white man. The more menial his behavior, the better his pay.

It's all right to play games. The danger is that the racial game became the truth to a lot of white and black people. Black parents had their inferiority beaten into them so firmly that they sometimes told their children: "Child, you're just a nigger. You're nothing but a nigger, and you've got to behave when you go around white folks." When the black child hears this from white people and then goes home and hears it from his own parents, he begins to believe he's not as good as whites simply because he's black. "I'm only a nigger," he concedes, and lowers his aspirations.

Jim Crow Days

I will remember scenes of injustice and brutality the rest of my life.

"DON'T SIT IN THE CROW'S NEST." That's what my daddy used to tell me when I was a boy in Columbia. The crow's nest was what he called the balcony where Negroes had to sit when they went to the movie theater. "If I catch you going down that back alley to go up those back stairs to get to that balcony, I'll skin you alive!" he warned. So I never saw one of those silent Western films other children talked about at school. I saw my first movie when I was nineteen and attending school in Knoxville. There I went to an all-black theater where I could sit anywhere I wanted to. Even today I can hear the echo of my father's voice. "It's wrong to go down that alley. Lyman, don't let the white people degrade you that way. I didn't raise my children to sit in the crow's nest."

The colored movie balcony was just one of the ways I was reminded over and over that I was a Negro. There are dozens of childhood incidents that I remember vividly and painfully. When I was very young, I didn't always understand what they meant. I remember one time I was walking with my two older sisters uptown. Although we lived next to a white neighborhood, we were seldom harassed if we stayed within a block and a half of home. We walked through that "safe" block and a half. When we got farther away and closer to town, we passed a bunch of white boys— young men—seated out on the porch of a grocery store. Here were two Negro girls—attractive young ladies, about seventeen or eighteen—and a little boy just tagging along after them. It never occurred to me what those white boys meant till much later, years later, and when I thought of it, it made me mad. One said: "She's too pretty to be a nigger. She oughta be white." When I finally realized what they were saying, I put two and two together and understood why my mother always told me, "Lyman, when your sisters go into town, I want you to go along with them." I understood why she wanted me to go with them when they went beyond a block and a half of our house.

But we Johnson children had our white playmates. We played games with little white boys and girls after school till six or seven or eight o'clock, depending upon the time of year. My brother Charles, who was just a little older than I was, often played with white children. Charles was a handsome little cuss, but he was a sickly fellow. He died when he was eighteen, but he wanted so much to play with us. It was rough on him because any exertion would affect his heart. He was a good pitcher, but if he played more than two innings, he'd have to pay for it with ten days in bed.

Oh, but Charles was so handsome. He had blond hair, straight blond hair. When he'd hold his head over, his hair would fall down front, and when he'd shake it back, it'd lie down like he'd combed it. Ah, he was hard on the eyes of the little girls—the little white girls. I was about fourteen when he was seventeen, but I was getting old enough to begin to understand boy and girl conduct and language. One little white girl about a block up the street from us was sweet on my brother, and one down the other way was also sweet on him. But no matter what kind of hair he had. No matter if he had blue eyes. No matter what his complexion was. He was still a nigger. And those Ku Kluxers down there would lynch a Negro boy if they caught him looking at a white girl. I used to ask, "Why, Charley?" And he'd say: "Don't worry, Lyman. I don't want the girls. I don't want them." I said: "But, Charley, when you play with these two girls, they fuss because of you. Keep on and you'll get lynched out here in the street." He said: "Well, what can I do about it? I can't insult either one of them. That'd make things worse."

Every time I saw them with him, I'd get scared. They were so sweet on him, hugging and kissing him, playing with him and showing him special favors. When their mamas baked a pie, they'd save a piece of it for Charles. I suppose the mamas knew what was going on. When Charles died, the mother of one of the girls came down to our house to pay her respects. In those days we didn't leave the body at the funeral parlor but brought it back home. She and I were the only ones in the room, and she reached over and kissed the dead boy and said: "This was the nicest young man in this town. I guess it's the Lord's will, but Lord, why do you have to take the best we have?"

Charles would maybe have lived longer if he'd had better medical treatment. But we didn't have much for white people and even less for Negroes. The black doctor was no good. He couldn't have made it in a city. But it was our custom to start with him, though he didn't know what to do. Then we'd send for the white doctor, who couldn't do much more. White doctors had either a separate waiting room or separate hours for their black patients. White doctors always had separate entrances for whites and blacks. For blacks it was anything that looked like a back door. If anybody saw a Negro going to a white doctor, they saw him going in the back way. The white doctor would do whatever was necessary to keep his white patients. If he thought they would object to him seeing a Negro patient in his office, even at separate hours, then he would arrange to see him somewhere else.

Most white dentists had a chair for whites and a chair for blacks. The white dentist who had only one chair had a big problem. No matter what he said, it was obvious he was using the same chair for both races. White patients would want everything scrubbed up and sterilized. And they really didn't like to think about having to sit in the same chair where a damn nigger sat.

I grew up with these patterns of segregation, but I never accepted them. I've known, however, many black people who did—some in my own family. I have a niece who lives on the campus of Tuskegee Institute in Alabama. As a young lady coming up, she was reared in comfortable circumstances by her grand-aunt in Rochester, New York, and had no interest in anything southern. Before she finished high school, she had made three cultural visits to Paris. In school and out of school, she'd had very few contacts with other blacks.

When she finished high school, her grandaunt said: "Now I will pay all your expenses through college, but you must go to a southern Negro college. You've had almost no experience with Negroes, and I want you to know what it's like to be a Negro." They settled on Fisk University in Nashville. All four years in college, she was determined that as soon as she could get out of the benighted Southland, she'd head back up North. But sometimes young people's fancies are turned by love, and they forget their resolutions. About four or five blocks from Fisk is Meharry Medical School, where she met a young man who was graduating at the same time she was finishing college. In 1945 they married.

Their first big argument was over leaving the South. "You've got to start your practice up North," she said. "I just can't stand the South. It's too hot in the summertime. The white folks down here are mean. They make me ride in the back end of the bus. They won't let me go to the regular theaters. There are so many more things open to us Negroes up North." Her new husband argued: "Look, my daddy is a big-shot professor at Tuskegee. If I go and hang up my shingle there with my name and an M.D. behind it, I've got it made. And that's what I'm going to do, and you are going with me. You're already hooked."

About ten years after they set up in Alabama, I went down to visit them. I was in my heyday of civil rights activity. In the meantime she had gotten addicted to college life. Her husband was campus physician. As long as she stayed on campus, she had culture, refinement, and everything else she wanted. It was high living. Her husband was a doctor, and her father-in-law was a professor, and she meandered through that cultured society on campus. She knew, however, not to go into town and not to go to Montgomery. If they wanted anything outside the college community, they would wait till they were in Chicago, Detroit, Cleveland, or New York, where they would be treated decently. She had been thoroughly acclimated to the southern way of life. When I arrived, the first thing she said to me was: "Now, Lyman, I know all about your civil rights work up in Kentucky; but whatever you say inside this house stays here. When you get out on campus, I'll be your mouthpiece. I'll tell the people what a great man you are and how brave you are and all that kind of stuff. But I'm not going to let you start talking your civil rights rabble down here. Leave us alone. We're doing all right."

I was not convinced. At that time, when a white person—especially a white woman—came to the campus for a conference or a lecture, she would have to be put up in one of the downtown white hotels. She could not stay on the campus overnight with Negroes. Not long before my visit, a white woman had come to Tuskegee for a three-day workshop at the college. On the second day of the conference, officials from the town of Tuskegee came on campus looking for her. They knew she had arrived in town the day before, but they had checked all the hotels and rooming places for whites, and she was not listed. What they demanded to know was where in the hell did she stay. Apparently she was the guest of a white family in town. If she had stayed on campus, she could have been arrested for violating Alabama's Jim Crow laws.

Those were the conditions that even educated blacks had to live under. And here was my niece telling me: "Don't open your mouth, Lyman. We are going over big. We are adjusted here. I don't want you to spoil it all. My husband is going to build me a nice house with air conditioning. I'm going to stay in my nice new house, and I'll enjoy all that he brings in here." I reminded her that the shoe was now on the other foot. "Honey, you once said you could never live in the South, but you're condoning what you once objected to. How can you bottle yourself up in a house—even a new one with air conditioning—and make your home into a penitentiary? The whole world lives outside your house, and you're missing it!"

Soon afterward, when Rosa Parks took her stand over in Montgomery and refused to give up her bus seat to a white man, this niece invited me back for a visit—and an apology. She said: "Uncle Lyman, I know now just how stupid you must have thought I was when I said for you to keep your mouth closed. I was wrong." And I said: "Darling, I don't need an apology, but Rosa Parks deserves one. She doesn't have a father-in-law who is a college professor. Her husband isn't a doctor. She's just a plain domestic servant. I doubt whether she finished the eighth grade. Yet she has become your emancipator. *You* should feel ashamed."

I have always felt that when you go along, when you cooperate, when you don't protest unfair treatment, you are tacitly agreeing with your adversary. When I came to Louisville, Negroes couldn't use the main public library at Fourth and York. If you were a black janitor, you could go in to clean up, of course, but you couldn't go in to read a book. We were told, "You have your *own* library." So about sixteen of us Negroes, including two black Ph.D.'s from the all-black Louisville Municipal College, went to a Board of Trustees meeting at the main library.

The board was courteous and invited us in. Of course, they escorted us through the building to make sure we didn't wander out into the reference room or the reading room or the rest rooms. We were herded through the main reception area, around a corner, around another corner, and then into the Trustees' Room. We asked, "Why can't Negroes be permitted to use the 'free' and 'public' library?" They said, "We just can't afford it. For one thing we don't have enough money to provide you with any toilet facilities. Anyway, Negroes have never complained before. We thought everybody liked it the way it is." That's my point: As long as we blacks don't raise complaints, "they"—whoever "they" are—can assume that everything is all right.

Unfortunately, even high-principled blacks have had to compromise. Certainly I have. When I left Columbia to go to boarding school in Knoxville, I had to either ride a Jim Crow coach or walk. I didn't want to walk, so I allowed myself to be segregated in the "colored" section of the train. In order to survive, I learned that at times I had to cooperate with a system my parents had taught me to detest. There have been times when I was hungry as hell, and my choice was to eat in the café's kitchen or to go hungry. I ate in the kitchen.

In 1930 after I had finished my degree, two college friends and I were driving from Richmond, Virginia, to Kentucky. We drove all day without any food. When we reached a little mountain town in eastern Kentucky, the pangs of hunger were just about to eat us up. We decided we had to stop. We drove up to a little café, parked, and walked in. "You have such an enticing sign outside," we said to the white man behind the counter, "we just had to stop and try out your food." He said, "Oh, yes, I think we can accommodate you all." He then took us down the side of the big dining room, past the serving counter, and opened the door into the kitchen. To one of the waitresses, he said, "Clear a table back here and put a tablecloth on it for these fellows." To us he said: "Have a seat here, boys. You didn't think we were going to feed you out there in the dining room with white folks, did you? Back here, you'll get the same food and the same service at the same price. You just can't eat in the dining room. By the way, when you leave, I'd appreciate it if you'd go out the side door." Here we were with our new college degrees, and we had to eat in the kitchen. But we were hungry, and we knew we wouldn't find any better place to eat. At least they gave us a clean tablecloth, nice silver, dishes, and napkins, and good food. They gave us everything but respect.

In those days travel was inconvenient for Negroes, especially when we used public transportation. In the fall of 1931 after I'd spent a month in Columbia, I was getting ready to go back to the University of Michigan to begin the fall semester. When I boarded the bus in Columbia to take me north, I suddenly decided that I would not sit in the back. It was hot, crowded, and bumpy back there. Buses weren't cushioned very well in those days, and every time we hit a pothole in the road—and there were a lot of them on Route 31-W north—the people in the back seats were bumped up and down. It was as rough as riding an old mule. The only halfway comfortable seats were in the front, and that's where I decided to sit. So I sat down with the white people. I was light skinned and perhaps could have gotten away with it somewhere else, but my family was known in Columbia as black. My sitting down in the front of the bus raised a ruckus. Suddenly, there was a big, burly bus driver standing over me, threatening, "If you don't go to the back of the bus or get off, I'll throw you out." I sat still. I was getting my satisfaction, sitting in that off-limits seat. I could hear black voices in the back, saying: "That yellow nigger is nuts. Come on back here with us and stop raising all that Cain." And I could hear white voices, saying: "Who is that uppity nigger? Get on back where you belong!" But I knew that some of the white people were saying, at least in their conscience: "Oh, isn't it a shame? Why do we make him sit in the back? He paid as much as we did to ride this bus." Finally, my father came on board. He was an old man, now speaking to his last child to leave home, pleading, "Son, will you please move to the back of the bus?" And I said: "Yes, Papa, for you I'll do anything. I'll even move to the back of the bus."

The bus route north took us from Columbia to Franklin to Nashville, then up to Franklin, Kentucky, to Bowling Green, Elizabethtown, and Louisville, from Louisville to Cincinnati, to Dayton, Akron, Detroit, and finally Ann Arbor. We Negroes had to ride in the back seats all the way through Tennessee and Kentucky until we got to Cincinnati, where we could take any seat that was vacant. I never minded sitting in the back of the bus—even when the roads were bumpy—if that's where the only empty seats were. That's the democratic way: first come, first served. The first people on the bus should be able to get the best seats, black or white. But I didn't like having to pass empty seats in the front to go to the colored seats in the back!

The rest stops were another great humiliation for Negroes. We couldn't go in the front door. We'd have to go around to the side or back door to go to the toilet. No mixing allowed. Maybe they even had separate sewers to take our body wastes to the river! Or maybe once they left the body, black and white wastes looked the same, so it would be all right for them to go down the same sewer! It was an absurd system.

The most inhumane separate-but-equal toilet arrangements I ever saw were in Birmingham. As the bus drove into the city, we'd see a big welcoming sign: "YOU ARE NOW ENTERING THE CITY BEAUTIFUL, BIRMINGHAM." The bus arrived at the station. The whites were in front and got off first. They walked in the front door by the ticket counters into a neat, clean waiting room. Then we blacks walked down a ramp and past a greasy bus garage to get to a bunch of dirty rooms that served as our waiting room. At the back of the waiting room were two signs marked "Men" and "Women." I went into the men's room. I was shocked. It was dirty and smelly, and flies swarmed everywhere. And it might as well have been one big toilet for both men and women. Separating the two toilets was a thin piece of plywood that started about a foot from the floor and rose to about six feet. It was then open to the ceiling. There was almost no privacy. Through the wall I could hear all the bathroom noises and every toilet flush. And I thought how brutal white people are to make us use facilities like this. They must think we're no better than a bunch of dogs.

I always knew that the white accommodations were better—separate and better—but I wanted to see for myself. Because I was light skinned, I could pass for white in a bad light. So sometimes I'd pull my hat down a bit, straighten up my tie, brace myself, and walk directly through the white waiting room at a bus or train station back to the white rest rooms. I wanted to be sure I knew what I was talking about when I raised hell about separate-but-equal laws.

One time I checked out the white facilities at the old L & N station in Louisville. Oh, it was beautiful as a cathedral, with huge stained-glass windows in the waiting room and six feet of white tile lining the walls of the men's rest room. It was immaculate, floors spotless, no trash anywhere, no bad smells. Then I walked around to the "colored" facilities. In one corner were mops spread out on the floor to dry, mops the Negro janitor had just used to clean the white rest rooms. The place was dirty, stinking, and crowded with custodial supplies. The washbasins were grimy and chipped. The latrines were smelly and filled with cigarette butts. The white inspectors would have fired the janitors on the spot if they had found the white toilets in this filthy condition, but they simply didn't care about the black toilets. I had the evidence. I knew what I was talking about when I said: "Even a blind man can tell that this is not separate but equal. Anybody who says so is a damn lying son of a bitch!" As I got older, I got bolder, and I've always tried to be diplomatic and polite till I got my foot in the door. Once inside, I'd explode. I knew I couldn't do any damage to the system if I exploded out on the street—or in the "colored" toilet.

Riding the Jim Crow trains was just as bad as the buses. It was humiliating to ride from Detroit to Tennessee. When we arrived in Cincinnati, the white conductor would parade through the coaches and remind us: "All right, now, we're fixing to cross the Ohio River. All you Negroes—you colored people—will have to move to the colored coach." We knew we were just as cultured and refined as the white people around us, but we were herded like cattle back to one coach. "We could no longer eat in the dining car. Of course, we knew we'd have to provide our own food once we crossed into Kentucky, so we'd take out the lunch boxes we'd brought to do us till we got home to Nashville or Birmingham or Mobile or Columbia, Tennessee. Here's a good example of people behaving the way they're treated. We seemed to feel that it was no use to act refined anymore. We were being treated like niggers, so we might as well act like niggers. We'd kick off our shoes, unfasten our belts, open up our boxes of fried chicken and whatnot, and eat with our fingers. Gradually, we'd settle down and go to sleep in our seats. We were not allowed in the Pullmans. Not even the old or the sick. It was a disgrace. I know what I'm talking about. I saw it. It still hurts. The scars still bleed.

For a southern city, Louisville had good race relations. To be sure, it was a segregated community. But somehow it seemed that blacks and whites had a progressive relationship here that they didn't have in most other southern cities—and even in some northern ones. There was even some relaxing of segregation. At least as long as I've lived in Louisville, blacks have been able to ride streetcars and buses and to sit anywhere they pleased. State law required segregated seating on intercity buses and trains, but in Louisville we were integrated. Maybe segregated transportation was simply too inconvenient to bother with. In the morning when a streetcar came out of the West End, it would be full of black servants going to the East End, with maybe two or three whites. Later, when a streetcar went from the East End to downtown, it would be filled mostly with whites. Maybe it was just too complicated to mark off white and colored sections. This was one of the ironies of life in Louisville. Restaurants, schools, hotels, libraries—even the parks—were all segregated. But not the buses and the streetcars.

Until the 1970s Fourth Street was the retail and entertainment center of Louisville. It had all the dime stores—Woolworth's and Newberry's. It had the Taylor and Walgreen drugstores. It had all the fashionable department stores and the first-run movie theaters. We Negroes could not go into any of these stores and sit down. We could not go into any of the movies. We were allowed to do business with the department stores like Stewart's, Selman's, and Kaufman-Straus. We could buy anything these stores sold, but we could not try on any piece of clothing. Not even a hat. Some of the stores even discouraged Negro business. On the other hand, a few stores offered charge accounts to Negroes, though it was considered a favor. When Stewart's sent my wife and me an invitation to open an account, I wrote back to say that I would wait till Negroes as Negroes would be welcomed as charge customers. I didn't want a special privilege because I was an "exceptional" Negro.

There were, however, two clothing stores just off Fourth Street at Third and Market, where Negroes were reasonably well treated—Levy Brothers and Loevenhart's. At these stores we could try on anything and charge it. I tried to give all my business to them. I think they figured that since they were not on Fourth Street they didn't have to be so exclusive. They also knew it was good business. Negroes had to buy their clothes somewhere. And there weren't many Negro-owned retail businesses because of the high capital expense, the high overhead, and the limited market.

Negroes were not allowed in the grand movie palaces on Fourth Street. The two big Negro insurance companies, Mammoth and Domestic, had movie theaters on the first floor of their buildings. But compared to the Fourth Street theaters, the Grand and the Lyric were small and cramped. Negroes couldn't pay big admission prices, so when movies cost one dollar on Fourth Street, they were thirty-five cents in the Negro theaters. With smaller auditoriums and lower prices, the Negro movie houses couldn't afford to give us the big first-run shows. But we took what was available to us, and from Thursday through Sunday, the Grand and the Lyric would be crammed to capacity. They would show a lot of Westerns and stick-'em-up gangster pictures as well as so-called colored movies. Sometimes they could even afford to show first-rate films a year or two after they had run in the white theaters.

I remember when *Gone with the Wind* was playing on Fourth Street. After it had been showing for weeks and weeks, one of my white teacher friends said: "Lyman, have you seen *Gone with the Wind* yet? You'd better see it before it closes." I said, "Now, where in the hell do you expect me to see it?" She said, "Well, isn't it running also at one of your theaters?" I said, "Hell, no, it's not running at one of our little theaters." She said: "Oh, I thought that all the movies that ran on Fourth Street also ran over on Sixth Street. It's a shame you won't be able to see it." About a week after the film closed, she said, "Lyman, I do think it's a shame you didn't get to see *Gone with the Wind*." I said: "Yes, I saw it, and it is a shame. My wife, two kids, and I drove all the way up to Cincinnati to see it. And it wasn't worth the trip. It's just another shameful glorification of the fantasy known as the Old South and the myth that such a fine civilization was shamelessly destroyed by a damnable bunch of nigger-loving Yankees!"

Black people were not allowed, of course, to patronize any of the big Louisville hotels. We were only allowed to go inside if we were servants and in a servant's uniform. I once, however, got into old J. Graham

Brown's hotel as a guest. It was back in 1946 when the Brown Hotel was a show-off place, and John L. Lewis, who was in his heyday as a labor leader, came to town for a conference. The phone rang in the principal's office at Central High School, and a voice asked to speak with "Mr. Lyman Johnson." "Mr. Johnson is in class," the secretary said. "But I can take a message, and he'll call you back when he's free. Yes, I'll tell Mr. Johnson that he's been invited to a meeting at the Brown Hotel." The principal overheard the call and asked: "What's that? Who's inviting Johnson to the Brown Hotel? He knows he can't go there." The secretary said: "It was Mr. Ed Weyler, the executive secretary of the AFL-CIO. He's getting together some local labor leaders for a meeting with John L. Lewis, and Mr. Johnson is invited."

When I got the message, I called to make sure it wasn't a joke. Then I said: "Mr. Weyler, you know J. Graham Brown's policy on Negroes coming into his hotel. And I'm not going down the alley and sneak up in the freight elevator. And I'm not going to put on a white jacket so I can go in the front way." He said: "Mr. Johnson, you come right on. The meeting is at four o'clock, but you come about ten minutes to four, and we'll have five men waiting for you at the Broadway entrance. You get in the middle of them, and all of you will go in together, get on the elevator together, and get off at the fourth floor together. You'll be in the meeting before J. Graham Brown knows you're anywhere near." I said: "All right. Just remember that I'm not going in the back way, and I'm not going to put on a white jacket."

Everything worked just as the man said till I got ready to get off the elevator. In those days Negro girls operated the hotel elevators. Just as I was leaving the elevator, I felt as if I'd caught my coattail on a hook. I looked back, and there was a Negro girl holding my coattail so I'd be the last one off. She whispered: "Mr. Johnson, I like you. You were one of my best teachers at Central, but my job here is to operate this elevator. And I can't let Negroes ride it. When you came on, I recognized you, but I decided not to say anything about it because the white people didn't seem to care. But, please, Mr. Johnson, please, don't tell anybody what number elevator you came up on. I'd lose my job. And please don't take this one when you go back down." When the meeting was over about half past six, I remembered her plea. I got in with the same bunch of white people, and we all went down another elevator. Again, the same thing happened. As I was getting off on the first floor, the Negro elevator operator was tugging at my coat. "Mr. Johnson, please don't tell anybody you rode down on my elevator. I'll lose my job if you do."

I can't blame those girls. I'm sure they were working for minimum wages. They had little education. They were the kinds of people who needed someone like my Tuskegee niece to lead them out of the wilderness. I couldn't expect much leadership from people like them, but I did expect it from my niece. That's why I condemned her for trying to muzzle me. Yet she has benefited from the work of less privileged people like Rosa Parks. There's a new day in Tuskegee. The voting rights laws have put a black mayor and black councilmen in office. The mayor is even married to a white woman! It's a nice place to live now—even for blacks.

When I moved to Louisville, the only park open to blacks was Chickasaw, a little area south of Broadway. Negroes from all over the city and county who wanted to use a park had to go there. On a big holiday like the Fourth of July, people were elbow to elbow. There weren't enough tables for people to spread their food on, so most of us had to sit down on the ground and eat there. It was a tiny little park. All the parks for white people—Iroquois, Cherokee, Seneca, and Shawnee—were so spacious. Negroes would drive by those parks and see how nice they were. We could even drive through the white parks, but if we got out of our cars, we would be arrested for disorderly conduct. A lot of Negroes on their way to Chickasaw would drive down Chestnut Street, which empties into Shawnee Park. They would go on through Shawnee out to Chickasaw. I don't know what a Negro would have done if he'd had a flat in Shawnee. I guess he would have kept running on the flat till he got out to a public street open to Negroes. Then he could have stopped to change his tire.

We used to envy all the tennis courts the white folks had in their parks. I'd drive out to Iroquois, stop my car near the tennis courts, and if I didn't see a policeman or a park guard, I'd get out and walk around a little. If I stopped my car and a guard came up to me, my excuse was that I was just turning around. As long as our cars were moving, we were not technically violating the law.

Chickasaw is still open and is still practically all black because whites have never gotten used to the idea that it's open to them also. Although blacks now go to all the parks, to many people Chickasaw is still the Negro park.

Times are so much better today, but the scars remain. And sometimes they bleed like raw wounds. I'll never forget the fear that Negroes lived under all the time—our feelings of paralysis and helplessness. Here is an incident I must put on the record. I can never forget it. One afternoon when I was in school at Virginia Union, about five of us young men went over to visit with some sorority girls in their rooming house. We were all spruced up, and the girls were dolled up. We thought we were hotshots. It was about six o'clock in the evening—still light enough for us to see. We were just a bunch of boys and girls sitting around on the front porch. The house was located where a main street dead-ended into a side street. Suddenly, our talking and laughing was interrupted by all kinds of car noises—motors gunning, brakes squealing, tires spinning—and we real-ized that somebody was being chased by the police and that he was zigzagging all over the neighborhood trying to escape. Then we saw an old Ford ripping down our street, and we knew he was not going to make the ninety-degree turn. Sure enough, his car flipped over a wall and into a ravine, landing upside down. The police car pulled up in a cloud of dust, and two policemen jumped out and hollered: "Come on, nigger. Get on up here. You thought you could get away. Get your black ass up on this road."

This happened during the days of Prohibition, and the Negro was a well-known bootlegger. But now he was helpless. "I can't move," he screamed. "My legs are broke and one arm." We students still sat on the front porch and saw it all. We were afraid to move. We saw the police go down into the gully where the injured man was lying. They began to beat him with clubs as they pulled him up on the road. He was hollering all the time. And we were watching and didn't move. The sorority housemother came out on the porch and said: "Don't let them treat that man like that. He's helpless. They'll kill him." But we all sat still. So she walked off the porch, down the steps, and out to the gate, where she was just a few feet from where the police were still beating the man. She said: "Officers, don't you see that man can't help himself. Please don't beat him anymore. Please don't." We watched as the police turned on her and said: "Nigger woman, you tend to your own goddamn business. You better shut up and go back in your house, or you'll get a taste of this same medicine."

They began calling her all kinds of crude names. She turned around and came back up on the porch. She looked at us, but we couldn't look at her. There we were—five healthy young black men—and there wasn't a thing we could do. Just a few minutes before we had been bragging with those girls, making them think we were the saviors of civilization. Now we were cringing in fear. Not one of us opened our mouth. In less than five minutes, our manhood had been stripped from us. We felt completely impotent as the police threw that poor injured man into the police car and drove away. We were afraid of what would have happened to us if we had tried to interfere. We were afraid they would have shot us or beaten us up. We were like helpless aliens in our own country.

It was nothing new to me. I'd witnessed scenes like this all my life. One Sunday afternoon when I was a boy in Columbia, I was sitting on my father's front porch reading the paper. I heard a car racing down from off the highway, past the city limits, down to the foot of the hill where we lived. I could tell the car hadn't slowed down, and I thought, "Good God, why would anybody be driving that fast?" Just as he was trying to make a wide right turn, he got on the wrong side of the road and plowed smack into another car. When he crawled out of his car, I saw it was a Negro. Well,

I thought, this Negro is in for it: speeding, driving on the wrong side, and hitting another car. Sure enough, the first thing the police did when they arrived was to start beating on him. "Nigger," they said, "what in the hell do you mean driving like that? We'll just have to teach you a lesson."

The black man pleaded: "Officer, I know I was speeding. I know it was all my fault. But please don't beat me. Please get my insurance papers out of the car pocket." The police didn't pay him any attention. They had him down on his knees, clubbing him, and he was trying to protect himself with his arms. And I was sitting up there on my father's front porch and saw it all. It broke my heart that I didn't have the guts to go out and try to stop them. I would have gotten hurt. I would have made trouble for my family. And it wouldn't have done any good anyway. I knew I was helpless.

That's the system black people used to live under. It's a wonder we didn't break and go crazy. It's a wonder we survived. Oh, yes, if I wanted to, I could really unload some guilt. I got all hell packed up sky-high ready to unload. I will remember scenes of injustice and brutality the rest of my life.

Lunch Counters & Flaming Crosses

It's hard to make history if you spend too much time reading it.
You've got to focus on what you're doing.

WHEN I CAME to Louisville I had a Deep South accent, and the people were a little suspicious of me; but gradually they began to accept me. "Maybe this fellow from Tennessee is a go-getter," they said. I've tried not to disappoint them.

I got involved in controversy soon after I arrived. I was a civil rights activist before I ever heard the term. One of the first times I raised my hand as an activist was around 1935 when some white people were trying to help Negroes raise money to reopen the black YMCA that had closed several years before. At an all-black public meeting, I asked: "Why are these white people so eager for us to have a YMCA on Chestnut Street? Are they afraid we'll try to come to dinner at the main Y at Third and Broadway? If that's their motivation, then they ought to take the word *Christian* out of their name and just call it 'Young Men's Association.' It's good to have a branch in our neighborhood, but it's not good if the price for that branch is a white-only door at the main YMCA. I don't want to use the facilities of the Y in St. Matthews. It's too far from where I live. I don't expect a man in St. Matthews will want to come to a branch in the West End. But it seems to me that the main branch ought to be for everybody, regardless of his race or where he lives."

They pounded me down. "Lyman," a black man said, "don't insult those white people who are trying to help us open our Y. Keep on like that, and they won't give us any money. Now, you keep quiet and keep away from Third and Broadway. We want a Y in our neighborhood, and this is the only way to get it. So keep your opinions to yourself." I looked around me and saw that everybody was agreeing with him. I got angry as hell. "Well, damn all of you," I said. "If you go along with this sort of thing, you're as bad as the white folks."

When I began teaching at Central High School, I was an upstart, but I tried to fit into its excellent faculty. Many of them had degrees and advanced study from such schools as Columbia, Harvard, Chicago, Iowa, Illinois, Indiana, and Western Reserve. Starting in 1931, the principal spent thirty-two consecutive summers studying at the University of Chicago, not to get a Ph.D., he said, but so he could be a good principal. He knew that regardless of how much education he had he could never get any higher in the education hierarchy. He knew he could never become an assistant superintendent. To become a superintendent was unthinkable!

At the first faculty meeting in the fall, he would ask the teachers to tell about their summer school experiences. One time after the faculty had made their reports about summer study and travel, he turned to me and said: "Lyman, you haven't told us where you went this summer. You haven't said what you've done to become a better teacher." I said, "Yes, I went out and improved myself at the University of Wisconsin." I could have told them about my classes or my campus activities or how nice the young chicks looked in their swimsuits on the beach or how sometimes they'd come to class with water dripping off and a robe barely covering their nakedness. Instead, I said: "Now, I don't know whether we ought to be sitting here, beating our chests and praising ourselves. It reminds me of the caged chimpanzee that I heard about in psychology class. Somebody forgot to bring his food one time, and he got very hungry. Then someone came along and dropped a banana a short distance from his cage. The hungry chimp reached one paw out toward the banana but couldn't quite reach it. He started prancing around in his cage, eyeing that banana and crying because he couldn't get it. He kept on and on, and his appetite got keener and keener, and he got more and more frustrated. Finally, he saw a stick over in the corner of his cage. He went over, got the stick, reached out, and raked the banana close enough to his cage to reach it with his paw. He snatched it inside, peeled it, and looked at it for a few seconds. He got so elated at his accomplishment that he jumped up and shouted in his animal language. But, sorry to say, he was already so hungry and exhausted that he died before he had a chance to taste that banana. Now, here's the moral," I said. "I hope we don't get so carried away with our accomplishments that we fail to get to the meat of the matter—to pass on our learning to our students. Let's not fail to eat the banana. And let's not forget that we're still confined to a cage. We're still teaching and living in a segregated, caged society." For many years after that, somebody would be sure to say: "All right, all this bragging about our summer accomplishments is fine, but let's not forget to eat the banana. Let's not forget that we live in cages."

I tried to teach my students history, but I also wanted to help make changes in society that would ensure that some parts of history would not be repeated. And I used my position as a teacher to get my students involved in the struggle for their human rights. I was called on the carpet so many times by the board of education for my civil disobedience that they convinced me that what I was doing was right. It was refined in the fiery furnace. I taught my students that they are morally obligated to disobey laws that are wrong. At the same time, I warned them to think of the consequences and to ask three questions: How much penalty will I have to pay for violating this law? How much good will I accomplish by violating this law? When I weigh the good and the bad likely to result from violating this law, is the violation worthwhile?

One time a school board member said, "Mr. Johnson, if it's against the law for blacks to go to Iroquois Park and you tell your students to use the park anyway, don't you think you've done wrong?" I answered: "No. No. It would be wrong if some vicious policeman cracks open your head before he gets you to the police station. And it would be wrong if you're jailed or fined for using a public park that should be open to everyone."

I've used civil disobedience tactics, and I've used my students in my operations. Back in the late 1950s when we were demonstrating to open up the ten-cent store and drugstore lunch counters on Fourth Street, I was warned by the school board not to use kids in my classes in the demonstrations. A judge even told me he'd hold me in contempt of court if he found me using schoolchildren. So I told my students: "Well, young folks, the superintendent says he'll fire me. The judge says he'll hold me in contempt of court. So I'm not going to ask a single one of you—I'm not even going to invite you—to help with the demonstration this afternoon at Walgreen's at half past three. School will be out at three o'clock, which will give you plenty of time to go home and tell your mothers that Mr. Johnson will not invite you to participate in the demonstration that he'll be leading at half past three at Walgreen's on Fourth Street." By half past three, I always had more than enough students for the demonstration.

Those of us who demonstrated around Louisville followed a pattern that was set up in Chicago around 1946. We demonstrated to open up facilities and jobs to black people. We boycotted stores and made a nuisance of ourselves by occupying segregated facilities. We found out that most companies were not really concerned about segregation. "We're here for business and profit," they said. "We're not here for race relations. Whatever brings in money suits us. It doesn't matter whether we like black people or hate black people. We want to do whatever is profitable."

Our plan was to concentrate on one project at a time. First, we'd open up the parks, then the universities, then the lunch counters, then the hotels and restaurants, and so on till we had a society accessible to everyone. Although our focus would be in one area, we insisted that it didn't mean that we were not concerned about all the other patterns of segregation. It simply meant that we only had the forces to mount one front at a time. Once a battle was won, we went on to another opening.

My students were very useful in helping to open up the ten-cent stores, the drug stores, and the big department stores downtown. With from about ten to thirty students, I'd go to my target store. One time I remember we went to Woolworth's. The lunch counter was L-shaped, with about ten seats on one side and fifteen on the other. I was number four on the short side. One of my little girl students was number three on the long side. She was coal black. She was wearing a blue skirt and a pretty white blouse. It was such an attractive combination: blue skirt, white blouse, black arms, and black face. She looked so good sitting there with all her beauty and grace and dignity. In front of her were a napkin, some silverware, but no plate. The white waitress stood there but made no move to serve her. Suddenly, a white kid comes up from behind her and pours red tomato ketchup on top of her hair. Her hair had been straightened and pressed and combed down, as Negro girls did in those days. They didn't go in for Afros or naturals then. She was looking so refined and attractive, and here comes all this red ketchup pouring down her hair and down across her face and dripping on down her spotless white blouse.

She looked across the counter at me as if to say, "Shall I kill this bastard or what?" But she knew what I had told them. "No matter what they call you, you don't say one word back—not one. No matter what they do or how much vulgarity they spew out at you, sit there and be the picture of dignity and self-control." This little girl was being put to the test. She looked at me. I smiled at her and said, "Darling, you look lovely." Then she smiled, and I knew she was all right. Her dignity was so beautiful. Even the little white girls on the other side of the counter looked like they would cry. It was embarrassing even to white people to see how mean other white people could be. They seemed sorry for what had happened. I said to her, "Take a napkin and wipe if off your face." She wiped her face, then looked at the two red streaks all the way down her white blouse. I said: "Don't wipe that off. Let that show." Within seconds the manager of the store came up and said, "I'll serve all of you." I had told the kids to bring twenty-five or thirty cents, so they bought a hamburger and a coke.

After a while most of the drugstore and ten-cent store counters were open to us. So we started climbing the ladder by integrating the lunch-rooms at the big department stores. One day about thirty of us went into the first-floor counter at Kaufman-Straus. We took every seat. It was always understood that I would be the spokesman at the sit-ins. Nobody in our group would speak to anyone except among themselves. The manager came up and started arguing with me. "If you don't get out of here, I'll call the police," he threatened. Soon a policeman came into the store, leaving three others at the door on Fourth Street. "Arrest them all," the manager said. "Or at least get them out of here." The policeman didn't say anything. He just listened. Finally, the manager shouted, "Well, what are you going to do?" The officer said: "Everything seems peaceful and quiet to me. I don't see any violation of the law." The manager was enraged and said, "If you don't throw them out, I will."

I think this was the only time I ever came close to losing my cool. But I looked around and saw all my students I had preached to about self-discipline, and I knew I couldn't afford to violate my own rule. I said: "All right. Go ahead. Throw us out. But don't lay a hand on these people." The manager knew I was calling his bluff. He looked at the policeman, who said again: "I can't arrest them till they do something. You're the only one ranting and raving around here. You're the only one creating a distur-bance." That made the man mad, and he yelled over to the restaurant workers: "Clear the tables. Clear the tables. Take everything back to the kitchen. Shut down. Close up." And that's what they did. They took all the food back to the kitchen. They cleared the tables. They cleaned off the steam tables just like it was the end of the day. The waitresses were dismissed, and a waiter came along and turned off all the lights. We were still sitting there. Then the manager put up a big sign that said "CLOSED." Then I said to the children: "Everyone get out of here as fast as you can. If there is no food here, if there are no waitresses, if the lights have been turned out in the food section, and if there is a sign up that says "CLOSED" and you are inside this section, then you are trespassing. And when you go out on the street, hold your hands out flat like this so that they can see you brought nothing out. Don't go close to any counter. Quick! Quick!" Very quickly we were all out. The discipline we had practiced at briefing sessions paid off.

Usually, I had a handful of other adults who helped with the sit-ins—but not many. One black pastor who was very active in the demonstrations was Bishop E. Eubank Tucker. Many people considered him a nut. But he had guts. He had been a lawyer before he became a preacher. Once he was pleading a case when the opposing lawyer said to the judge, "Your honor, I will prove this nigger is guilty." Tucker said, "Your honor, I object!" The judge said, "What is your objection?" Tucker said: "I don't like that lawyer's language. He referred to my client as a nigger. He is not a nigger. He is a black man or a Negro. He is not a nigger." The judge said, "Objection overruled." When the lawyer kept referring to Tucker's client as a "nigger," Tucker finally said, "Call him that again and I'll knock you down, you son of a bitch!" The judge said, "Mr. Tucker, I hold you in contempt of court for using vulgarity in this court." Tucker laughed out loud and said, "The son of a bitch who called my client a nigger was the one using vulgarity." The judge had the last word. "Double the sentence for contempt," he ordered.

Tucker was a preacher and a lawyer—and a Nixon Republican. People said, "You see, that just proves the man is crazy." He nevertheless did a lot for blacks in Kentucky by raising hell as a civil rights advocate. As a bishop of the African Methodist Episcopal Zion Church, he was a powerful man. But he was so unrestrained that sometimes he had trouble getting parents to let him take their kids out for demonstrations. Sometimes he'd call me and say: "Professor, I can't get these parents to let their children go with me unless I can get you to go along. Will you please come?" I'd say, "All right, Mr. Tucker, what do you want to take on today?" Maybe he'd say, "I want to picket the phone company." Then we'd all go down and picket the target for that time.

Each breakthrough would give us encouragement. Each success gave us courage to tackle something more difficult. We went from the lunch counters to the Blue Boar Cafeteria and finally to first-class restaurants like Hasenour's. That was a rough one! They sent us word: "Tell the niggers not to come out here. They'll get their heads bashed in if they do. This restaurant is for white folks in a white neighborhood. Negroes don't live around here. And you can't pay the price we charge here. You don't belong here. We don't want you. Don't come." We held off on Hasenour's till the time was right.

Finally, we got up enough nerve to go against J. Graham Brown—his hotel, his theater, and his restaurants. Brown swore that any Negro who came in his hotel or restaurants had to come in the back alley, and as soon as he got in, he had to put on a white jacket. "Dressed like that," he said, "we will not only see your black face but know you're here as a servant." We started on the Brown Theater in December of 1959. A road show from New York was performing *Porgy and Bess*, but Louisville Negroes couldn't go to see it. We said, "This is hell on wheels," and we picketed for the whole run of the play. We cut into their attendance, and rather than let Negroes in, they stopped the play early.

One day a very affluent Negro and his wife drove up to the curb in their big Cadillac near where we were picketing and called me over. "Lyman," he said, "why don't you come away from that theater? You're just embarrassing us Negroes. Don't you know that J. Graham Brown doesn't give a damn about your picketing? Don't you know he'll never let Negroes in his theater?" I said: "One day Negroes will be free to go into this theater. I may not be able to afford it, but I can park my little Chevrolet across the street and watch rich Negroes like you stroll in with your beautiful, expensively dressed wives. And when you come out, I'll come up to you and ask: 'Did you like it? Did you like it?' "

I've been to the Brown several times since it was opened to us, but I didn't much care for what I saw. I never was very interested in the shows there. My wife was too timid and sensitive to take the kind of abuse and vulgarity we took on the picket line, but she would always go with me once a place was opened to us. I would usually get bored stiff after about thirty minutes of a two-hour ballet, and I'd say to her, "Let's go find another place to open up." My objective was to have the option to go anywhere I wanted. I was satisfied to be able to walk off the street and not have an usher tell me I couldn't go in or ask me whether I wanted the right or left balcony. I just wanted to be able to buy a ticket. If he had come down out of his penthouse, I would have told Mr. J. Graham Brown, "Until you let me in, I will mortgage my house in order to have enough money to stay in your hotel one night or to eat one meal in your restaurant or to go to one show in your theater." But after I had proved my principle, I might say: "Now you can have your damn place. I'm not interested any more."

Back in the early 1960s, we were trying to get the NAACP to hold its national convention here, and we asked how many hotels would take Negroes. The national office said they couldn't hold their meeting here because they had outgrown the practice of putting delegates in private homes, and there weren't enough hotels open to Negroes. The Sheraton said they would save a few rooms for regular customers but would let us have all the rest. We also got permission to use the Watterson Hotel. Even the Chamber of Commerce helped us to get more rooms, but we still couldn't round up enough for the convention, and it went to another city. Perhaps we would have had enough if the Brown Hotel had been open to us. I once said, however, that when a federal law is passed opening up all hotels to all races I would lead a picket at the Brown to keep our people out. The Brown has now reopened, and blacks are welcome if they can afford it. But ironically, when the NAACP did come to Louisville in 1979, the Brown Hotel was closed for lack of business. That's poetic justice.

Residential segregation has been one of the most difficult racial patterns to destroy. Whenever blacks got too close to whites, the whites would flee. This so-called white flight has been going on for a long time. In the mid-1930s, I was visiting my sister in Montgomery, Alabama, and went to a social gathering in a fine home on Jeff Davis Avenue. The Negroes were so proud of their fine quality. "White people used to live here," they said, "but they're all gone now. See what wonderful homes they left us." In a fit of outrage, I said, "How in the world can you Negroes brag about living in what were once white people's homes on Jeff Davis Avenue?" They said: "Oh, we don't care about that. We enjoy living in Montgomery's best homes on one of Montgomery's best streets named after one of the South's most illustrious sons!" And I said, "What a change is going on."

In earlier times, especially during slavery, blacks lived near whites because they were servants. They lived in quarters in the backyard. After they were freed, many of them stayed on and lived in their old cabins. This system was true in Louisville as well as elsewhere in the South. When the fancy mansions were being built on Second, Third, and Fourth streets in Louisville, most of them had spacious stables built out back. The servants lived upstairs. We now embellish the past and call these structures carriage houses, but most of them simply had lofts where the blacks lived.

But as time passed, whites became more sensitive to having blacks close to them, especially blacks who were not servants. About 1940 I caught on to the master scheme for the development and control of downtown Louisville. At that time Fourth Street was the business center of Louisville, and people thought it always would be. White business leaders decided they would keep blacks from moving into the downtown white areas by creating a vacuum or a buffer zone between the black community and Fourth Street. In those days the Negro business district was centered at Sixth and Walnut. A couple of Negroes then bought some pieces of property on Fifth Street. A corporation of Negroes decided to buy the National Theater at Fifth and Walnut on the west side—just across the street from the Kentucky Hotel, which was owned by J. Graham Brown. When Brown found out that a Negro corporation was about to buy a building across the street from his hotel, he got hopping mad. He said it would be an insult to his hotel guests if they had to look out and see a Negro outfit across the street. Somehow he forced the owners of the National Theater to rescind their offer to sell to Negroes. Then he bought the building, tore it down, and wiped out the whole block with a parking lot. He said he'd rather see the block covered with asphalt than with Negroes. Well, old man Brown is dead now and probably rolling over in his grave at all the blacks going in and out of his places.

Brown was simply a part of the master plan to keep blacks away from Fourth Street. They were already close, just two blocks from the hub of the white business district at Fourth and Walnut. That intersection had four of the biggest white concerns in town: the Seelbach Hotel on one corner, Selman's on another, the Starks Building on another, and Stewart's on the other. "We've got to be more careful," the white leaders were saying. "The

Negroes are getting closer. We'll just have to move them away." So the blueprint was to clear out from Seventh to Fifteenth streets and to push the Negroes west toward the Ohio River. Eventually, it made the West End a black ghetto.

The master plan put together principally by the Chamber of Commerce was to build an industrial and warehouse corridor between the blacks in the West End and the grand, glorious business district called Fourth Street. So they bought up the shacks of the Negroes living from about Seventh Street to Fifteenth Street, and Urban Renewal demolished them. Laws and attitudes changed. So what do you have now between Seventh and Fifteenth streets? Mostly a void. As the poor Negroes from Sixth, Seventh, and Eighth streets were pushed out and started moving west close to white residences, the whites panicked and moved to the East End suburbs. It was the beginning of white flight. The whites gave up beautiful houses on nice residential streets with sidewalks and trees and good drainage. They moved into cheaper-built houses that soon began to crack and fall apart.

So what happened to the beautiful homes vacated by the whites? A lot of poor Negroes displaced from their downtown homes by Urban Renewal moved in. Since they couldn't afford to pay rent for a whole house, the white slum landlord would put in two or three Negro families. He would squeeze every penny he could out of the renters. He didn't keep the houses repaired, and the renters didn't have the money or the desire to keep the places up. The houses began to deteriorate, and the grand homes of the West End began to look like shacks. When a house became unlivable, the tenants would move to another and bring it down. That's why there are so many run-down and torn-down houses in the West End right now. It's one price we've had to pay for racism.

On the other hand, blacks who can afford to own and keep up those homes live in dream places. Drive up and down Southwestern Parkway, for example, and you'll see black people sitting on those big front porches just like they've been there for ages. It's hard to believe that twenty-five years ago they were afraid even to go down there.

Residential segregation in Louisville, of course, goes back a long way, but it wasn't till about 1914 that the Board of Aldermen passed the Residential Segregation Ordinance. It provided that if a city block had a majority of one race living on it, no additional members of the other race could move into it. It meant that if a city block had a majority of blacks, no more whites could move there. If there was a majority of whites, no more blacks could move in. It hemmed Negroes into a few blocks near downtown Louisville. It meant, for example, that no Negroes could move west of Eighteenth Street because in practically every block beyond Eighteenth whites were in the majority. There was a church owned by Negroes that had two entrances, with the main one opening onto a white majority block and the other opening onto a black majority block. The blacks had to use the street of the smaller entrance as their official address because it was a Negro block.

In those days there was a black Louisville postal employee named William Warley who decided he was going to fight the ordinance. He bought a house on a white majority block. The white people living there said: "No, you can't move in. It's against the law." The police said, "You move in and we'll arrest you." The man from whom Warley bought the house said, "Pay me for my house, or I'll sue." The case went to court, and finally in 1917 the Supreme Court handed down its *Buchanan* v. *Warley* decision. The Court declared the ordinance a violation of the Fourteenth Amendment and therefore unconstitutional.

Warley won his case but lost his job in the post office. He couldn't get a job anywhere. He tried to put out a paper, the *Kentucky News*, but he had no money and couldn't get subscribers. It was poorly written, poorly edited, and poorly printed. He had some kind of old printing press, and he cranked out the papers himself. He even had to get out on the street corners and sell the papers himself. There was little other Negroes could do for him. They didn't have any jobs to offer him. When I knew him, he had gone down. He put the last nail in his coffin when he started drinking. Sometimes I would see this man who had once been a top-ranking black leader wobbling down the street drunk as hell. He was as shabbily dressed as any derelict and hadn't shaved for days. It was a pitiful sight. But we all benefited from the groundwork he had done.

Nevertheless, despite Warley's success in the courts, until the 1960s blacks could not live in most white neighborhoods in Louisville. In the 1950s we decided to push for open housing. About 1953 a Negro moved into a house in a white neighborhood off Crums Lane in the southwestern part of the city. The man behind the move was Carl Braden, a white man who had a reputation for being a Communist. He bought the house and let a Negro electrician, his wife, and two children move into the house with the understanding that they would make the monthly payments. Even before the black family moved in, the loan company discovered the strategem. When the black man went to the office to make a payment, the white clerk said, "Huh?" He called in the head of the mortgage company and said: "What's this Negro making this payment for? He doesn't live down there." They checked and found out that the house was sold in Carl Braden's name. Then they tried to stop the plan by bringing a legal charge against Braden that he was attempting to transfer property that he didn't own. Braden was just as clever. He said: "Oh, it's not an official transfer of property. I'm just letting this man use my house if he makes the monthly payments. Actually, I'm tricking this Negro! The house is in my name, and when he pays the house off, it'll still be mine, and I can put him out!"

When the black family moved in, they caught their white neighbors by surprise. Here were a deep yellow-colored Negro and his wife, a little darker than he, and their two little colored children suddenly living in their white midst! The whites said it must be a Communist plot to stir up racial strife. They began to parade in front of the house with signs like "Nigger, Get Out" and "Nigger, Leave While You Can" and "Stay Here, Nigger, and You're Dead." And when the man was at work, they would yell vulgar names at his wife. Finally, it all got to be too much, and the Negro woman got her two kids, locked up the house, and ran over to her mother-in-law's. When the man got home from work that evening, he found a note from her and two windows that had been broken out. All this time the police had been conspicuously absent. But the black man said he wasn't moving. "They'll have to shoot me out," he said.

When word got out that he was going to stay, some white agitators sent him a message. "Nigger, if you come back down here, we're going to blow up the house with you in it." When that threat spread to the black community, several of us agreed that we would go and help him stand guard. We set up a guard duty roster. My turn was from six to nine at night. I was armed with a .38. Another guard had a Winchester rifle. Each person had his own weapon, and we had ammunition stashed in a corner for general use. At six o'clock I started my duty. I sat on a sofa in front of a big picture window reading the afternoon paper. I was nervous, and if anybody had said "Boo!" I expect I would have jumped out the back window. But nothing happened. No one came by shouting any obscenities. I began to wonder if the situation was as serious as people thought, but there was that ugly thing still written on the window: "Nigger, Get Out!"

The changing of the guard came at nine o'clock, and I was relieved. By that time about fifteen blacks had been by. They had come in large numbers for protection. All of us left, except for three men who were to stand guard from nine to twelve. One fellow was sitting in a chair away from the window. Another was in the back room. The third man decided to lie down on the sofa in front of the picture window. About ten minutes to eleven a volley of bullets came breaking through the window and riddled the top part of the sofa. When he heard the first bullet, the fellow on the sofa rolled off onto the floor. If he had been seated upright, he'd have been cut to pieces. If the shots had been fired when I was there reading the paper, I'd have been killed.

That wasn't all that happened that night. Later on the foundation was blown out from under one corner of the house. If the dynamite had been pushed under the house far enough, it would have blown up the whole building. Other damage was done. Nobody was hurt, but the house was practically wrecked.

The black community pressured the city and county to investigate. Finally, after what they called a thorough investigation, law officials arrested Carl Braden! They said it was all set up. They said he had set the bomb himself and had the fellow lie down on the sofa so he wouldn't be hit when Braden fired the shots through the window. It was part of a Communist plot, they said, and the state began to prosecute him on a charge of sedition. After a trial he was found guilty and sentenced to fifteen years in the state penitentiary. However, he only stayed about six weeks. A similar case in Pennsylvania found that a single state cannot prosecute for sedition. That upset a lot of people. "We found the man guilty of sedition," they said. "We gave him a fair trial with a jury of his peers. He was sentenced to fifteen years in prison. Now he's been turned loose!"

So Carl Braden was generally thought to be a Communist. And the FBI wanted to know who else was in the "cell" with him. They looked in my direction. "We think Lyman is a good fellow," they said. "He's just naive. He's still an unwitting tool of the Communists. Maybe he'll give us evidence about who else is behind all this agitation." Shoot, I wasn't fighting for any Communist cause. I was fighting for myself and my children's right to go to Cherokee Park or to eat at the Walgreen's lunch counter or to live anywhere they wanted when they got grown—just like the white kids.

I know the FBI started keeping a file on me before 1942. It's the law now that if I demand it they have to open up my file to show me what they have. But I'm not curious enough to bother. I expect if I should see what's there I'd get so mad I might become violent. I'd rather let bygones be bygones. But, dammit, I don't want the government to treat me like that again. From here on in, I don't want them to harass me. I've done a lot of mental therapy on myself about a lot of things—from Columbia, Tennessee, to Louisville, Kentucky. Things are a lot better now. I'm willing to let the bones stay buried. By God, there may be trouble if anybody digs those bones up!

Open housing was a hard battle to win. We were still fighting it when we enlisted the aid of Martin Luther King, Jr., in the mid-1960s. It was always our policy to keep in touch with the national movement. Our strategy was to bring in national leaders whenever we wanted to shake up the town. King came to bolster our morale. I met him at the home of Frank Stanley, editor of the *Louisville Weekly Defender*. About twenty of us so-called Negro leaders met in Stanley's recreation room on his third floor. The meeting started about half past eleven at night and ran till about three o'clock in the morning. King was the center person. He spent most of his time encouraging us. "Don't back down," he said. "Don't water down your objectives. Let people know where you stand and be determined. People of goodwill all across this country and people around the world are supporting you. Don't give in and be intimidated. Don't become despondent. Don't become hopeless. Keep encouraging other blacks as well as your white supporters, but don't let anyone get to the point of committing rash acts of vandalism, rowdyism, and violence."

I agreed with King on nonviolence. There were even times when I would advise that we cancel a demonstration because of the likelihood of violence, from either blacks or whites. When we had racial disturbances in Louisville in 1968, a lot of blacks armed themselves with sticks and rocks and guns. I said to them: "Fellows, you can't win with these weapons— not even with your little guns. As soon as you shoot up all the bullets you've got, you'll have to go to the white man to buy more. There's not one black man in this town making bullets! As soon as you need a new gun, you've got to go to a white dealer and buy one. And he'll say, 'Black boy, what are you gonna do with this gun and these bullets?' And you'll say, 'I want a gun and some bullets so I can shoot whitey.' So you've got to buy a gun from whitey to shoot whitey! Now, do you think that white man's going to let you have one—even if he's in sympathy with you? Or maybe he'll say, 'Fellows, I just sold out to whitey, and he's standing over there on the corner waiting for you to come out.' "

But the damn fools did it anyway. Two of them got killed. Two of them got sent to the penitentiary. And a whole business section in the black neighborhood went out of business. Most of the stores were owned by whites, but they gave work to blacks and provided a convenient place for them to shop. Now all those places are boarded up and vandalized. It's a disgrace. I tried to talk straight to them. "You can't win," I said. "You'll make things worse." That's what they did.

We learned a lot from King about using nonviolent tactics. I liked him personally. He was a cordial, warm person and a spellbinding speaker. I heard him speak five or six times, and I talked with him in small groups and one-on-one on three occasions. His brother, A.D. Williams King, was pastor of Zion Baptist Church at Twenty-second and Muhammad Ali, about a block from where I live. Martin preached there from time to time. His brother A.D. left Louisville to become one of the pastors of his father's church in Atlanta. One day he was found dead in his backyard swimming pool.

King was a good model to hold up to young black people. I could say to my students: "Here is a young man who went through high school and got his lessons. He had good morals and good conduct. His mother and father didn't have to make him behave himself. He was smart enough that his parents didn't have to make him be good. He excelled in college. Then he did his university work and got top degrees. But he never became so sophisticated, so elegantly conditioned that he couldn't meet and mingle with common people. He did a lot of good things for the common people. He was a great man and a good example for you to follow."

Left, Lyman Johnson's father, Robert Graves Johnson (seated), with his brother John William Johnson and sister Mary Johnson (Williams), c. 1914. Below, the Johnson children in front of their home in Columbia, Tennessee, c. 1915 (Lyman is standing).

Unless otherwise noted, photos are courtesy of Lyman Johnson.

Above, Queenie Moore's second grade class at College Hill School, Columbia, Tennessee, 1915; Johnson is in the second row, 9th from left. Below, Johnson (third from left) at Alpha Phi Alpha Fraternity House while attending graduate school at the University of Michigan, 1930-32.

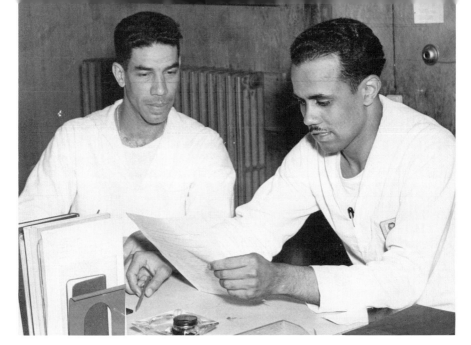

Above, Johnson (left) teaching in the U.S. Navy literacy program, 1944. Below, schoolteacher Johnson at Central High School, March 1947. Courtesy of the *Louisville Courier-Journal.*

Above, the Johnson family in the early 1950s: wife Juanita Morrell, son Lyman Morrell, and daughter Yvonne Johnson (Hutchins). Below, Johnson (right) and the president of Kentucky State College, R.B. Atwood, leaving Federal District Court in Lexington after victory in Johnson's suit to gain admission to the University of Kentucky graduate school. Courtesy of The Herald-Leader Company.

Above, an Alpha Lambda Alpha Fraternity banquet honoring Johnson as 1950 Man-of-the-Year. Below, Johnson as business manager of the Central High School football team with the coaching staff, c. 1952.

Left, demonstrators
protest segregation laws
at the corner of 4th and
Chestnut streets in
downtown Louisville.
Below, protesters waiting
for service at a Louisville
restaurant before being
arrested for delinquency
and breach of the peace.
Both photos, 1961;
Louisville Courier-Journal.

Above, segregation protesters during the first Louisville sit-in in front of the Blue Boar cafeteria, 1961; *Louisville Courier-Journal.* Below, Johnson receives a bust of Dr. Martin Luther King, Jr., awarded for community service, from *Louisville Defender* publisher Frank L. Stanley, Sr., at the Plymouth Congregational Church. At extreme left is Mrs. Johnson. Courtesy of the University of Louisville Photographic Archives, Louisville Defender Collection.

Above, Johnson and
a student at Lyman
Johnson Middle
School, Louisville,
1978. Below,
Johnson at the gate
to his home on
Muhammad Ali
Boulevard where he
has lived for more
than thirty years.
*Louisville Courier-
Journal.*

A lot of people have been blinded by his charisma, especially since his assassination. They look to him as the Messiah, the Savior, the One-and-Only. I don't hold to that opinion. To me Martin Luther King, Jr., was an important black leader but just one among many others. I think King, like Lincoln, was on the scene and available when a leader was needed. Both of them had daring leadership qualities. Rosa Parks's refusal to give her bus seat to a white man in Montgomey opened the door for King. Without her he would have been just another young black intellectual preacher whose influence wouldn't have gone much beyond his own congregation. But he was there and was prepared and he rose to the occasion. He was just the man at the time for the job that needed to be done in Montgomery.

King's death was a great loss to the civil rights movement. When we had our meeting at Frank Stanley's house, I told him: "Dr. King, you are too reckless with your young life. We need you alive. You're more value to us making your speeches. If you get killed, it'll be a long time before we can produce another Martin Luther King. We need leaders like you on the battlefield for at least the next twenty years. You're educated for the job; you've proved yourself; and you've gotten high up on the mountain; but that's just when some nut may try to bump you off. Please be careful. The way on up is steep. Help us get to the top of the mountain." And he said: "I'm not worried, Lyman. If it is my fortune or misfortune to have to leave this world tonight, there's no hesitancy on my part. I'm ready to go."

I don't think King's work was finished, but I'm not sure how much more he could have accomplished by himself. He was a solo player. He ran the Southern Christian Leadership Conference; he *was* the SCLC. With King gone, the group has almost fallen flat. It's not like the NAACP, which is run by a board. Their executive secretaries like Roy Wilkins and Walter White had their shots called by this board. King was always bigger than his organization, so he was under no board discipline. In the long run, this kind of discipline is important. Thurgood Marshall is a model of the disciplined leader. He didn't have the religious fervor or charisma of King, but he's accomplished as much.

I don't mean to low-rate or to underestimate King. He patterned his methods after Gandhi and was very effective. Like Gandhi he would whip people into an emotional pitch, then say: "Now hold it. Wait just a minute. Cool it." I saw him do it once at Kentucky State when he delivered the commencement address in the mid-1960s. He had the whole audience shouting: "Amen! Glory Hallelujah! Tell it like it is!" Then when they were at a fever pitch and he had them eating out of his hands, he quit his preacher twang and said: "Now, come on down out of the clouds. We've got to walk on the streets. Don't waste all that good energy you've got. Use it constructively tomorrow and the next day. You want good jobs. You want good housing. You want good schools. You want all these good things in life, but you're not going to get them up there in the clouds.

Come on down and let's talk about how you can get them." Then he began to lecture like hell about the cold economic facts of why black people are at the bottom of the pile.

Like all good leaders, he knew he couldn't solve the problems himself. The work had to be done by the people themselves. King knew how to put them on the road to a better life. He was a good general and a pretty good foot soldier. He'd get out and walk with the people. He'd get his head beaten in. He'd have police dogs sicked on him. He'd get jailed. He'd take a lot of ugly words people threw at him. And all the time he'd be praying for his tormentors' salvation from prejudice. He proved that fighting back is unproductive. I don't think he could have done any more.

I never heard King preach in his church in Montgomery, though I was a visitor to the Dexter Avenue Baptist Church many times in the 1930s when my brother-in-law was pastor. King had arrived by the time Rosa Parks decided not to give up her seat to a white man. I expect my brother-in-law could have done what King did. But he had no Rosa Parks.

I was also involved in the local school busing controversy. The Democratic Issues Convention met in Louisville in the midst of the antibusing agitation. A bunch of people had taken over the parking lot across the street from Louisville Gardens, where the hearings were being held. They were howling and chanting and hooting, saying all sorts of ugly things. The city sent police down to try to protect the Gardens and the visitors from any violence. On one side of the street there was a line of police, and on the other was a mob of people. The police were armed with sticks and pistols. They said: "Now, you people, you stay on that side of Walnut Street, and we won't bother you. But if you come over here where the convention is going on, you'll get your heads cracked."

The mob kept making so much noise they were embarrassing the city administration. "Here we have all these visitors in town and look how these white people are carrying on," they said. It wasn't black people raising all that hell. It was white people embarrassing white people. In order to get them to pipe down, the program committee arranged to let one of their spokesmen come in to the meeting and explain why they were protesting busing. They were to be given five minutes. Then the program committee decided that in all fairness they had to have somebody represent the other side. So on Sunday morning at ten o'clock, the phone rang at my home. I said, "Yes, what is it?" Somebody said, "Lyman, get down here in twenty minutes." I said, "Get down where?" He said: "To the Democratic Issues Convention. You're going to make a speech on busing." I said, "I'm not registered as a delegate." He said, "Don't worry, and come on." Fortunately, I had just dressed to go to church, and I got to the Gardens in about twenty-five minutes.

At the door several people converged on me. One person pinned a big badge on my coat. Another one said, "Lyman, you've got five minutes to speak in favor of busing." By then it was about twenty minutes to eleven. First, the antibusing speaker talked for five minutes, and he was booed all the way through. Then it was my turn. I was cheered all the way. Because there had been so much cheering, the chairman ruled that I hadn't had my five minutes and gave me another three.

"Ladies and gentlemen," I said, "you heard all that noise out there in the streets all day yesterday. In Louisville we have grown accustomed to their [whites'] clamor and their violence. It is the price the black community still has to pay to live a decent life. We know that not all white people are mean and malicious. That's to our benefit because we know that we constitute such a small minority of the population that we could not win on our own. We have abiding faith that surely 60 percent of the white people in this country—that's a good majority—want to treat us fairly. But we wish that you people of goodwill would not hide your good wishes under a bushel. The black people of Louisville depend on the rulings of the federal courts to guarantee us equality of opportunity. We carried this county before the court, and it was found guilty of inequality. Now we are merely asking for the benefits the court said we are entitled to."

When I finished, they gave me a standing ovation and kept on cheering. Reporters from all around the country ganged around me, and the people were still cheering. The convention chairman rapped for order. "Ladies and gentlemen, we've got to go on with the program. Please take your seats." I said to the reporters: "They're not going to sit down till I leave. Let's go outside, and I'll talk to you." After I finished with the reporters, I went back in just as the candidates for the Democratic nomination for president were about to speak. Each had about ten minutes. Walter Mondale went on, then Jesse Jackson, and finally Jimmy Carter. Mr. Carter said in his ten minutes about what I had said in my five minutes. Right then I decided that if anybody from Georgia—and all that it represents—could come and say what I was saying I was going to support him. "Yes," I said, "I've made up my mind to support this man. I'm going to work hard for Jimmy Carter."

And I did. He got a man from Henderson to run his Kentucky campaign. Early in February of 1975, my phone rang. "Lyman Johnson," a voice said, "you don't know me. I'm Dale Sights calling from Henderson. Jimmy Carter has asked me to run his campaign in Kentucky, and he told me, 'Be sure you get Lyman Johnson on the steering committee.' " I served on the committee and worked hard to get him elected. I'm not sorry I supported him. He could have done some things better, but he could have done some things much worse. Overall, he was a good president.

There have been a lot of people in Louisville—black and white—who have stood up for civil rights.

I have made it a practice to cultivate both black and white friends in my civil rights work. One of my best white friends was Patrick Kirwan, who taught at Male High School and later at Atherton. He was active in the NAACP and other civil rights groups, but he was too liberal for his own good. He's a good example of what I tell my white friends. "Don't try to outdo me in civil rights. I get by because white people will tolerate me because I'm black, but if you do the same things, you will be cut to pieces."

Carl Braden, the man who helped push open housing, is another example of a white man who was too liberal for his skin color. He and his wife Anne were always getting themselves into serious trouble. White people would say to him, "Carl, do you mean to do all this with niggers?" He would say: "First of all, don't call them niggers. And the answer is yes. I believe in absolute equality in all things—no ifs, ands, or buts. I'm a Christian, and that's the only right thing to do."

Carl was from Louisville, but Anne was from Alabama. She was liberal when she met Carl, but he took her the last mile. She was a reporter for the *Courier-Journal*, and in the 1940s she would come down to the Negro business district looking for news. Around Sixth and Walnut on a Saturday night, the place was jumping. All of us couldn't go to Harlem, so we brought a piece of Harlem here. In those days a policeman would beat any Negro man caught walking down the street with a white woman. But Anne Braden insisted on coming down and walking through the Negro district on Saturday night. I used to get after her. "Anne," I'd say, "for your sake stay away. I don't want these white policemen downgrading you or accusing you of being a plain street strumpet. You are a fine woman. Black people are not going to say that you're a whore, but the police are. And if any of us get caught down here with you, we're liable to get beat up. I don't want to get battered because I was polite to you." She would say: "Lyman, I'm a reporter, and I have to go where the news is. I'm not afraid."

A lot of other white people helped with the civil rights work in Louisville, especially people from the Unitarian and Jewish communities—people like Arthur Kling, Kenton Atwood, Robert Reed, Mary K. Tachau, Suzy Post—and a number of Presbyterian ministers. I've always felt that Jewish support was a bit ambiguous and self-serving, though I've worked with Jews all my life, and I think they're more liberal on racial matters than other whites. Negroes could eat at the Young Men's Hebrew Association at Second and Jacob, for example, but I don't believe we could have stayed overnight. Jews knew they could get too close to Negroes for their own good. In matters of discrimination, they've been just a little above the Negro. They have helped the black man win his battles because they stand to gain too. In other words, they have helped blacks over the years fight the Jews' problems. By and large, they have helped the NAACP, the Urban League, and other civil rights groups because they're helping themselves when they help us. They know that when blacks—the low man on the totem pole—make progress, that progress will also move the Jews up.

In Louisville the Jews owned a lot of stores where we couldn't try on clothes. For them it was a business decision. They catered to white gentiles, and they knew they'd drive away their gentile business if they allowed Negroes to try on clothes. But we could sit down and eat at the YMHA because most of their business was with Jews. They weren't losing any white gentile business because the white gentiles weren't going to sit down and eat with a Jew—or a Negro.

Most of our local civil rights work has been done by black people—people like Dr. Maurice Rabb, a physician; J. Earl Dearing, a lawyer; Frank Stanley, a publisher; and several ministers—and that's the way it should be. We have always had the support of small numbers of white people, but most of them have not been very active or vocal. They've not taken a public stand for fear of being ostracized by other whites. In many cases they have helped but have done it anonymously. Our rocky road would have been smoother if more whites had supported us openly and politically. Back in 1949 at the University of Kentucky, one of the white professors came up to my table in the cafeteria and asked if he could sit with me. I said: "Now, professor, I don't want you to think I object to having you sit at my table. But I would appreciate it much more if you would stand up for me in a faculty meeting."

The *Courier-Journal* has supported much of the civil rights work that we've done. At times they've criticized me severely, but often their positions were identical to mine. Sometimes when I would get involved in an issue and chart a particular path, they would come out with an editorial and say exactly what I was saying. When they said it, it made the public think: "Well, maybe Lyman isn't so crazy after all. Maybe he's not so far wrong." When we were demanding equal pay for black and white teachers, the *Courier-Journal* said: "Why not? It's the only fair thing." When we were raising hell about keeping Negroes out of all the public parks except Chickasaw, they said, "Why shouldn't Negroes be allowed to go to all the public parks?" When we were trying to open the University of Kentucky to blacks, they asked, "What's wrong with it?" *Courier-Journal* editorials helped make my positions respectable.

Most of the local breakthroughs in civil rights have been started by a handful of people. We'd decide on a project, get it started, and then go to an organization like the NAACP or the Kentucky Civil Liberties Union. I believe in the KCLU. Through this group whites have been very helpful to the cause of blacks. But black groups have done the most good, beginning with the National Association for the Advancement of Colored People and coming down to the Southern Christian Leadership Conference. All the black progress organizations have done some good work, even the Black Panthers and the Black Muslims. The organizations that have advocated and tolerated violence, however, have done the least for blacks in the long run. I have always believed that violence is counterproductive. If any minority uses violence, it's eventually going to be wiped out by the majority. That happened to the Black Panthers. They got too bold, took matters into their own hands, started arming themselves with guns, and got wiped out. Anybody who thinks he can lick the U.S. Army or Fort Knox is crazy.

Since it was founded in 1907, the NAACP has tried to use the law to bring about social change. It focuses on enforcing the law of the land, and the law of the land is made up of the federal Constitution and the amendments that provide that all citizens will be treated alike. The NAACP says, "The law guarantees equality, and it's up to the courts to make sure it's done." That was the position of W.E.B. Du Bois. He'd say: "Don't beg for anything. You are an American citizen, and you're entitled to what every other American citizen gets. It demeans your citizenship if you beg. Demand the rights that the law guarantees you." Du Bois was sometimes too much of an idealist, and I temper his approach with a bit of practicality and common sense. I say: "I do not intend to beg, so let us reason together. Doesn't it make sense to give black people their rights so that they can be more productive citizens? Free, educated people are better able to compete and will therefore contribute more to the Gross National Product."

Some black people are embarrassed by the word *colored* in the National Association for the Advancement of Colored People. It doesn't bother me. I don't generally use the word *colored* to refer to black people, but the NAACP has done so much for black people or Afro-Americans or Negroes or whatever you want to call us that I'll take the "colored" part too. I don't have much patience with young blacks who've ridden the NAACP up the mountain and now want to scrap it because, as they say, "it's too conservative." In some ways it is more militant than the Urban League, whose main thrust has been to get jobs for blacks. The Urban League will go to a business and say to the president: "We see that you have 100 people working here but not a single black person. Don't you think it would be a good thing if you put in, say, ten or twenty blacks?" The NAACP will come along and say: "Hey, you don't have any blacks in that business. If you don't put some on in a hurry, we'll do what we can to hurt your business. We'll picket you or boycott your product. We'll make you wish you had hired some Negroes." The Urban League takes its inspiration from the economic policies of Booker T. Washington, while the NAACP is more inspired by the ideal of W.E.B. Du Bois.

The Louisville chapter of the NAACP was founded around 1914. Now we have twenty-five or thirty chapters all over Kentucky, but it was rough getting them started in small towns. If the Negro dishwasher at a white café started a chapter in, say, Elizabethtown, he'd likely have been fired. But in Louisville there were too many of us to fire us all. One time back in the 1940s when I was chairman of a membership drive for all of Kentucky, I received a letter from Lebanon, Kentucky, with eight one-dollar bills for eight memberships in the NAACP. The lady who sent in the money wrote: "Dear Mr. Johnson, please don't send any receipts. Don't answer this letter. Don't send us anything from the NAACP. It might be intercepted, and all of us would lose our jobs. Just use our little bit of money to the best advantage of us all. We feel that whatever you accomplish in Louisville will eventually be accomplished here in Lebanon." There are a lot of intelligent, educated, energetic young people who are now working with the NAACP all over Kentucky. If they keep on, they'll make us old-timers look like nobodies.

A lot of the leadership for civil rights in Kentucky came from ministers, but I believe teachers did a lion's share of the work too. Most of the teachers I knew kept the faith to the end. But some of them got tired and disgusted and gave up. One man I knew who taught at Madison Junior High said: "Lyman, I am convinced that the world does not want to be reformed or made better, so I'm going to leave the work to you. You can stay here and butt your head against a stone wall if you want to. I'm going to the University of Michigan to get a Ph.D. and to get myself a soft, safe job with a university." And that's what he did. I knew another local black teacher who quit his job, got a master's degree from Indiana University, and went to Los Angeles to become a school administrator. Another man I knew quit his job at Jackson Junior High and took a fine job in industry, advising a large company on how to reduce absenteeism and drunkenness among its black employees. When he left, he said: "Lyman, I deserve more than I'm getting here. Why don't you leave this rat race of education and civil rights and get what you can for yourself?" I said, "No, I've started this work, and I'll see it through. I believe a better day is coming."

And a better day did come. We didn't make much progress, however, till we got the federal government involved. The progress we have made would not have been possible, in fact, without their intervention. I don't like for people to say: "Oh, we don't want the federal government to come in and make us do things. We'll do them better if they'll leave us alone." That's a lie, and everybody knows it. This is what I say. "If it weren't for the federal government, black people wouldn't be going to decent schools; we wouldn't be eating where we can afford to eat; we wouldn't be seeing a movie anywhere we want or riding on a bus anywhere but the rear. Without this bad old federal government, we Negroes would still be robbed of our civil rights."

When I hear people at the Board of Education bellyache about federal interference in the schools, I say: "Damn it, if you were on your own, you wouldn't be providing decent schools for blacks. You wouldn't be paying black teachers but half of white teachers' salaries. If we hadn't taken you to court and accused you of gross discrimination, you wouldn't have been found guilty and sentenced to busing. It's a penalty you've had to pay for not having done what was right in the first place."

I don't get too enthusiastic about paying my local and state taxes, but I get a kick out of paying my federal tax. I laugh at black people who stay up long hours at night trying to figure ways to cut down their federal taxes. I say, "As good as this country has been to us, we ought to enjoy paying the full amount we owe."

Black people have learned to use whatever people, resources, and tactics are available at the time. We've also learned that a victory is not a victory till it's applied locally. We live on such-and-such a street in Louisville or Lexington or Bowling Green or Henderson—and that's where tactics have to be proved. Although we've always needed and welcomed help from the federal government and from outsiders like Martin Luther King, we know that the real trench work has to be done by the people living in their own hometowns. That's what I've tried to do for over fifty years in Louisville, Kentucky. One of my favorite methods has been to use the experts' expertise. I like to be in the presence of brilliant people, even if I detest their ideas. I've cultivated their friendship and talked with them about problems that need to be solved. I'd try to talk with a number of brilliant people about a particular problem, and then I'd sit back and say: "Now which one of these people has the best solution? Or which combination of solutions is the best?" Then I'd put their brilliance with my courage and action and try to get something done. If I was successful and people said: "Lyman, you're so smart. You're great!" I'd say, "Yeah, I'm so good because I'm using someone else's brain."

One night I was at a civil liberties union meeting with about four blacks and sixteen or seventeen whites. We were trying to decide on a legal course of action. Two lawyers suggested that we approach the case a certain way. When they finished, I said: "No, I don't think we should go that way. This is what I believe we should do." Then I proceeded to present an opposite course of action. One woman said: "Lyman, how can you contest the advice of these two lawyers? You don't have a law degree!" I said: "No, I don't have formal training in law, but I know a lot of competent lawyers. And it just so happens that yesterday I sought the advice of two lawyers just as competent as these two gentlemen, and they advised me that we should go a different route. So you see, I've now heard the expert advice of four lawyers, two on each side, and I'm the boss of all four of them. And I've concluded that the advice given me yesterday is better than the advice I've heard here tonight." Within six weeks, when we went to court, everyone had come over to my position.

It's always been my habit to checkmate when one person tells me with someone else's advice. Then I make a decision. My oldest sister, Cornelia Blue, came to Louisville before I did and was well established here before I came. When I arrived as a young man, I looked up to her and would often go to her for advice. One day I asked her how she would handle a certain situation, and she clammed up on me. I went back again. Still she wouldn't say anything. I asked her why. Finally, she said: "Lyman, don't ask me for any more advice. You never take it." I said: "Cornelia, I've always asked you what you would do in a situation. I've never asked you to tell me what I should do. I didn't ask you for orders. I asked you for advice. When I ask for advice, it means I reserve the right to do as I damn well please. It means I make my own final decision." It's a method I've used in civil rights work for half a century. I gather advice, make my own decision, and take the consequences.

Victories are won locally, but what happens in one city affects what goes on in another. No one lives on an island anymore. Whatever we were able to accomplish in Louisville eventually helped every little corner of Kentucky. When I'd go to Paducah or Ashland or Hopkinsville to speak, I'd say: "If the parks aren't open to you here, you can now open them up. If the lunch counters don't serve Negroes, you can now demand service. The laws and federal court decisions reach into every town in the state. What's legal in Louisville is legal in Paducah."

Although we had to focus our civil rights work on one front at a time, our aim was always to open up the whole society to full participation by blacks. Life is not compartmentalized. It's all one piece. It was good when we had a breakthrough in education, but what good was it when we were denied rights elsewhere? For so many years, for example, we were denied access to Louisville's cultural life. We couldn't go to the operas or concerts or plays in Memorial Auditorium like everyone else. Sometimes we'd have a section of the balcony set aside for us, and sometimes we were told simply, "We just didn't make any provision for you." When we asked about attending the so-called Kentucky State Basketball Tournament, we were told, "Well, we would like for you people to see the games, but we didn't make any provision for you."

In the 1930s and 1940s, one of the best coaches in Kentucky was William L. Kean, the head basketball coach at Central. He was known nationwide. One year he and his assistant wanted to see the games. They were told: "We know who you are. We know you coach one of the best teams in the country. But we just didn't make any provisions for colored people." At Central we suspected that the white teams were second-rate, but we wanted to see for ourselves. The white officials wouldn't let us.

A full life means full access to all areas of society. It means that if you want to see a ball game you can, regardless of skin color. It means that if you want to hear an outstanding soprano or tenor or baritone at Memorial Auditorium you can hear them there, without having to drive to Chicago or Cincinnati or New York.

If I want to close off my life to certain experiences, that's my decision. But it's not right for society to deny me an opportunity to make that decision. I may choose not to hear opera or to see ballet or to attend the St. Matthews YMCA or to go to the University of Kentucky or to play softball at Hogan's Fountain in Cherokee Park. But I should make those decisions. I remember the first time I went to the Sheraton Hotel Restaurant, which was in the basement of the hotel at Fourth and Walnut. It was in the early 1960s, and other Negroes were beginning to go there. As I walked down the steps, I thought of how many times I had passed by the little window that looked out from the basement onto Fourth Street. I had always thought it was a window of a storeroom or a junk room. When I opened the door, lo and behold, things were jumping. People were drinking and eating and lollygagging, having a good time. And I thought about how many times I had passed by without knowing what fun was going on down there below my feet! Instead of enjoying my first visit, I said: "I'm mad! Look at what I've been missing for thirty years!"

My most publicized civil rights work was as plaintiff in the case that opened up the University of Kentucky to Negroes in 1949. The state of Kentucky had maintained that Negroes were being adequately provided for at Kentucky State in Frankfort. At the trial, Thurgood Marshall, who had been sent to us by the NAACP, asked the president of the University of Kentucky, "Do you really believe that the educational facilities at Kentucky State are equal to what you have on your campus for white students?" Dr. Donovan shook his head. "So, your honor," Marshall said to the judge, "we will use the state's main witness to prove our point." The judge said: "Why drag this out? The state has won the case for you."

When I won my case, I thought I should show my good intentions and decided to register for summer classes. After I'd attended graduate school at the University of Michigan and the University of Wisconsin, I wasn't too thrilled about enrolling at Kentucky. When I went on campus, I said: "Isn't this some school? It's a dump. It's beneath me to even come to this place." But I stuck it out for the summer. Some people said, "Lyman, now that you're in, why don't you go on and get your doctorate at Kentucky?" I said: "I wouldn't cheapen my master's degree from Michigan with a doctorate from the University of Kentucky. If I get a Ph.D., I want to get it from a school I have some respect for."

Because of death threats I'd received, I decided not to stay on campus but instead roomed with a Negro family nearby. I didn't want to press my luck. My presence was enough provocation for some people. There were thirty-one other blacks on campus that summer, but my name was on the court order, and I was the symbol of integration. One of the professors pointed out to me a number of foreigners on campus who were darker than I and said: "Mr. Johnson, with your complexion you could have passed for white. You didn't have to raise all this hell to get on campus. You could have said you're from Argentina or Brazil or Chile." I said: "Yeah, I'll tell people I'm from the Chile part of Kentucky. I've been a Negro all my days, and I'm not thinking about changing my race now."

I didn't try to pass for white, and at least seven crosses—maybe more—were burned to intimidate me and the other blacks on campus. I was usually very punctual in going to my eight o'clock class on the Civil War taught by Dr. A.D. Kirwan, but one morning I ran a little late. When I arrived in class, most of the students were already there. So was Dr. Kirwan. I sat down, took out my notepad, and was ready to begin writing when I heard one of the students say, "Oh, it was such a shame to put that damn picture on the front page of the paper and to fan it out all over the country and all over the world." I wondered what he was talking about. I looked up at Dr. Kirwan. He said, "It's a disgrace." They kept on talking, and I began itching to know what they were talking about. I waited and didn't say anything. It got to be ten minutes after eight, and the class hadn't started. I began to notice that the students kept glancing over at me with embarrassed looks. Then Dr. Kirwan said, "Mr. Johnson, did it disturb you?" I didn't know what he was talking about, so I said, "No, not at all." He looked all around. Everybody was looking squarely at me by now. Then he said: "Well, if it didn't bother Mr. Johnson, we'll just say it was a shame and leave it at that. But I will say that Mr. Johnson has more courage than anybody I know." He then launched into his lecture on the Battle of Chickamauga.

In the meantime I had gotten so curious to know what the class was talking about that as soon as class was over, I jumped out the window—I didn't even wait to walk down the steps—and grabbed me a copy of the *Lexington Herald*. There on the top half of the front page was what the class had been talking about. It was a picture of a half-burned, charred cross in front of the administration building. It had fallen over and scorched the shape of a cross in the grass. At last, I knew what the classroom excitement had been about. That burned grass cross remained for several days. Then it was removed and replaced with fresh sod. The fresh green grass accentuated the shape of the cross for the rest of the summer.

There were other problems. People began telling me that a radio station out of Versailles, Kentucky, was broadcasting warnings that I'd better get off campus before I had to be carried off in a sack. The threats didn't bother me. I intended to stay on campus till the summer was over, and I did.

Even though I was black and therefore conspicuous, I tried to keep a low profile. In the morning my usual pattern was to get up, perform my toilet duties, get dressed, and walk over to the campus cafeteria. I'd pick up a morning paper at the vending machine outside, walk in at my usual speed, and get in line. I wanted to say: "See, I'm just a man, a gentleman even. I'm just like you except I'm a little older and I'm black." I'd get some coffee, toast, and jelly and walk over to a table as inconspicuously as I could. I never sat at a table with white people unless I was invited, but I never obviously segregated myself by going over to a corner table. I said to myself: "I don't care whether I sit with them or not. Here I am with my paper, my coffee, and my toast—and I'm at the University of Kentucky. A black man at the University of Kentucky—something new under the sun. That's all I need."

There wasn't a lot of opposition to my being on campus from the faculty, the administration, or the students. Most of the trouble came from racists outside the university. A lawyer from Henderson wrote the university to say that the federal court had not killed the Day Law, which required separate racial facilities. All the court had done was require that the university admit me, he said, because black schools were not equal. Once on the campus, the lawyer said, the university should provide segregated facilities for me—a separate toilet, a separate table in the cafeteria, and so on. It could easily be proved, he said, that the toilets and tables thus provided for me were equal to those being used by white students. It was, of course, a lot of malarkey. But it wasn't till 1954—five years later—that the Supreme Court ruled in *Brown* v. *Topeka Board of Education* that "separate" was ipso facto "unequal."

Most of the faculty treated me decently if not cordially. Dr. Thomas D. Clark, who was head of the History Department then, was as courteous to me as he could be. Recently, Dr. Clark wrote to me and said: "Mr. Johnson, when you came to the university, you and I had cordial relations. I treated you as I would any other student on campus. I was, therefore, grieved to hear you refer to the university as a dump." I wrote right back. "Dr. Clark, I can remember the cordial relations we had. You took quite a beating for having treated me and my fellow blacks as you would want to be treated. I appreciate that. But, Dr. Clark, until I won my case in federal court and came up here, you raised not one finger against the status quo. Like everyone else you went along with the mores. I repeat: Until the university was forced to do right by us blacks, the place was a dump. I'll even say it was a goddamn dump."

I don't know what effect the presence of black students has had and will have on the formerly all-white colleges. It certainly has changed the composition of their sports programs and has improved them. It may even improve the schools academically in the long run. One of the Kentucky professors told me the summer I was there: "Your being here is one of the best things that could have happened. The white students have already started studying more. Although they're saying that Negroes can't handle real university work, they're afraid that one of you might make a better mark than a white student. It's shaken up the white students."

I'm now over any ill feeling I may have had against the University of Kentucky. In fact, on May 12, 1979, they conferred on me the honorary doctor of letters degree, and I was there to accept. I was one of four people to receive honorary degrees at the commencement ceremonies. The others were Congressman Carl Perkins, writer James Still, and a mathematician named Shah. In the library we were shown showcases with clippings and materials about our lives. It was very flattering. I admit I liked it. In my showcase they had a picture of me shaking hands with the president of Kentucky State College. It was taken when he was apparently dressing me down for trying to enroll at the University of Kentucky before I checked with his school to see if he had the program of study I wanted. Actually, I was dressing him down for assuming I should have come to him first. There were also pictures of me doing things around campus. There was a clipping from the *Lexington Herald* describing the biggest cross they burned for me.

My sister Mary had come from New York. My son and daughter and their families had come for the ceremony. They all stayed with me. I fixed up a lot of food and put it in the refrigerator and told them to help themselves. I cooked chickens and ham and stocked up on bacon, sausage, eggs, doughnuts, and bread. And I said: "If you don't like what I've got here, you can go to a restaurant—any restaurant in town. Louisville is integrated now, and you can go where you please. But it may cost you more to eat out at a fancy restaurant than to eat in my kitchen. Integration, you know, has a price!"

After breakfast we drove over to Lexington in two cars. While the others scouted around town, I took my sister to a reception for the four recipients of honorary degrees. It was at two o'clock in the library. That's where the showcases were. I felt good about it all. Paul in the Bible says you must be careful not to think more highly of yourself than you ought to. I try to play down honors like that Kentucky degree—and others I've received since then—so I won't look too gooey and giddy and gaddy. But I don't think I have enough discipline not to be proud and elated by such awards.

The ceremonies were in an auditorium. Down one aisle marched the professors and down another came the high-ranking brass, led by the vice-president, Dr. Lewis Cochran. I was after him, followed by Congressman Perkins, Mr. Still, and Mr. Shah. We all went up on the stage with the president. It was the smoothest graduation of a big bunch of people I've ever seen. There must have been a couple of thousand graduates, but they had chosen a few symbolic graduates to actually receive diplomas. The rest would get their sheepskins as they went out the door.

Then they called for the honorary degrees. I was sitting two seats from President Otis Singletary. He went to the podium and said, "Mr. Lyman Johnson, please come forward." The vice-president next to me said, "All right, Mr. Johnson, follow me." I followed him and stood on an "X" marked on the floor. Another vice-president or dean at the end of the stage began to read a lot about me, saying that I was a man who had dedicated his life to comforting the afflicted and afflicting the comfortable. I began to feel too somber and decided I was disciplining myself too well. So I let the people know how much I appreciated what was being said and looked out at the audience and smiled broadly. Then the president said, "By the authority vested in me . . ." and so forth, "I hereby confer the degree of doctor of letters on Mr. Lyman Johnson." The vice-president reached over and put a stole over me and adjusted it across my back. It felt good. They went through the same procedure with the other three: Mr. Perkins, who was called the most honest man in Congress; Mr. Still, who had written so many books; and Mr. Shah, who was a genius in mathematics. I felt I was in tall cotton with those men. It had been raining in the morning, but by graduation time it was clear, cool, and comfortable in those gowns. But I would have smiled even if it had been raining.

At six o'clock my daughter went with me to the buffet Dr. and Mrs. Singletary had for the honorees in the president's home. I wasn't expecting anything fancy. I said, "I'll go on in, get me a sandwich, and ease on out." I found out it was an elegant affair—invitations only. Dr. and Mrs. Singletary came up to me three or four times during the evening. He said, "Dr. Johnson, we're honored to give you a degree."

It's remarkable that so much has changed in the space of thirty years— from the time I forced my way into the university on a court order to the day the university gave me an honorary degree. It's progress that I keep telling young black people about. I say: "Just look how far we've come. Don't worry about how far we've yet got to go." I don't think they understand what I mean. Maybe you have to be as old as I am to see. When I was a student at the university, I never thought race relations would get to the point where they would make such a big ado over such a spunky and cocky fellow like me.

On the Sunday after I received my degree, I left my house full of people and drove back to Lexington to speak to a little Negro Baptist church. I had agreed to speak to them before I heard about my degree, and I knew it wouldn't be right for me to cancel out. I knew that little handful of people would be disappointed if I didn't come. They would have said: "Yeah, look at that big shot now. Dr. Lyman Johnson! All that attention has gone to his head. He's too good for us now. He's been carried away by all the honors from these white folks, and he's told us damn niggers to go to hell."

I was invited to speak at the eleven o'clock service honoring senior citizens. They were all sitting in a special section in the church. But there were also two-year-olds, five-year-olds, ten-year-olds, teenagers, mothers, and fathers—people of all ages. So I talked to the old people but included everybody. After all the singing and praying and announcing, I got up to speak. Sometimes I have a prepared speech, but I'll take it out of my pocket and look at it, then fold it up and put it back and say: "If anybody wants to know what I've prepared for this occasion, you can read my speech later. Now here's what I want to say now." So I got up in the little church and said: "Now, you older people sitting over here, I'm one of you. Like you, I've paid my dues. We have all somehow survived. Some of us had pretty good sense when we started out, and some of us added a little education to it as we went along. But through all our years, we have been getting experience that all these younger people *need*. They need our advice and our wisdom. We have a wealth of information they need. Even when they don't think they need us, they do. They can benefit. So, my fellow senior citizens, let's not think that we have run our course and that we're no longer of any use." I talked along those lines for about twenty minutes, and I had every eye in the church looking at me and every ear listening.

After the service a very elderly man came up to me and said: "Mr. Johnson, I've been following you ever since you came to Kentucky. I want you to know how much I appreciate what you've done to benefit us Negroes all over the state." I didn't know the old man, but what he said made me feel good. In his way he was also awarding me an honorary degree. Unlike the one I'd received the day before, this one came from the heart of a black man whose life—in my small, limited way—I had tried to make better.

My civil rights work has not been without a price. In addition to its toll in terms of time, money, and nerves, I was kept under FBI surveillance for some twelve years. When I returned to Louisville after spending summer school at the University of Kentucky, I found McCarthyism running rampant. In the early 1950s, people who had encouraged me suddenly began to caution me to be careful. My friend, Dr. Lattimore, a highly respected Louisville doctor and member of my fraternity, called me aside one night after we had dinner at his home. "Lyman," he said, "watch yourself. The FBI has been to my office five times asking about you. I've told them that so far as I know you're as clean as a whistle. Now, Lyman, I'm your friend. You can be honest with me. Do you have anything to hide? Are you masquerading as an innocent teacher and deacon at Plymouth Congregational Church? Are you hiding behind the false facade of a dutiful father and husband? If you're doing anything subversive, don't let me be the last one to find out. I don't want to tarnish my own reputation by polishing yours. Are you keeping yourself clean?" I said: "Dr. Lattimore, I appreciate your friendship and your kind words about me. Don't worry. I've not done anything to hurt you—or me."

Other people said: "McCarthy is chopping down people all over the country. Be careful or he'll get you. Lay off the controversial issues." The more they told me to lay off, the more I showered down on them. That's when the FBI started to visit me. In the spring of 1950, an agent called me at Central High School. "We'd like to talk with you sometime soon," he said. I said: "What about today? I can be ready any time after a quarter past three." He said, "What about half past three at your house?" I had talked with a lot of people over the years about my activities but never anybody from the FBI. I knew they were trying to find out to what extent I was a Communist or Communist-supported. They assumed that somebody with an alien ideology to promote had pounced on this poor black school-teacher and was using me as a dupe. I was nervous but tried not to let it show.

That day I got home at 3:29. I had hoped to beat the FBI men home so that I could tell my wife what to expect, but they were already there. Some years before, my wife had rearranged the house and put the kitchen near the front so she could cook and see the street at the same time. The two FBI men arrived, she told me later, a few minutes after three, parked in front, and sat in their car a few minutes. She could see them from the kitchen and wondered who they were. At twenty-five minutes after three, she said, they came to the front door, rang the bell, pulled out their FBI badges, and said, "We have an appointment to speak with Mr. Johnson at half past three." She was nervous and didn't know what was going on but said: "Well, come on in. If he said he'd be here at half past three, he'll be here." They sat down, and she went back to the kitchen and watched for me to drive up. When I started up the walkway, she opened the side door and motioned for me to come that way. "Lyman," she said, "I don't know what you've done. But you go on out the back way, jump over the back fence, and go up to the head of the alley, and I'll bring the car around to you. You can explain later what trouble you're in now."

I said: "Honey, I haven't done anything. There's nothing to be afraid of." She said: "Don't treat me like this. You've always been bullheaded. All right. Go in there and let them take you and put you *under* the jail." I went on in, and the three of us talked for almost two hours. We talked about birds and bees and trees and ball games and the navy and parks and playgrounds. Finally, I said: "Gentlemen, I'm not stupid. We've taken up almost two hours of my time and your time, and we've just been shooting the breeze. Now, what in the hell did you come down here for?" One of them said: "We have a file on you in our office about two inches thick. We were assigned to come here and get acquainted with you and make sure that there is flesh and blood that goes with the file labeled 'Lyman T. Johnson.' Now we've met you. You've been very cordial. We've met your wife, and she has been very gracious and polite. That's all we're supposed to do right now."

I said: "Now, you can go back and tell your superiors that you saw me. But before you go, I want to ask you a question. Do you have any children?" One man said he had two, and the other man said he had one. I said: "Now, tell me this. If you carried your kids over to Cherokee Park and somebody stood at the gate and told you not to bring your children in, wouldn't you want to know why? Wouldn't you fuss with anybody who wanted to keep them out? Wouldn't you berate the government that kept the park closed to them? Wouldn't you feel like a heel of a father if you didn't try to get your children into that park? That's all I'm trying to do! Put that in your file! And also put in that any goddamn government that won't protect me in protecting my child is no good. Say that I'm standing on the very best principles of American citizenship when I say that my children have a right to go to that park. And say that until they can go into that park and play like other children I'm not going to worship a government that keeps them out! Be sure to put that in the files too!"

They said: "Mr. Johnson, it's all been taped—everything you've said from the beginning. And we commend you. You're a strong man."

The same two men continued to visit me, but over the years the visits dropped. I think what they wanted was for me to slip up and to give them leads to the big shots they believed were using me. I'm sure they thought I was honest and sincere but dumb. They were certain that I was being used by the Communists, and sooner or later they thought I would name the name of someone who was pulling my puppet's strings. That's why I think that for the twelve years they visited me they never closed in on me and never suggested that I stop doing anything I was doing. They thought I had been set up by the Communists to go to the University of Kentucky, to demand equal pay for white and black teachers, to picket white cafés and cafeterias and lunch counters, and to generally stir up trouble between the races. We got into some arguments when I refused to back off my principles and beliefs and when I refused to defend myself against something I was *not*. In those days you could smear a person you didn't like simply by calling him a Communist. You didn't have to prove anything. I said: "You think I'm a Communist. Now prove it." Of course, they couldn't. But they said: "Johnson, you're an agitator. If you don't like this country, why don't you leave it?" I said: "Because this is where I was born and where I live. If my house is leaking, I don't get mad and move out. I get a ladder, climb up on the roof, and patch the leak. That's what I'm trying to do for my country. I love my country, and when I see its leaks, I'm not going to move out. I get irritated enough to try to repair them."

The love-it-or-leave-it kind of mentality promoted by McCarthyism is provincial and idiotic. It leads you to think that what you represent alone is right. You start with your nation. Then you move down to your state, your race, your club, your church, your family. Finally, you can get to the place where you think that maybe even your parents, brothers, and sisters are all wrong. Maybe you're the only one who's right. You're like the out-of-step soldier who thinks that everyone else is out of step. It's the mentality that leads to witch hunts and persecution. If not checked by reason and common sense, such hysteria can destroy individuals and victims. Thank God this country freed itself of McCarthyism before it was too late.

During our demonstrations and sit-ins, hundreds of people were arrested and jailed in Louisville. The cases were finally dismissed because the judge found that our people hadn't violated any law—maybe some city or county ordinances, but not the Constitution of the United States, the law of the whole land. I agreed with the view of W.E.B. Du Bois that any local or state laws that did not square with the U.S. Constitution were invalid; they weren't laws at all. When I tried to enroll at the University of Kentucky, the man said: "Hold it. You can't come here." I said, "Why not?" He said, "It's the law." I said: "Your so-called law violates the Constitution of the United States and is therefore no law. It is simply an expression of local prejudice." I value the Constitution very highly. Without it I'd still be picking cotton right now. When it's correctly interpreted by the Supreme Court, it's a remarkable guarantee of human freedom.

I've never been in jail, and that's been something of an embarrassment to me. Back in the early 1960s, there was a young Presbyterian professor who used to come help us with our demonstrations. Almost every time he'd get arrested and jailed. Finally, his wife said: "Honey, why do you keep on going back? All they'll do is arrest you again. I agree with what you're doing, but I'm afraid people will start shunning me because I'm married to a jailbird. Why do you keep helping Lyman? He never gets arrested." A lot of people close to me were arrested. I never was. I don't know why.

One time my daughter came home for a visit after she had finished her master's degree in psychology at Ohio State. When she came in on the bus, she saw some kids picketing at one of the downtown stores. When I picked her up, she said, "Come on, Papa, let's go and help." I couldn't join her, but she changed her clothes, put on her walking shoes, and demonstrated. When she came home, she said: "Papa, the police came and arrested a lot of people. But they stopped before they got to me." It seems that no one in the Johnson family could get behind bars!

Why have I worked so hard to open up hotels, schools, restaurants, libraries, parks—even rest rooms—for me and my people? I've worked because we're American citizens who deserve equal treatment under the law. I've worked not so much for those of us of the older generation. We won't be here much longer. I've worked for our children and the children to come. It was so humiliating to be denied access to public facilities. It's still vivid in my mind how often my daughter would say, "Papa, I've got to go to the toilet." It was difficult to tell that little girl: "Honey, you can't go to the toilet. It's only for white people." Or "You can't drink from that fountain because it's marked 'White Only.' " Or you'd see little white kids putting down their nickels and dimes and getting a hamburger or a hot dog. They'd look so tempting. They'd look like the most delicious things in the world. And your child's mouth would be watering, and she'd want one more than anything. Just a humble little hot dog. How do you tell your child: "Honey, that's not for you. That's for other people"? They don't understand.

Down in Columbia I used to hear Negro mothers and fathers tell their children: "You ain't white. That's for white folks. You ain't white. Get that in your head and behave." I didn't have the gall to tell my children that, but I had to find a way around saying what I had heard as a child, a way to avoid having to say: "Honey, you ain't white. Honey, you ain't nothing." That's the worst thing a parent can tell a child. I learned something different from my parents. My daddy used to say: "Son, despite the way you're treated, don't ever get the idea that you're nothing. God created you. And if God created you, no matter what you are, you are something. You are God's child." But I had a hard time convincing my own children when I said, "You are something." How could they believe me when they couldn't get a drink of water, couldn't go to the toilet, or couldn't go into a ten-cent store and order a hamburger? Yes, we opened up these things for our children.

Life is friction. Where there's no more friction, no more resistance, you're dead. Whatever pricks you, whatever makes you move, also makes you alive. The problems I've faced as a man and as a black man have been my friction. My civil rights battles have been my special friction. My friends used to warn me: "Lyman, you've got a wife and two kids and a house. You don't make much money, but you make enough to take care of your basic needs. Be careful or you're gonna lose that job." That's advice I never took. Finally, I reached the point where I could say, "I just don't give a damn." That's when I became a free person. The more risks I took, the more friction I felt and the more alive I became. My actions made me free.

I have a niece living in Connecticut in a comfortable home. Her son has a Ph.D. from the University of Connecticut. For years he's tried to get me to move up there. "Uncle Lyman," he says, "why don't you come on out from down there? You got stuck down in Kentucky when you were a young man. Now you can leave it. Come on out and let those fools down there go to hell!" I said: "Son, you have to live your life your way. I have to live my life my way. I like it down here. Living here has been a challenge."

Black Heroes

Evil is color blind.

ONE DAY in Sunday School when I was about six, the teacher was trying to get us little kids to look to the future. He asked, "Lyman, name some grown person you want to be like." I said: "I want to be like Mr. Armstrong. He's fat. He always stands up straight. He wears good clothes. He throws his shoulders back and puts his hands in his pockets and rattles money all the time."

Back then I thought a leader was a big man with a lot of money. In fact, I found out that most black leaders have had very little money, despite the fact that it costs so much to be a leader. I know what I'm talking about. The life I've tried to live and the standards I've tried to set have been very costly. I know why so few people can live the life of Martin Luther King, Jr., or W.E.B. Du Bois—or even Lyman Johnson. It just costs so much. That's one reason we've had few consistent black leaders—I mean people who are active in the black struggle for not just five or ten years but forty or fifty years—their whole life. I've seen a lot of young men come along and wax eloquent in the movement for six or seven years. Then the white establishment says, "Here is a person we can use." And they buy him off with a good job. You ask him, "Won't you help us with this unfinished business?" He says: "Hell, no. Why should I jeopardize my nice job?"

But we've been blessed with some fine leaders in black American history. Frederick Douglass, Nat Turner, Harriet Tubman, Du Bois, King, Booker T. Washington—to name a few. I've always held them up to my students as models. Maybe I've spun a little fantasy when I've talked about them, but I was trying to give my students black heroes to look up to. I made sure young blacks respected Frederick Douglass, who was almost a messiah for black people in bondage. I'd say: "He wanted freedom so much he ran off from his master many times. Every time he was caught he'd be given terrible beatings. The last time he ran off he said, 'I bet I'll go so far this time you won't catch me.' He didn't quit running till he got to England. And there he told a good story about his slave life, the people anted up enough money to send him back over here and buy himself free. Then he became a great spokesman for the abolition movement and advised almost every president till he died."

Nat Turner is another hero I held up to my students. I used him as the example of the slave who hated slavery so much and loved freedom so much he organized a revolt that led to a lot of bloodshed but showed the determination of the slaves to be free. I didn't forget black heroines either. I told about Harriet Tubman, who would slip into a slave state, organize a bunch of slaves, and help them get to a free state, then go back and get another bunch.

After emancipation, two of our greatest leaders were Booker T. Washington and W.E.B. Du Bois. They were very different in how they worked for Negro advancement. I like them both, and I won't argue which one did the most good for the Negro. Each one served a good purpose in the progress of civil rights. Around 1900 Du Bois began building the foundation on which many of us stand today. He was the cornerstone for black rights. He was courageous and gallant and dominated the civil rights movement for forty years. He was a powerful writer and editor—he headed the NAACP magazine, *The Crisis*—and showed how the freed Negro was still enslaved by discrimination. He was a smart man, a scholar with a Ph.D. from Harvard. He considered most southern historians a bunch of hogwash peddlers. Sure, he was an agitator, especially if you compare him with Booker T.

Oh, yes, old Booker T. was an Uncle Tom. He was always playing footsie with the white folks. He was always sucking up to them for favors and benefits. But I can't be too hard on Uncle Tom. It was the only way he could build a first-rate school in the South for Negroes. Uncle Tom has always known how to manipulate white folks. "Mr. White Man, you're so nice, so good. But you sometimes treat us cullud people so bad, and we work so hard. Can't you give us something now? Jus' a crumb will do." So Uncle Tom comes away from Mr. White Man grinning and smiling from ear to ear and says, "Look what I got." As much as I detest that humiliating subterfuge, I have to admit that it's better than nothing. It's gotten results, even if they've been crumbs from the white man's table. So old Booker T. played Uncle Tom up to the hilt. He'd take his hat off in the presence of white men as well as white women. He'd drive his buggy up to the white man's house, around to the back door, and he'd knock gently, hat in hand. And he'd come away with maybe $100,000 from that rich white cat, take it back to Tuskegee, and spend it on first-rate professors and facilities.

I say to young blacks today: "Sure, Booker T. was an Uncle Tom. But look what he did. He built Tuskegee Institute. He got white people to give him money to build it and to run it. It was a private school, but he even got money from the state of Alabama. The president of Alabama A & M, the Negro college in Montgomery, was supposed to go to the legislature and beg for money. He wouldn't get much, even though A & M was a state school. But Booker T. knew how to play the game. He'd go to the legislature with his hat in hand and come away with a satchel full of money. Back at Tuskegee he'd bring in the best black professors with the money he'd gotten from the whites. He put up with a lot of humiliation to get what he wanted for his school. He knew that white people had all the money, and he knew what had to be done to get it from them."

Hell, no, Booker T. is not an embarrassment to me. I understand the position he was in. But I also know that he was a sly devil. In those days the traffic for keeping the black man down was to keep him ignorant. Washington knew that to educate a person was to unfit him to be a slave—or a second-class citizen. On the other hand, he believed that education for full citizenship had to be done step by step. "Black people first have to learn useful trades," he'd say. "Learn how to lay bricks. Learn how to put down concrete. Learn how to build a house. Learn electricity. Learn how to farm more productively. Learn so much that you are an asset to whoever hires you and to yourself." So Tuskegee emphasized the trades, not an intellectual education. Even when I was college age, a Negro who wanted a literary education would not have gone to Tuskegee. But Booker T. and his successors knew that if he had emphasized intellectual pursuits, he wouldn't have gotten white money to support the school. His appeal to most whites was that he was preparing skilled laborers who would be of more benefit to the South than if they were ignorant and unskilled. But the white man believed that the Tuskegee graduate would still work for him, and Booker T. let him believe that. "The more the Negro knows about agriculture, the better he'll handle your farm. The more he knows about bricklaying, the better house he'll build for you." So Booker T. said.

Washington was always careful never to suggest that he was educating black people to be white people's equals. He was careful never to intimate that he was educating black men who might want to take out the white man's daughter or who might expect to eat in the same dining room with him and his family. Those were private matters where the fingers stayed separate. The fingers would come together only when the country's work was being done. That was Booker T.'s favorite metaphor. "People are like the separate fingers," he'd say, "that collect to make a hand." It was his graphic way of saying to the white power structure: "Although all races of people are important and have their unique gifts, I don't advocate social equality. You help us, and we'll help you. We can come together as a hand, but when the work is over, you go your way and we'll go ours and be as separate as the fingers."

Du Bois thought Booker T.'s strategy was just too demeaning. He would say: "I'm a human being. I'm as cultured and as refined as most white people. I have a Ph.D. from Harvard University. What else do I need to be respected? I've done all I can. I certainly had nothing to do with the skin color I was born with. So if you call a white Ph.D. 'doctor,' then, damn it, you call me 'doctor' too. If you call a white man 'mister,' then call me 'mister' too. If a white man can go to a certain hotel and get a room and eat in the restaurant, then reserve a room for me and prepare a dinner for me too."

Booker T. would say: "Oh, let's not worry about sleeping in white folks' hotels and eating next to white people. Let's educate ourselves so we can hold down good jobs. The world will respect us for our know-how." To which Du Bois would respond: "I am a man with a lot of know-how. How much respect do I have?" I'm going to give Booker T. the last word because his way may have worked better back then. "I take off my hat and go to the white man's back door. You keep on your hat, walk straight up to the white man's front door. You knock hard. He won't even talk to you, and he'll give you nothing. He may even shoot the hell out of you! Now, I come away from the back door with $100,000. I've got a good school. What have you got, Du Bois?" Du Bois would say, "I've got my philosophy, my principles, and my self-respect." Booker T. would say, "Hell, you can't eat that."

I think both men and both ways were needed back then. Washington took the pragmatic approach and learned to work within the system to improve the economic lot of his people. Du Bois agitated outside the system and kept us aware that blacks would not tolerate permanent second-class citizenship. Through my life Du Bois has been my hero, but I've tried to mix in some of Booker T.s practicality with Du Bois's vision. I've tried not to be as blatantly insulting as Du Bois to my adversaries. I've tried to educate them and not strike them in the face to get their attention. At the same time, like Du Bois, I've tried never to compromise my principles or my long-range goals.

Right here in Louisville we've produced a good number of black role models. The most famous, of course, is the Louisville Lip—Cassius Clay or, as he calls himself now, Muhammad Ali. He was a student at Central when I taught there, but he was never in any of my classes. He claims that he came to my classroom door one time, looked in, and said: "That man's not for me. I don't intend to study as much as I'd have to if I took his class."

But I knew and liked Cassius Clay. He was a playful, mischievous young fellow—always wholesome, even when he was playing tricks. He came to school to have a good time and did have a good time. He was a school clown, but he was bright. He has to be intelligent to make up poetry as he goes along. Everything he says is rhyme. He starts off jiving, and the stuff begins to rhyme. When he's in front of a microphone, what he says makes sense. He couldn't possibly just stumble into what he's saying. He was simply not a good academic student. But we're proud of him in Louisville. We like it when he says: "I've been in places where they've never heard of Cleveland, Ohio, or Omaha, Nebraska, but they've heard of Louisville, Kentucky. That's because I just opened my big mouth, and Louisville lived."

He has been very thoughtful of his family too. I know both his parents. One day before my wife died, I took a bus out to visit her in a suburban nursing home. I had made my visit and was waiting by the bus stop reading the afternoon paper when a long, black Cadillac drove up and stopped. A man rolled down the window and said, "Lyman Johnson." I looked up from my paper but was blinded by the hot afternoon sun and couldn't see who it was. The man said, "What in the hell are you doing out here?" I said, "I've just been to visit my wife, and I'm waiting to catch a bus home." He said: "Oh, hell, even when the bus gets here, it'll be two weeks before it gets to town. I've got nothing else to do. Get in, and I'll drive you home." When I hesitated, he said: "You don't have to be afraid to get in my car. You know who I am. I'm Cassius Clay, Muhammad Ali's daddy." I said, "Oh, I recognize you now," and stepped into that beautiful car, thinking, "This is a different sort of ride from the one I had coming out here."

Clay said, "Do you mind if I stop by my house and tell my wife I'll be a little late?" They lived in one of the expensive suburbs nearby. In the driveway was another Cadillac. Inside the house Mrs. Clay was sewing on a dress she was going to wear to one of Muhammad Ali's fights in New York. By that time Ali had made millions as a boxer and had shared it with his parents. He had given them a fancy house, two Cadillacs, and everything else they wanted. "Stay for supper," Clay said, "and let me show you around the house." They showed me trophies, pictures, and art pieces they had picked up all over the world where Ali had fought. When we'd finished the tour, he said: "Now let's have something to eat. You like soul food, don't you?" I said I wasn't hungry, so he brought in some food from the kitchen, sat down in his plush den surrounded by expensive furniture and finery, and ate his bowl of collard greens and cornbread. I had a fine visit in the home that Muhammad Ali had given them before they took me to my home on the street named after their son. I've not approved of everything Ali has done, but I've always held him up to young people as an example of what a dedicated, talented black man can achieve.

When I talk about heroes for black Americans, I must not forget the white people who have championed our cause since the days of slavery—from John Brown to Franklin Roosevelt. Evil is color-blind. Idi Amin was a black leader, but it certainly didn't make him good. On the other hand, a lot of white people have risked their fortunes and lives to help black Americans. I greatly admire the abolitionist Charles Sumner of Massachusetts. He was cruelly beaten in the Senate by Preston Brooks of South Carolina, who didn't like the way Sumner was attacking slavery and slaveowners. Sumner said that one of the reasons slavery was popular in the South was that an owner could walk out in his backyard and down to the quarters and have a different girl every night. That infuriated Brooks. "You're talking about the people who elected me to this Congress," he shouted.

Right here in Kentucky a champion of black people was Cassius Marcellus Clay, who supported emancipation and even published an antislavery newspaper called the *True American*, which was wrecked by a proslavery mob in Lexington. And, of course, I can't forget John Brown, that crazy wild man from Kansas, who surely knew that his insurrection at Harper's Ferry would be crushed. It is said he picked up a little black child on the way to the gallows and said: "I'm doing this for you. One day you and your people will be free. But now I must die." He kissed the child, handed it back to its mother, and went on to be hanged.

It's hard for me to figure Abraham Lincoln out. I think he stumbled into the right place at the right time. But once he got into his high position, he measured up to its requirements; as president he came on strong. Once when he was a young man visiting New Orleans, he is supposed to have been so disgusted with slavery that he said, "If I ever get the chance, I'll hit this evil a hard lick." Then when he became president, he said if he could save the Union without freeing any slaves he would do it. So let's not give him too much credit for emancipation. It was purely a political act. In fact, the Emancipation Proclamation didn't free the slaves in four states, including Kentucky. We have to remember that he came from the class of poor whites in Kentucky.

Lincoln understood the problems of the poor white. I wouldn't be surprised if he hadn't hoped to get rid of the slaves so they wouldn't be in competition with his own class of people. I think he wanted to ship them back to Africa; then the poor whites could come down from the hills and mountains—where they had been pushed by the plantation owners—and could have done the common labor. Despite what he may have said in New Orleans, I believe that he was more interested in helping the poor whites, even if it was at the expense of the slave. The freed slave stayed in this country and started competing with the white laborer—and there was hell to pay.

I have to give a lot of credit to those unselfish Union troops who fought during the Civil War to preserve this nation and thus prevented the Confederacy from going its own way with slavery intact. Let us also not forget the hundreds of free Negroes who fought to free their brothers and sisters in bondage and the slaves who ran away to join the Union army.

After the Civil War, many, many white people from the North came south to help the freedmen, who were mostly illiterate, ignorant, and unable to care for themselves. I'm talking about the hundreds of teachers who taught in southern black schools, like Lyman Tefft, after whom I'm named.

There are, of course, many other white people who can be heroes for black people. Take Dr. Albert Schweitzer, the master physician and musician who left France to dedicate his life to poor Africans. He said: "When I see how the white people of Europe—the Dutch, French, Spanish, German, Portuguese, English—all have exploited the black African people, I am embarrassed and want to do something for them. Maybe I can atone for the meanness of some of my people by donating my medical knowledge to these poor, exploited Africans."

Some of our presidents can serve as heroes for black Americans. To me our greatest presidents have been Washington, Jefferson, Lincoln, Franklin Roosevelt, and Truman. I think Eleanor helped to make Roosevelt humane. As a man of great wealth, he had benefited from the capitalist system, but he knew that something was wrong with it, so he set about trying to do something about it. He went as far as he could get away with. He knew we couldn't go from a purely capitalist society to a socialist one in one decade. But he knew that the old system had to be, if not scratched, at least somewhat dismantled. What he did to improve the lot of the poor, unemployed people generally benefited black people too.

When Truman got to be president, I said, "He's not the caliber that we'd like to have in a president, but he's muddling through pretty well." In fact, he did even better than that. I liked his dogged determination to do what he thought was right. If you told him you didn't like what he was doing, he'd tell you publicly to go to hell right quick. I liked his presidency because he used his power to do what he thought was right.

I would like to put Wilson in as a great president, but I can't. When he was president of Princeton University, he was reported to have said that no more blacks would go to Princeton as long as he was there. He rose to heights, however, at the end of World War I when he wanted us in the League of Nations. And his Fourteen Points just about gutted the Beatitudes of the Bible. Why do some people want to do what's morally right and some don't? I think goodness is not something you just stumble into or something that just happens. I don't think there is an inborn drive to be either good or bad. Virtue is a way of life that has to be cultivated. I remember a philosophy professor I had back at Virginia Union who said: "The best way to cultivate virtues like honesty, truth, and justice is to let no exception come. Never allow yourself *one* exception. If you let yourself be dishonest one time—with the assurance that 'I won't do it any more'— you'll find that the second time it'll be easier to be dishonest and your dishonesty will be more serious too." I know I've failed many times, but I've always tried to live that way—never to let an exception occur. That's the way I believe the people I admire in history have tried to live.

Blacks at the Ballot Box

Socrates could never have been elected to any office.

THE NAME of action in this country is politics. It has taken black people a long time to learn that justice begins at the ballot box. As long as we had no political power, we had no rights in this society. When we began to be a factor in electing mayors, governors, senators, and presidents, the politicians began to take notice. We've come a long way from no political voice to electing our own people to positions of leadership.

I've been active in politics for a long time, from 'Happy' Chandler in the 1930s to Jimmy Carter and beyond. I worked on the precinct level soon after I came to Louisville and got a job teaching. I thought my social studies classes would be enriched if I could have some practical experience. I could talk about vote buying and selling because I had seen it go on.

The first time I voted was in 1928 in Columbia. Except for my family, not many Negroes voted in Columbia. My father voted every election day. So did my uncle. Tennessee had a poll tax, but it was not as vicious as in some states. In Alabama the tax was cumulative—that is, it was retroactive back to the age of twenty-one. If you were forty-five and tried to vote for the first time, you had to pay the back poll tax for twenty-four years. You also had to interpret the Constitution to the satisfaction of the registration judge. Most Negroes failed. Almost all whites passed, unless there was someone the judge wanted to wash down the drain. There are always some people who can't matriculate into first-rate society regardless of their race! But generally the feeling was this: "Niggers got no business in politics. Politics is white folks' business. The polling booth is for whites. The cotton field is for niggers."

Since I've lived in Louisville, blacks have voted in pretty heavy numbers. White candidates would come into the Negro neighborhoods and put on rallies and forums to get the Negro vote. Sometimes all it would take would be a drink of liquor or a dollar bill. Some black people turned the other way and said: "After all, it doesn't make any difference anyway. Both candidates are white, and they're both against us. So let's not begrudge the poor Negro his drink of whiskey or his dollar." I knew a fellow from Memphis who said he'd sometimes get ten dollars to vote ten times for certain candidates. "I always voted," he said, "against the man who paid me. That way I got him twice; I took his money, and I helped elect the other man."

I've been to polling places on election day and have seen white candidates in the voting line with Negroes. They'd pull out a bottle of whiskey, take a drink, then hand it to a Negro. He'd drink, and then the white man would drink again to show that he didn't mind drinking after a Negro. Then the Negro would go in and vote, and when he came out, the white man would hand him a dollar bill. Sometimes I'd go around to half a dozen polling places and see the same Negroes showing up.

That kind of corruption has been going on, of course, since the freedman got the right to vote. The Union soldiers who occupied the South after the war have been criticized for helping the former slaves take over the elections. I'm sure there were many abuses, and I'm not excusing them. Some blacks were carted around from poll to poll and told who to vote for. But one thing is certain. If the Union soldiers had not been present, southern whites would not have let the Negroes vote. As soon as the soldiers were removed and Reconstruction was officially over, the black voters were systematically disfranchised. It was done through changing voter laws—adding poll taxes, literacy requirements—and through intimidation.

Imagine this. A man who used to be a slave goes up to the polling place. He sees a white man standing there holding a gun. The white man says: "Nigger, don't your corn need plowing? You don't have time to come up here and vote today, do you?" The black man looks at the pistol. He thinks about the half-dozen Negroes he's known who have been lynched for little or no reason. He realizes that both candidates for sheriff are white men who are against him. So he turns around and heads home to hitch up Ol' Beck to plow that corn. The next election day he won't even bother to try to vote. Not voting becomes a habit. To his children he'll say: "Don't raise Cain around here trying to vote. That's for white people."

My grandfather, Dyer Johnson, was the first member of my family to vote, and we've voted ever since then. In fact, there have always been some blacks who managed by hook or by crook to exercise their citizenship rights, despite the obstacles put in their way. I was told one time about a Negro college professor down in Alabama who put on some faded, washed-out, patched overalls, a ragged shirt, and worn-out shoes and went down to the polls one election day to vote. He shuffled up to the voting place. The white clerk said, "You can't vote here unless you can recite the Constitution of the United States." The man said, "Ah, Mr. White Folks, you sho is hard on us colored people." Then without batting an eye, he launched into a recitation in perfect English. "Fourscore and seven years ago, our fathers brought forth on this continent a new nation, conceived in liberty and dedicated to the proposition that all men are created equal. . . ." He went on till he'd finished Lincoln's famous speech. The white man was astounded. He said: "Nigger, you know you're the first man I've ever known who could recite the Constitution from beginning to end. You go on and vote."

I'm a Democrat, but I was born into a staunch Republican family; my father and uncle never voted Democratic. In 1944 when my uncle was eighty-six, he went to the Republican National Convention in Chicago. The Tennessee Republican party wanted to pay his expenses and send him as a delegate. He said: "I want to be a delegate, but I want to be independent. I'll pay my own expenses." He wanted to be a national Republican because by 1944 southern Republicans were second cousins to southern Democrats. Roosevelt had changed blacks into Democrats, and Republicans were trying to get them back. But every time a liberal Republican like Wendell Willkie showed up, the other Republicans froze him out; and when they did, they froze out the black vote. Today there is no real affinity between the masses of blacks and the Republican party.

I'm a Democrat, but the first time I voted it was for Hoover in 1928. By 1932 the poor people were in such a fix and the Republican party was the party of the big boys, so I changed over. When I voted for Franklin Roosevelt that year, I had to apologize to my father and my uncle. They said, "We understand, but don't forget that you have turned your back on the party that freed you." I said: "Yes, Papa, yes, Uncle, but your generation has already paid back the Republicans for what they did. You've kept buying from them after they've stopped giving you good service. When you stop getting good service, you should shop in a new store. You don't keep on buying shoes from a man who *used* to sell you good shoes."

In fact, the Republican party began turning its back on the Negro in 1876 when, in exchange for the presidency, it let the rich southerners regain control over the poor whites and the Negroes. Till then, the Republicans had done a good job of freeing and protecting and helping the black man. But in 1876 a bargain was struck between the bankers and the industrialists of the North and the East and the upper-class southern whites—plantation owners, bankers, businessmen—and it gave control over the South back to those people who had had it before the war.

When I supported Adlai Stevenson and John Sparkman in 1952, I took a terrible beating from black people. They said: "Lyman, how in the hell can you stand for John Sparkman? Stevenson is a good man, so why don't you say you volunteered for him and had to take Sparkman in the deal?" I was on the steering committee for Volunteers for Stevenson and Sparkman, and we had our headquarters in a little storefront near Third and Jefferson.

One day in October I got a call at Central High School from our headquarters. "Senator Sparkman's in town. Come on down and meet him." I said, "Oh, I don't think I want to meet him." Finally, I agreed to come down about four o'clock. Six of us local people—I was the only black—went into a back room to talk with Senator Sparkman. After refreshments two people excused themselves. Then two more disappeared. As the fifth one eased by me, he said, "OK, Lyman, he's your boy now. Whip on him as much as you please." That left just Sparkman and me in the room. I suddenly realized the meeting had been arranged so that I could tell him the problems blacks were having in supporting him.

So I decided to unload. I said, "Well, Mr. Senator. . . ." He said: "Don't call me senator. Call me John." I said: "Hell, OK, I'll call you John, but I don't think that's going to change who you are. John, do you know how much it's costing me in the Negro community to have my name linked with yours in this campaign?" I held up a Stevenson-Sparkman pamphlet we had sponsored. "It's costing me like hell every time we pass out one of these little papers. People are saying: 'Lyman Johnson is supporting John Sparkman. He's a racist. He's from that hell of a place called Alabama.' " I went on piling up my objections, talking to him like a preacher to a sinner. After I had finished and sat back, he said: "Lyman, I'll do the best I can to defend myself. I've had a rough time getting through high school and college and law school. But with my education and a little pull and a lot of pluck, I got into politics and worked up to be a senator. I love being senator. Now, how did I get to be senator? I was elected by the voters of Alabama. And who votes in Alabama? Most Alabama voters are white, and most of them don't want Negroes to vote or to have other citizenship rights. If I were to campaign in Alabama on a platform that is opposite to the thinking of most Alabama voters, I'd never get elected. So long as I'm in Alabama and so long as I want to be in the Senate, I've got to do what the white voters in Alabama say for me to do. As long as I'm at the mercy of the present voters in Alabama and as long as I want to be a senator, I've got to run on a white supremacy platform."

Then Senator Sparkman said something that impressed me deeply. "But help me get out of Alabama, and I'll be another Hugo Black. Leave me in Alabama, and I can't do any good. I'll have to do what will get me back in the Senate." I understood what he was saying. He wasn't going to change his politics—he couldn't change his politics—as long as he had to live and run in Alabama. Like a lot of white southerners—a lot of white liberal politicians in the South—he was a victim of the racial system too. Nobody can defy the social mores and expect to be accepted and supported—and voted for—by his neighbors. Now, of course, federal laws and the courts have freed southerners to be men of conscience. When Hugo Black was appointed to the Supreme Court by President Roosevelt, it didn't change Black's character and inclinations. It simply freed him to do what he had always thought was right. Now men like Black and Sparkman can live in the South and do what's right.

I had given Sparkman a good shellacking, and he had come back with a good presentation of himself. I liked that. I don't break down and cry very often, but I did some symbolical crying when he was telling me about his travails growing up. After we had spent more than thirty minutes together—just the two of us—I told him I would be pleased to continue campaigning for him.

After that meeting with Senator Sparkman, when my black friends would start ribbing me about him, I'd say: "Man, what do you know about him? What do you know about the real man he is?" Then I'd ask, "If you were running for senator from Alabama and wanted to be elected, what kind of platform would *you* have to run on?" After that soaked in, I'd say: "Somebody's got to be senator from Alabama. Isn't it better to have a basically good man in the Senate from down there, a man who will vote the right way on a lot of bills, even if he has to vote against direct civil rights laws? When he votes for other kinds of social legislation, like the Hill-Burton Hospital Act, it helps everybody, even blacks in Alabama. It's better to have a good man who will do the right thing when he has a chance than a person of bad intentions to begin with." Then I'd mention Hugo Black as a prime example of the good man from the South who simply needed to be extricated from social mores in order to do good.

I remember the hullabaloo when Black was nominated by President Roosevelt for the Supreme Court in the late 1930s. We had a meeting of the local NAACP chapter to talk about a special telegram we'd received from the national office. It said, "Do all you can to keep your Kentucky senators from voting to confirm this Alabama racist." I stood up and said: "Yes, his voting record on civil rights is not good. But I hope we'll not forget Mr. Black's other qualifications. Look at the other liberal laws he's championed in Congress, laws that have helped Negroes more than the wrong he did them by being a member of the Ku Klux Klan. I can remember when Negroes couldn't make more than ten cents an hour. Black has helped us get federal legislation that raises that to around thirty cents. I believe he knew those two extra dimes were going to benefit black people as much as poor whites. When he gets to be a Supreme Court justice, we may be surprised what Mr. Black's true color is!"

My NAACP friends turned on me. "Lyman," they said, "if you're going to stand there and fight for that damn Ku Kluxer from Alabama, maybe you ought to go back down South where you came from. We don't need you up here!" After Black was confirmed and turned out to be one of the best friends black people ever had on the Supreme Court, I loved to remind my NAACP friends in Louisville how they had attacked him—and me. My knowledge of history has helped give me a long-range view, which keeps me from being too shortsighted. So many brilliant people can see only the present, and their perspective on history is short and shallow. They wear blinders and see only one little spot, and it gets smaller and smaller. Finally, they imprison themselves in myopia. Unfortunately, a lot of black leaders have been afflicted.

Despite our mistakes, however, Louisville Negroes learned a long time ago how to use their political power effectively. In the late 1920s, the public school board wanted to float a bond to build some new school buildings. The referendum had to be approved by public vote. When Negroes found out that all the new buildings would be for white schools, they said: "Wait a minute. We want some new schools too." The school board said, "Help us pass this referendum to build schools for the whites; then we'll float another bond issue to build schools for Negroes."

The Negroes said: "Oh, no. We've been tricked this way before. Put something in this issue for us. Then we'll support it." The school board refused. The election was held. A lot of Catholics voted against the bond issue because they didn't see any reason to support schools their children didn't attend. A lot of rich people sent their children to private schools, and they voted against it. A lot of Negroes voted against it because it contained nothing for them. So the bond issue was defeated.

Two years later the school board again asked the Negroes to support a bond issue. The Negroes said: "Didn't you learn your lesson two years ago? Unless you put in some money for our schools, we'll team up with the Catholics and the rich people and vote it down again." Finally, the board agreed, and Negroes supported the referendum. It passed. We got Madison Junior High and Jackson Junior High, two of our nicest schools.

A few years later the University of Louisville wanted some city money for a project. The Negro community said: "Did you get the message we sent to the board of education and the politicians? Count us in, and we'll be for you. We don't see any reason for helping a college that won't allow Negroes on campus unless they've got on white aprons or white coats." The university got the message and said: "We'll start a Negro municipal college. We'll call it the Municipal College of the University of Louisville, and we'll hire first-rate Negro professors and put in first-rate facilities." The university bought the buildings owned by a private black school, Simmons University, and opened their "colored" division. It developed a good reputation among Negro colleges, though none of the public colleges for Negroes were first-rate. We blacks who went to private Negro colleges in the South thought we were going to miniature Harvards and Yales, and we looked down our noses at the public colleges. Finally, the university opened its doors to blacks—about a year after I won admission to the University of Kentucky—and Municipal College was closed down. At first, the University of Louisville maintained that they were a private institution because they received only about 15 percent of their income from public sources. Therefore, they felt integration rulings didn't apply to them. "OK," we said. "We'll just have to sue you for the 15 percent." They opened up instead.

In Louisville we also learned to use the two-party system to our advantage. Back in the late 1950s, for example, the Democrats wouldn't give us the public accommodations law we wanted, so we helped elect William Cowger and his bunch of Republicans. They did such a good job that another Republican administration was voted in after Cowger, headed by Mayor Kenneth Schmied. When he came into office, we said: "Mr. Schmied, we find that Negroes cannot buy homes outside the West End. We want you to put residential segregation to an end." He said: "Well, now, that's a new wrinkle. You're getting into people's sleeping habits, and that's going to cause a lot of problems." We said: "Mr. Schmied, you're in office to solve a lot of problems. We want you to pass an open housing ordinance." He said: "Mr. Johnson, we Republicans have given you your public accommodations law. You can eat and go anywhere you want to. But now this housing business—we can't do that."

So we helped kick the Republicans out and put the Democrats back in. We told the Democrats: "Remember two terms ago you wouldn't pass a public accommodations ordinance, and you paid for it. In a 65 percent Democratic community, you had to put up with two terms of Republicans." The message got across. The Democrats passed the open housing bill, and we've been with the Democrats ever since.

Although I'd run in and lost several elections for alderman and the State Senate, in 1977 I ran successfully for the Jefferson County Board of Education. That year we knew we had a chance to elect a black to the board because we would vote by districts and not countywide. Several people asked me to run. I said: "No, I've had my day. I'll help find a capable person to run." As the filing deadline approached, however, we had no viable candidate. Time was running out. Several days before the deadline, the doorbell rang, and two young men were standing at the door with a petition signed by thirty-three people. It said, "We, the undersigned, request that Mr. Lyman T. Johnson once more put his services to the use of his community by submitting his name as a candidate for District One of the Board of Education." It was a beautiful gesture, and it catered to my vanity. I said: "Well, now, this is something. But I can't run. I'm old. I'm tired. I'm worn out. Senility is just around the corner. My wife has just died. What little time I have left I ought to spend with my relatives and my children. I might even go back to Columbia, Tennessee, to wait the end of my time. Tell these people I appreciate what they've done, but I just can't run."

The next day another group came to the door with the same petition but with thirty new names on it. Finally, I said, "I'll have to think it over." The next day still another group came with more names on the petition. There were names of big shots and little shots, white collars and blue collars and no collars, white and black, doctors and lawyers, professors and dropouts, housewives and prostitutes. I said: "I've thought about this race. You know I've been defeated for every office I've run for. I'm getting old, and I don't want to close out in defeat. Anything I go into now, I've got to be elected." They said: "Mr. Johnson, you won't even need to campaign. We'll do it for you. And you'll get elected." I said: "All right. It's wrong to have to beg anybody to do what he should do. I know what I should do. I'll go down tomorrow and file." I was elected with 1,000 more votes than my four opponents put together. The people knew my record and gave me a clear mandate. I told the superintendent, "I've got a mandate to give you hell, and I'm going to do it!" It was a sweet victory because I was elected by my own people and because I was elected to the same board that gave me so much trouble when I was teaching. I was now in a position to give orders to the school superintendent whose predecessor said I was a no-good cuss and rabble-rouser.

At one of the first board meetings I attended, I said to the other members: "If you condone what was done in the past, if you try to continue the inequities that you inherited, then I must be a gadfly and sting you like hell. Don't let me catch you trying to underpin a collapsing set of mores. The mean and ungodly days of your elders are done with. I warn you: The old people have eaten sour grapes. Now I look at you and wonder if your teeth are also on edge."

During my tenure on the board, I think we made a number of progressive moves, but I would sometimes get frustrated at how slowly we acted. After a proposal was presented, a board member might say, "It sounds good, but we need to study it some more." I'd blow my top. "Ladies and gentlemen," I'd say, "you people sound like you've got a thousand years to fix up this project and make it perfect. Well, it's never going to be perfect. We're never going to be absolutely sure about anything till we try it out. Let's try it and change it if it needs changing. Let's do the best thinking we can in the light of what we now know. Then let's act. If we make a mistake, we can correct it. If you buy a brand new car and then find out the carburetor won't work, you don't take a sledgehammer and bust up the whole car or return it and get a new one. You take it back to the shop and say, 'Man, fix my car.' We're never going to get anywhere if we're afraid to take the car out of the showroom."

As was always my custom, I spoke out loudly for what I believed. I tried to take positions that were good for all the schoolchildren—not just the black ones or the white ones. I don't think many people resented a Negro on the school board, but they often resented my outspoken opinions. I was frequently threatened—even my life was threatened. One time five men ganged up on me after a board meeting and suggested what might happen to me on the way home. I said: "Hell, if you're so courageous as you claim to be, why don't you do it right here in the open, in front of all these people. Now do it! I'm ready. I call your bluff!" They didn't do anything. Another time just before a board meeting a man called me on the phone. "Nigger, you better resign from that board if you want to stay alive. You go to that meeting tonight and resign, or the undertaker will have to carry you away. You understand, nigger?" I said: "I'll be there to see the show. I'll be there to see what you've got to offer. I'll be looking at you." Nothing happened. I've been threatened so much I've learned to live with it. But I'm getting old. I wish I could use some of those threats as therapy for my arthritis!

I don't think I would have made a very good professional politician. Maybe I'm too conscientious about what's right and what's wrong. Maybe I don't always do what's right, but I do have a conscience that won't let me compromise the way politicians do. I fancy myself something of a philosopher, and a conscientious philosopher can never be elected to office. Somebody once said that a philosopher should consider himself a failure if he ever becomes an elected official. I agree. A philosopher has to be something of a gadfly and a visionary. He should always be up on the mountaintop pointing out to the people below something even higher than the mountaintop. He can't stay on the mountaintop and win popularity contests. To win a public office, he would have to lower his high philosophy to the level of the average person below. To be elected to office means that he has become more like them than they have become like him.

That doesn't mean that we can't have people who will try to lead in public office. It does mean, however, a temptation to compromise. When I was on the board of education, I tried to lead from principle, not from expediency. One time somebody from the *Courier-Journal* called me and said: "Mr. Johnson, your vote on such-and-such an issue was contrary to what we expected. You let us down. You know we endorsed you." That kind of stirred me up, and I said: "Let me tell you right now that when you endorsed me, you didn't make me your slave. I do my own thinking." He said, "Well, we're going to have to blast you to hell." I said: "Go ahead. I live on blastings."

I know I've not been the soul of diplomacy when dealing with the opposition. Back in 1975 at the height of the busing controversy, I was invited to be a member of the platform party at the big Louisville Defender

Exposition held at Louisville Gardens. The governor, the mayor, the county judge, and Congressman Ron Mazzoli were there. Just before nine o'clock in the evening, when we were supposed to go on stage and make little speeches, we were rounded up and taken to a side room. The auditorium was full of people. At a quarter past nine, we were still in that little room and were beginning to get anxious. Finally, ten minutes later we were led out to the stage and told that there had been calls stating that bombs had been placed under the platform. I took advantage of the time we spent in that little side room, however, to lecture all those leaders on their lack of leadership. I said: "People, you're all in positions of leadership, but you have failed to lead. You've acted like demagogues, catering to the lowest levels of the people." I must have been pointing my finger at them when I said that because the next day in the *Courier-Journal* there was a picture of me doing that. I guess I was a bit rough on them. If I had been one of them, I couldn't have pointed my finger the way I did. A democratic society needs its philosophers and critics, and they have to stand apart from the political process. Socrates could never have been elected to any office.

At the same time, I know we live in an imperfect world. I used to tell my wife: "Honey, the difference between you and me is that you want to do a job perfectly, and I'm willing to settle for something less than perfection. It's like settling for a good passing grade on a paper. I'd like to get 100 percent, but I'll take 85—or even 70, if I have to. Then I'll go on to something else." While a person who demands a 100 on a paper is still working on it, I've already gone on to other projects that I was trying to bring from 0 up to 70 or 85. "This house," I'd tell her, "is an 85 percent house. It's not perfect, but it keeps you warm and protected. If I had insisted on building a 100 percent house, I'd still be outside planning it. And we'd both be freezing."

I know I'm not a profound thinker. But I do believe I'm blessed with a moral sense that makes me try to do what's right. I also try to seek out brilliant people who can help me do my thinking. Finally, I believe I have an impetuousness for action. I want to see a job done. I try to be a catalyst and a gadfly. I suppose you could say I've tried to be a bit of both—a thinker and a doer.

Uncle Tom & George Wallace

A new day has come.

WHEN I WAS a short-term student at the University of Kentucky in 1949, there were two young professors there who would ask me to go out and have a beer with them late at night. They wanted to show how much they respected me. One was from Mississippi and the other from Ohio. The Ohio professor said, "Now, Lyman, you understand I am from the North, and we've never had any kind of troubles with Negroes in my hometown?" I said, "Mr. Professor, how many Negroes live in your hometown?" He said, "None." I said, "All right, when half your town gets to be black, I'll find out how pure your motives are, my friend."

The man from Mississippi said: "Lyman, I admit white people down home sure have treated black people miserably. I was also brought up to give black people hell. We used to get great sport out of throwing a half-dollar in front of a poor Negro, and just when he reached over to pick it up, we'd kick him as hard as we could in the seat of his pants. He'd land on the ground, and we'd recover our money and laugh uproariously." Then this converted Mississippian would plead: "But, Lyman, I have overcome all that cultural conditioning. If you find me mistreating you or any other Negro, just tell me so. I aim to treat you right from now on." After both men had pleaded their cases, I looked them straight in the eyes and said: "Now let me unload on both of you fellows. I don't give a damn about your cultural conditioning. You can't undo anything that happened in the past. You can't square the difference. You can't pay reparations to the dead. It only makes for hard feelings to bring it up. The past is past. Just let it stay where it is. What I'm concerned about is how you treat me today and tomorrow."

Frankly, I've been treated very well in my old age. I only wish it had come sooner when I was young enough to enjoy it more. Conditions aren't ideal yet, but they're better for all blacks. Before my wife died, she and I would drive down to Columbia and visit other little southern towns just to marvel at the things we could enjoy that we couldn't when we were growing up. As a youngster I would never have believed it could happen in my lifetime. I'm elated with race relations in Columbia today. A new day has come. Several years after my father was refused treatment in the Columbia hospital, my uncle had to have an operation. By then the Hill-Burton Hospital Act had been passed and had begun to bear fruit. The county had built a new hospital with federal money. When my uncle was admitted, he was treated just as courteously as a white person.

One of my nephews is on the police force down there. When I was a kid, the most despised person in town to the black community was the policeman. When he would go down into a Negro neighborhood to arrest a person, the first thing he'd do was to put handcuffs on him. Then he'd beat him. Yeah, he had to beat him. No matter how willingly the Negro would surrender, the policeman would beat him before he took him to jail. He seemed to get a kick out of beating the poor Negro. Thank God, it's different now. Nowadays if a policeman hits a Negro—or a white man—he'd better have a good reason. Nowadays my nephew arrests blacks and whites and doesn't beat them up.

On the other hand, racism is so deeply rooted in American society it will take a long time to eliminate it—if ever. Great progress has been made since World War II, but it is always possible to go backward. Look at what happened between 1865 and 1876. The slave was freed, made a full citizen, and given rights he'd never dreamed of. He was on his way to being a full partner in American society. Then about 1876—our Centennial year—the trend was reversed, and the freedman began to go downhill politically, socially, and economically. From about 1890 to 1915, almost all the progress the black man had made was wiped out. He was almost back to being a slave.

I know there will always be people who won't like me because I'm black. That's all right as long as they don't abuse and mistreat me. One day I was walking across the University of Michigan campus with a young white man from Birmingham when a fellow in my history class walked right by me and didn't speak. After we passed, my companion said: "Lyman, don't you feel like a misfit up here? Doesn't it bother you when a man who knows who you are won't even speak to you in public?" I said: "You see that tree there? I pass by that tree every day, and it hasn't spoken to me yet, and it hasn't run into me yet. Now if that white boy doesn't want to speak to me, that's all right. And everything will stay all right as long as he doesn't run into me." I can take being ignored. Treat me like an invisible man if you need to. Just don't think you can spit on me and get away with it.

More nails are being hammered into the coffin of white supremacy every day. The energy crisis that made a lot of brown-skinned Arabs wealthy has also made a lot of white Americans realize how dependent they are on the goodwill of nonwhite people. When dark-skinned people buy hotels in New York and Atlanta, factories in Chicago, and horse farms in Kentucky, they put more nails in the coffin. When basketball and football teams from the University of Alabama or Georgia Tech or Ole Miss have more black players than whites, the old white supremacists start digging their graves.

I don't mean to suggest that everyone in the South has always been racist. There has always been a moral minority of southern whites who've wanted to do right by blacks. They've had to pay a terrible price, however, for their liberal morality. I know of a man in South Carolina who was appointed a federal judge in the early 1960s. He said: "I'm a white southerner, but I'm a man of conscience. Now that I have a federal judgeship I'll render my decisions on the basis of right and not race." He made so many decisions favorable to black people, the white people ran him out of town. He thought he was safe because he couldn't be fired. He thought he couldn't be intimidated. He was wrong. He was ostracized. He was shunned. Even at church people turned their backs to him. Almost every day he'd have to go out and wipe off eggs from his front door and windows. They'd put mayonnaise on his car doors, and he'd get it on his hands and clothes. Finally, he had to leave. He moved to New York.

Even members of my own family—my brothers and sisters who moved North—have been amazed by changes in the South. Several years ago my sister who lives in New York came down for a visit, and I took her around to various places about town—restaurants, libraries, hotels, parks, schools. She said: "Lyman, I'm amazed that all these places are open to Negroes now. They were off-limits to us when we were growing up in Tennessee." I said, "Yes, Sister, but did it ever occur to you that if so many of you educated Negroes had not gone up North, we would've accomplished this sooner?"

Shortly after I won the case against the University of Kentucky, another sister, my wife, and I drove over to Lexington and ate dinner in the campus cafeteria. My sister was incredulous. "Lyman," she said, "you mean to tell me they're not going to put us out of this place?" I said, "No, Sister, this is what I stayed and worked and fought for." When I see the opportunities blacks have now in Kentucky and throughout the South, I feel so pleased that I stayed and helped remove some of the racial barriers. I'm glad I didn't tuck tail and run like most of my kinpeople. To them I say: "You ran away from the problem. You ran to Detroit, Chicago, New York, and Philadelphia. But when you arrived and opened up your suitcase, the first thing that jumped out was the problem you thought you left behind. Now look at all the ghettos spread all over the North. You ran from the problem down South and took the problem with you. White people are the same everywhere."

Not one of my father's children ever got over his bitterness toward the South. I haven't. When I go back to Columbia, I try to forget. I try to be tactful. I say to my hometown whites: "I won't bring it up, and you'd better not. If you rub me the wrong way, I may snap at you like a mad bulldog. We'll look to the future and try to forget the way your grandpappy treated my grandpappy, the way your papa treated my papa, the way your older brother treated me as I came up." It's sort of a truce we're working under. I think—I hope—that most whites believe that if they stop trying to hold the black man down, then black and white will rise together. When the white man holds the black man down, he has to stay down with him.

We black people want a piece of the pie. If you don't let me have my piece, I'll put my big foot square down in the center of the pie and mess it up for both of us! Either we share it, or there won't be any pie for anyone. We're going to sit down at the table and divide the pie. I may not like you, and you may not like me. That doesn't matter. What matters is that in order for the pie to benefit either of us we're going to have to share it. Like it or not!

Uncle Tom is dead. Even white people would spurn him. Yet we haven't emancipated ourselves to the point that we don't sometimes use his tactics. Take the black man who works for an affluent family on their suburban estate. They like him and give him all sorts of tips, handouts, and tokens—enough, say, for him to splurge and buy himself a Cadillac. When he gets back to his end of town, he can ride the streets in his shiny, big car and put on the dog. He's probably going to be smart enough to buy two cars, a Cadillac and a Chevrolet, so that when he goes to work he drives the Chevy. The black man says: "Look at me. I don't work hard, and I make more than a schoolteacher. Why shouldn't I make it easy on myself?"

Race relations have changed in the South, but blacks still have to be wary. Take the Negro who drives a fancy new car back home to the South. See him pull up to a filling station. The white attendant comes out and says, "Yeah, what can I do for you?" The black man says, "Fill 'er up!" The white man knows the tank will hold maybe thirty gallons, so he fills it up, gets paid, and maybe gets a little tip. The white fellow gets out his cleaning rag, runs it over the black man's car, and gets another tip. A black man tipping a white man in a filling station! It's all right now. It's now a matter of economics. The white man is anxious to get all the tips he can, even if they are from a black man. He looks around, and when he doesn't see any white people, he begins to do a white man's version of the coon act. "Now what else can I do for you, sir?" he says. "You don't need any oil, but I'll be glad to put some water in your radiator. I can put some freon in your air conditioner. Yes, the rest rooms are open, and they're clean." While he's talking, he's shining the chrome on the car door. He gets another tip. Just as the black man is about ready to drive off, the white man says: "Tell me something. You black people go up North broke and come back riding a Cadillac. How did you do it?"

Suddenly, the Negro remembers where he is, and he remembers

what happened to his daddy and granddaddy, and he thinks, "Maybe I better be a little careful." Aloud he says: "Well, you folks had all the land. You folks had all the money. You folks had all the brains. So there was nothing for me to do but to go up north. I got a job, saved my money, bought me a car, and thought I'd come down to see how my folks were doing here in Mississippi." He gets a little bolder and says: "No, I can't explain what happened. You all had everything—the brains, the land, the money. Now you figure it out." By this time he's already headed down the road. He's made his point, but he's been careful not to make the white man mad. He could still be lynched. A black man still has to remember who he is and where he is.

Despite the South's lingering racism, however, it is a good place for black people to live today. For many blacks it's better than the North. When I visit my relatives in Philadelphia or New York and see how poor blacks live in the ghettos, it breaks my heart. I want to say: "Oh, people, why don't you move back down South where you can have a better life? You're sitting on the curb with nothing to do. You live in hot, steamy tenements with just enough in government handouts to keep you alive. You have no quality of life. It's a disgrace. You can go south and get a little fifty-acre farm and have ham year-round. You can raise your own chickens. You can have strawberries. You can have fresh air. And when you walk into a store, no one will call your wife 'auntie.' They'll call her Mrs. Johnson. If you work and save enough money to buy a car, the salesman will say: 'Good morning, Mr. Johnson. Let me show you this car, sir. Yes, we'll be glad to let you test-drive it.' The salespeople will be so polite and courteous. You know the white people up here don't care anything about you. They won't even give you a job. They're cold. If too many of you move into a neighborhood, they'll move out. Now you know the truth: The only reason white people up here haven't been too bad to you is that they didn't have very many of you black people to get bad to."

Many years ago a black friend of mine drove up north to New York, then to Niagara Falls and over into Canada and all across Canada from east to west. He said: "Lyman, you wouldn't believe how nice those white people up there were to us. I just hated to come back into the states and back South. People in Canada are a different breed." I let him finish and then said: "Man, has it ever occurred to you why the white people in Canada were so nice to you? Do you know that they, like their American cousins, killed off the Indians when they started their manifest destiny expansion west? They got the Indians down to a handful and have kept them under control ever since. How many blacks do you think they have up there? When you were on your trip across Canada, you may have been the only black family passing through. They certainly weren't going to build black and white rest rooms when only one black family comes through every week or two. Of course, they don't have a race problem with blacks or Indians. They've got them both down to small numbers and under control. That's the reason they were so gracious to you. They're not a different breed of people. Take a dozen of your country cousins up there and move into a neighborhood, and then see how they treat you. No, they won't *treat* you anymore; they'll *mistreat* you." I was trying to show my friend that Canadians can't be given credit for being any better than anybody else. Before the Civil War, they had a reputation for befriending the slave and giving him a safe haven. But they had already tried slavery in those cold climates, and it had failed. Black people have always been able to pick up long-distance friends.

Canadians are like white people in the American North. Some people have always tried to harmonize their Christian religion with good works and fair play for minorities. Some people were closet racists who never had a chance to show their true color because they had never come into contact with minorities. But when blacks began moving into northern towns, cities, and neighborhoods in the 1920s and '30s and '40s and '50s, they said: "We don't want no damn niggers up here. Get out or we'll run you out." A lot of people have been racists all along but never had a chance to prove it.

The white people of the South now know that the best way to free themselves for a better life is to get off the back of the black man. They are beginning to realize that the black man only wants what any human being wants. Together the white man and the black man can go higher than either one could go alone. White people are at last being emancipated from their own traditions.

I believe there is a reservoir of good feeling between southern whites and blacks, even though it is rooted in an assumption of white supremacy. As long as the black man admitted that he was subordinate and allowed the white man to assert his superiority—as long as this special relationship wasn't tampered with—the two races would die for each other. In this new day in the South, there is still that special feeling of closeness. To tap that reservoir of good feeling and to make race relations healthy and mutually beneficial, we must root out the concept of racial superiority and inferiority.

Give the South due credit. It may have been jerked kicking and screaming into a new era, but in many ways it has accommodated itself with grace and dignity. When a fellow like George Wallace, who stood in the schoolhouse door to keep Negroes from attending the University of Alabama, who defied federal authorities on black voter registration, who became a white racist symbol—when you see a man like that at the end of his career courting black votes, shaking black hands, and kissing little black babies, you can see what a transformation has been wrought.

The Battle's Not Over

Eliminating racism isn't going to bring Paradise down for black people.

BLACK AMERICANS can trace their ancestry farther back in this country than most white Americans. Blacks have been in this "land of opportunity" for a long, long time. But we still live under worse handicaps than the newest immigrant. Even a Mexican still dripping with water from the Rio Grande has a brighter future. When a white immigrant arrives in this country and speaks no English, he has a handicap. But it's not a handicap till he opens his mouth. If you see a boy a block away from you, you can tell that he's black. You don't know what kind of English he speaks, but the black boy is already handicapped because you see his color. If you speak to him and find out that he is educated and speaks good English, he's still black. When the white immigrant learns English, he's eliminated most of his handicap. The black boy can't learn his color away.

The white immigrants who came to America fifty or a hundred and fifty years ago—after all the Africans had been brought here—were eventually assimilated into American society because they had white faces. They quickly learned correct literary English in the schools. But not the black man. When he arrived, he was a slave and had to pick up English any way he could. He couldn't learn it in school. His fear of the lash was his only teacher. The white man said: "I told you to bring me a *hatchet*, and you brought me a *saw*. You dumbhead! After I finish whipping you, you won't make that mistake again!" So the poor slave tried to pick up on what the white man meant when he said "plow" and "cotton" and "work" and "come here" and "harness that mule." The lash was a brutal, primitive teacher.

When I look ahead, I do so with some fear. I'm afraid that black people in this world and in this country will not be as passively resistant to an unjust society as we have been. I see the threat of violence. A society that will tolerate having 40 to 50 percent of its young black people unemployed in big cities is a society sitting on a powder keg. When I visit my daughter in Philadelphia or my sister in New York, I sometimes say, "I think I'll go out to get the morning paper." I leave their nice, comfortable homes, get in my car, and drive around to the black ghettos. Sometimes I think they're plotting to get even with a society that will not allow them an honest job to earn their own keep and a few luxuries from this affluent economy. I know that my fears are not merely nightmares. I've seen the future right here in Louisville. I saw it in 1968 just two blocks from where I live when young blacks rioted and destroyed property. I tried to stop a bunch of young men about to break out a large plate glass in a store. "Young fellows," I said, "if you start a race war, you'll lose everything." They said: "Mr. Johnson, we love you. You've done a lot for us in school and out of school. But, Mr. Johnson, you have a good education. You had a decent job. You are now retired. Your children are educated and grown and have good jobs. We don't have any of those things. We have nothing to lose!" One of the young men said: "I've been to the penitentiary three times. It's better in the pen than it is out here. They treat us mighty rough, but at least they give us work. We've got a place to sleep. We've got something to eat. So move on, Mr. Johnson." They pointed toward my home, and I walked away.

That was the talking stage of violence. A few weeks later it got to the acting stage at Twenty-eighth and Greenwood. My wife and I were eating dinner in a little restaurant a block away. We began to hear noises, and my wife said: "What's going on? People are gathering outside and talking loud." I said: "Oh, they're getting a little bit stirred up. I'll go to the door and check." When I came back, I said: "It's getting pretty rough out there. You finish up, and I'll take you home." She said, "Lyman, why did you bring me here when you knew things were getting out of hand?" I said: "I wanted to see the show. It's getting dangerous now, so I'll get you on home."

I drove her home and went back. I parked and was walking toward the action talking to young blacks, trying to get them to disperse. A young student at Parkland Junior High saw me and went inside. Her father came out and said: "Mr. Johnson, I live down here, but I'm staying inside my house. I've got my gun and my ammunition stacked inside. If anybody comes into my yard, he's a dead duck; I don't care who he is! Anybody crosses my yard, I know he's up to no good. I don't believe you know how serious this thing is, Mr. Johnson. And with your light skin, you may not be safe either. When the thing really breaks out, it's gonna be dangerous for any white person—or any white-looking person—around here. So you'd better turn your car around. Don't turn your lights on. Drive in the dark till you get a couple of blocks away and then drive like hell to get away." I took part of his advice, drove my car about five blocks from the danger zone, then walked back. I got there in time to see a Yellow Cab get its windshield smashed in by two bricks. The white driver had his white passenger in the back seat fall down on the floor. I said: "People, don't do that. These white people are not responsible for what's wrong." They said, "Goddamn all white people," and went on throwing bricks. The driver somehow managed to peep up over the broken-out windshield, made a quick left turn, and race on down the street. Before he got away, every window in his cab was smashed out. I had tried to show the black rioters how futile, how useless, the violence was. At the same time, I understood their frustration at a government that could be so concerned about what goes on in Iran and Egypt and the Persian Gulf, in Nicaragua and Chile and every little corner of the world—and not be aware that we're sitting on a powder keg right here at home.

I knew how those black rioters felt. I knew their frustration and their anger because I'd been in a similar situation. I was at the University of Michigan when the bank there failed. I didn't have but twenty-seven dollars in the bank, but it was all I had. I had only fifteen cents in my pockets. I couldn't borrow any money from anybody, and I couldn't buy anything on credit. I couldn't buy a decent meal for fifteen cents. It was a hell of a situation. Simple survival is not an academic or a theoretical matter with me. I know how these people without work or money or hope feel. I've been there.

Young black men feel especially frustrated and helpless. Historically, the male is supposed to be strong enough to protect the female. But the black male in this country has never been able to do that. His manhood has been denied him! He's been emasculated! The black woman knows the score. She knows there's almost nothing her boyfriend or husband or any black man can do to protect her. The black male has seen evil done to him and to his women, but he's had to look on passively. He's looked on the tragic history of his race in America as an impotent bystander. Since the 1960s such men have gotten so desperate they feel they have nothing to lose. "I don't give a damn if I'm shot down in the street," one of them told me. "I've heard how white people treated my ancestors. Well, the white man may not give me a job, but he's not going to make me bow and scrape before him. He made my daddy into an Uncle Tom, but I'll behave the way I please." It's a sad, dangerous situation when a man gets that low. He knows he can't win when he fights the white establishment.

That's true everywhere in this country, not just in the South. Eldridge Cleaver and the Black Panthers found out what happens when they tried to resist. They got torn to pieces. Jump on a white man, and he will mow you down. Young blacks are beginning to understand why the old folks behaved the way they did. The technique of survival is still to keep your mouth closed and to hope for a better day. Young blacks won't accept that stratagem and even strike out at us old guard. When I've tried to put the soft pedal on, I've been called an Uncle Tom and a coward. "He called me a son of a bitch, and I'll not take it," a young black will say. I've replied: "They've called me a son of a bitch too, son. You can get killed. . . ." He will say: "Uncle Tom, your days are over. They can't get away with that anymore."

The pattern of black/white sexual relations in America was set in slavery times. The white female was pampered and pedestaled by her husband. Her role was to stay home and to keep her skin white, her eyes blue, and her hair blonde and to be available for occasional sex for her husband in order to provide him with heirs. For real fun and sex, he went down to the quarters and played with the Negro women. They never had any choice. They were his property. If they didn't give in, they would be beaten up and taken off their soft jobs and given field work. The Negro man knew he'd better not be caught slipping up to the cabin when the white man was there with his wife. When her Negro husband came back, she'd look at him and say: "Well, what can you do for me? I have sex with the master and don't have to work. You gottta go out and work in the hot sun all day long. I just have to sit around here and wait till the master comes, and as long as I'm nice to him, he makes it easy for me. So what do you have to offer, black boy?" The black man felt useless.

My own family has been affected by this pattern of sexual behavior. My maternal grandmother was an attractive colored girl—Indian brown, almost an olive color. Her owner up in East Tennessee was attracted to her. When she wouldn't give in to him, he sold her down the river. She was on her way to the cotton fields of Mississippi when someone bought her and brought her to his plantation in Middle Tennessee. She was afraid to go to Mississippi. It was a place that would break down and kill a frail woman like her. She knew that those Mississippi fields would be her cemetery.

I remember my grandmother very well. I remember her reddish-brown complexion, and I look in the mirror at my own light complexion. I didn't need to ask any questions. I knew the answers already. Questions would have been unnecessary and embarrassing. I don't censure her for what she did. If anyone casts aspersions on my color, I look upon him with utter contempt and say: "How ignorant can you be! You don't know or can't appreciate the situation she was in. In the first place, she was sold because she had scruples. A slave's not supposed to have scruples. A slave's supposed to have plain common sense. A slave's supposed to play ball. Maybe she started playing ball when she saw the cotton fields getting closer to her—or saw that she was getting closer to the cotton fields. Maybe she simply wanted to survive."

The poor black man has wanted to survive too, and sometimes that has meant that he's found it convenient to go along with the system. In a community near my hometown, a certain Negro man was principal of the black school. I wondered: "How in the world did this dummy get that job? He's not bright enough to plow a straight furrow." When I found out, I was embarrassed and ashamed for us all. A big white businessman in town was playing around with his wife. She had a car the white man had given her, and she'd drive to Nashville to meet him. The Negro husband was strutting around town like an Oxford graduate and didn't know beans about anything. But he apparently knew about his wife's extracurricular activities. People told me: "Sure, Lyman, he knows what's going on. He knows how he got his job. He just doesn't interfere." So the white man's wife doesn't interfere. The Negro principal doesn't interfere. The white woman is the cream of southern society. She gets what she wants and belongs to the arts societies. Her husband gives her money, and she gives him respectability. He takes his Negro mistress to Nashville and gets what he wants from her. The Negro principal gets what he wants and parades around in his fine car and nice clothes. Then he goes home and sleeps in a bed that some white man has given his wife! I could be charitable and say he was merely trying to survive. In the process, however, he sold his manhood.

This sexual exploitation of black women and the emasculation of black men are a part of underwritten American history and sociology. It is so common that case histories are found on every street in every black neighborhood. I find it disgusting, but I can't find fault with my brothers and sisters who are the victims. Sometimes—as in my grandmother's case—it was truly the only way to survive. In the case of a family in my hometown, survival was at stake. I knew a black man who worked at the city waterworks for two dollars a day. Since he couldn't support his wife and five children on that wage, his wife got a job as a domestic for a white family near where I lived. In those days I meandered between the white and the black communities. I played with boys of both races and knew how to conduct myself in order to be accepted by both. All my father's children were well schooled in how to play both sides of the game. I used to go to school with this black man's children and knew the family well. When I played with the white boys near our neighborhood, I could see the black woman working as a servant for the white family, cooking, washing, ironing, and scrubbing. When we played hard and got hot and thirsty, the white boys would say, "Come on, Lyman, let's go in and get a glass of water or some lemonade." So we'd all run into the house for refreshments.

One time we started down to the basement to get a baseball mitt. One of the white boys opened the door leading down the steps, got halfway down, and came rushing back. What he saw was a joke to him. "Papa's down there," he said, out of breath, "just working old Alice over. He's going to town on her." I don't know where the white man's wife was, probably up in the front room knitting or crocheting. I don't know whether she knew what was going on or whether she knew and didn't care or whether she knew and couldn't do anything about it. Maybe she knew if she complained, she'd be sent to the cotton fields too. There's more than one kind of cotton field.

I can't find fault with that black woman in the basement. Maybe she was looking out for her children the only way she could. I know that every morning she took a little pail with her, and every evening she loaded it up with the white family's leftover food to take home. There was never enough to eat at her house till she got in with her bucket. She made only about fifty cents a day, and it was understood that the table leftovers were part of her pay. She also understood that a part of her work was going down to the basement whenever the man said so. The food she took home wasn't worth a cuss, except to people who were hungry.

This is not the end of the story. One day the black woman gave birth to another baby. This time the baby was half-white. I didn't ask any questions. I knew who the papa was. The man who worked at the water company for two dollars a day—he didn't fuss either. Maybe he didn't like it, but what the hell could he do? The baby was simply a by-product of a situation they had to live under. The man used common sense. Maybe he ate some of the food his wife brought from the white man's house too.

These three stories show the black man's and the black woman's predicament in this country. One story occurred in the 1850s and the other two around 1915. They are quilts made from the same pattern. It hurts me, and I grieve that my people have had to degrade themselves so in order to survive. It has affected us all. When I was a schoolboy, I saw something that broke my heart. There was a black teacher—we'll call her Miss Alice— who taught three of us Johnson children. We thought she was the most darling, charming teacher we'd ever had. In those days Columbia had two main black communities, both built on hills—College Hill, where we lived, and East Hill, where Miss Alice lived. Separating the two neighborhoods was about a block and a half of white families. It was common to see black people walking across the white section to get from one black area to the other. No blacks we knew owned cars; very few even owned horses and buggies, and there was no public transportation. Blacks walked wherever they went in town.

One day I was out playing when I saw a white cashier in the town's leading drugstore driving down the street in his buggy. I saw him stop, pick up this beautiful woman who was my teacher, and carry her out the highway into the country. She didn't know that I saw her, and I didn't know where they went or what they did. But I was at an impressionable age and had heard the bigger boys joke about what went on when a white man picked up a black woman on the street. Now I was seeing my own darling teacher being picked up that way. My favor, my confidence, my respect for her went down to zero. I never regained it.

In my older days, I'm not so hard on her. As a Negro teacher, she could make only thirty dollars a month. By going with that white man, she could make a third that much in less than a day. She could sell her body for five or ten times what she earned as a teacher. Maybe she was using her head as well as her body.

The legacy of those times is still with us. It is enclosed in our national consciousness and within each of us individually. The black woman and the black man are facing serious personal problems in our integrated society. If a black man comes in contact with a white girl and begins to date her, he's likely to upset the pattern of race relations. Blacks begin to wonder why the black man is going with the white girl. Is he trying to emancipate himself from the old taboos? Is he putting blacks down? Is he saying that black girls are not good enough for him? White people ask questions too. Why is the white girl taking up with a black boy? Is something wrong with her? Two generations ago that boy would have been lynched and left hanging from a telephone pole. People also wonder if the couple is a white boy and a black girl. Will the white boy use the black girl up to a point and then ditch her? No one knows whether to approve, criticize, or be nonchalant.

Eliminating racism from society isn't going to bring Paradise down for black people. It'll just give us an even start with white people. "If you were to become white overnight," I say to blacks, "you'd still have to work like hell to make a living. Just being white is not going to save you!"

Some of the problem is, of course, with blacks themselves. Young people these days have electricity and gas and piped-in water. When they want to cook a hamburger, they don't have to go out and cut wood and cook in an open fireplace. They just turn a knob. Still they complain. I'm a link between this new generation and the people who lived in dire poverty and yet learned to become scholars and producers. Sometimes what I see floors me. I see young men driving up and down the street in big, shiny cars and flunking freshman English. They ought to be brought to their senses with a baseball bat!

Our educational system, on the other hand, has to find out why black students are such underachievers. We've got to know why black students who start out in kindergarten and the first grade about even with white children finish high school twenty or more percentile points behind. How can a person with a percentile score of thirty compete with a person whose score is fifty? He can't do it. In a technological society, if he gets a job at all, he'll get the most marginal, the most servile, the most menial, the lowest-paying job. Most of these low-achieving people will be condemned to perpetual idleness and unemployment—of no use to society or to themselves.

I certainly don't want a dummy—whether he's white or black—working on the carburetor of my little Chevrolet. He'll do more damage than good. So what can be done? Teachers and administrators will have to take the black education problem seriously and not try to deny or to hide it. They'll have to stop their "push-out" programs, which push out students with unearned and undeserved diplomas. They'll have to have more understanding and compassion. Yet they'll have to be just as rough on black kids as on white kids. They'll have to work out programs, approaches, and techniques that will equip all children with what they need to know to survive in a highly technological future.

Every person has to hoe his own row. No one can live on what Daddy or Mama did. Being born into a high-achieving family can be a benefit or a handicap. Everyone should try to add to what the previous generation has accomplished. I don't criticize a person for having a fortunate inheritance, but I will judge him on what he does with it. If a kid looks up from his cradle, sees his daddy's law degree from Yale and then grows up with the attitude that he wants to do at least as well as his daddy, that's all right. That's good. It's an incentive. But if it makes him think he's already somebody because of who his daddy is, he's dead wrong. Nobody is born great.

I have a nephew who is a good example of how advantages can turn out to be a handicap. His mother and father were both college graduates, and he grew up in a cultured home. He's one of the smartest men in this town. He's got a head full of brains. He's a mathematical whiz. I pay him no compliment to call him the most intelligent, best-read unemployed man in town. He's turned out to be of no benefit to himself or to anyone else. When I taught economics, I'd say to my students: "I know you're all consumers. That's obvious. But responsible people are also producers. They contribute to what we call the Gross National Product. While you're taking out of this national storehouse, remember you're obligated to put something in."

Children can also be discouraged by highly successful parents. Some people are so industrious that they stand in the way of their children. Their accomplishments rob them of incentives. "Look what Papa has done," they say. "I can't live up to that. I'd have to live on his reputation." Living on the old man's reputation won't get you far in this world. How much have Franklin Roosevelt's children accomplished? Their father set standards they couldn't hope to reach.

My daddy was successful, but he constantly reminded us that we had to make our own lives. "Son," he'd say, "you can't make it off me. You've got to make your own mark. I'll do what I can to get you started, but you'll have to work for what you get." Sure enough, we had to work for what we got. We got no unearned allowance. "I'll pay you $1.50 a day for plowing in the fields," he'd say, "but I won't pay you till the work is done."

I had a cousin whose parents treated him differently. He was older and went off to college three years before me. Soon after he arrived, he wrote his mother: "I don't like the food here. I can't stand all these beans they feed us." She replied: "Now, son, don't hurt your delicate digestive system. I'll send you some extra money so you can eat off campus." He dropped out of college in his sophomore year. He never learned to be independent and to hoe his own row. Three years later when I got to the college, they were still serving beans—I expect the same beans he didn't eat! But I got my Greek and my chemistry and my English off those beans and even got fat. If I'd written home complaining about the beans, my daddy would have said: "That's just too bad, son. Those beans are nutritious. They haven't killed any kids there yet, and I don't believe they'll kill you."

Because of his special circumstances, the black man still has a long way to go. Not all the battles have been won. We old-timers could look back and gloat over what we've accomplished. But we must be like the Apostle Paul, who said: "I've put all that behind me. Now I look out in front. I look forward to what is to come." I say to young people: "Just the business of living is exacting. No matter how far you've come, when you look ahead, you will see rugged mountains yet to be scaled. If you refuse to go on the hard way, it will be an easy slide back down the hill. And when you slide back, you will crush all the progress you've made. Don't ever think that the journey is over. Don't ever think that living is going to be easy. The problems you face today are just as agonizing and as difficult to solve as the ones we faced." I firmly believe that life is a struggle for all people. For blacks it is an intensified struggle. No one wants to live on beans his entire life, but we may have to eat them for a while till we can afford steak.

All Colors Are Beautiful

We all belong to one human family.

IN THE 1960s a lot of black people started using the slogan "Black is Beautiful." They said: "Let's stop denying we're black. Our skin is dark, and our hair is kinky, so let's accept it. Let's look the world in the face and say, 'I'm black and proud of it.' " Well, I've been a black man all my life and have always been proud of it. I'm glad that a lot of other Negroes agree now with a position I've always taken. I'm afraid, however, that some of the black-is-beautiful people went a little too far. They began to look as if they didn't care how they looked. They wanted a "natural" look. Even some whites started to ape the "natural" look. It got ridiculous.

One time I was in Frank Stanley, Jr.'s office at the *Louisville Defender* when a young black dude walked in to ask for a job. "Do you think," Stanley said, "I'd hire anybody to work at my paper who looked like you? You insult me by coming in here looking like you do. I'll hire you if you can do the job; but first you go home, take a real good bath, put on some conventional clothes, and do something about your hair. If you're attached to those dirty blue jeans and those dirty sneakers and all that uncombed, natural hair, then, damn it, don't come through that door again." That was rough talk, but Stanley was a businessman who wanted productive, decent-looking employees regardless of their color.

We Negroes get lost when we try to describe who we are. I'm skeptical of Negroes who boast: "We are somebody because of our heritage. Our grandpappy or great-grandpappy was governor of Mississippi!" So what? A few black people even try to cover up their African blood by saying: "My great-grandmother was a pure-blooded Cherokee. I'm mostly Indian." I say: "So? What does that make *you*?" The fact is that none of us really know what's in our bloodline—none of us, black or white. Sometimes when I'm talking to a white audience, I'll say: "I won't talk about my ancestors before 1865. If I do, I might embarrass some of my white kinfolks in the audience. If your great-grandpappy had kept away from the cabin and stayed up there with his wife at the big house, we wouldn't be cousins."

In Columbia I know there are white people who are blood relatives of mine. I say to them: "I don't give a damn whether you want to own your kinship or not. The simple fact is that in 1619 about twenty Africans were brought to this country, and every one of them was black. All the other Africans who followed were black. All the people who came here from England and other European countries were white. Now look at me. Something happened! Which one of your grandfathers is my grandfather too?"

I have cousins in Chicago who don't have much to do publicly with black people because they're passing for white. If they were shown to be black, they might be cut off from some of the amenities they have by being white. But still they're my cousins. On the other hand, I have some very dark-skinned cousins down in Nashville. They are known as Negroes. When people start talking to me about race purity, I say: "What do you mean? If I have cousins who are so white that white people can't tell they're not, how can any white person know he doesn't have some black blood? From history I know that a lot of black African blood got mixed in with white European blood when the African Moors conquered much of southern Europe. Not even the blondest, blue-eyedest German can be absolutely sure he doesn't have some non-Aryan blood!"

Pride can be good or bad. We have different kinds of pride: self-pride, family pride, church pride, club pride, national pride, racial pride. Pride can be good when it imposes a kind of discpline on you. You don't want to do anything to embarrass your clan, your tribe, your church, or your whatnot. You want to do good things to bring honor to your group as well as to yourself. But pride can be destructive. When you think your group is the best in the world, you take pride too far. You begin to think you're not simply *one* of the best, you *are* the best. Even before they were big enough to know what I was talking about, I told my two kids: "You don't want to be snooty, snobby, or mean. People will know that you're Mr. Johnson's daughter or Mrs. Johnon's son, and you'll disgrace us all. People will say, 'How can the Johnsons be such fine people and have such hellish, no-good children?' On the other hand, Mother and Father have to keep themselves decent too, or people will say, 'How can such fine children have such a derelict old cuss for a daddy or such a mean old woman for a mother?' Mama and Papa can't fuss and fight and get drunk and raise hell in the community because it affects you children. We all have a responsibility to each other in this family. You help the family and the family helps you."

It doesn't bother me at all that I don't have an "African" name. I know I have a slave name. I know that my granddaddy was named Johnson because he belonged to a white man named Johnson. But everybody has to have some sort of name. Maybe at one time the name reflected something about what a person did for a living or where he lived. A Mr. Taylor made clothes. A Mr. Barber cut hair. A Mr. Armstrong was apparently very strong. But people who bear those names today don't necessarily make clothes or cut hair; they aren't necessarily strong. What's in a name anyway? It's just a word. It's just something to be called by. "Hell," I say to other black people, "I don't know anything about African names. I'm not an African. I'm an American. I like it here, and I plan to stay. I like air conditioning, electric stoves, and airplanes. I don't give a damn who invented them." Like my name, these are all conveniences I use because I am an American.

I don't quite know what blacks mean when they talk about their blood identity. Normal black people in Africa don't study Greek, but I studied it for three years in college. I also studied Latin. I identify intellectually with Socrates, Aristotle, and Marcus Aurelius. Religiously, I identify with the Christian Bible. About the only African connection I have is my color— and not more than half of that. I suspect that about one-third of me comes from Africa, one-third from the Middle East, and one-third from Europe. I don't concern myself with my family tree. I shrug my shoulders and say, "Frankly, I don't give a damn."

It's all right with me if Cassius Clay didn't like his "slave" name and changed it to Muhammad Ali. A name is a name. Malcolm X may have wanted to dramatize his loss of African identity with "X," but even "X" is a name from the English alphabet. Regardless of your family roots, where you're born and grow up determines who you are. I don't care what a person calls himself, however, if it makes him a better person.

There's nothing about my African ancestry that embarrasses me. I have emancipated myself from all my racial ties. I don't want to be white. I don't want to be black. I don't want to be brown. My skin color is totally irrelevant. One time I was speaking to a white church audience at a fellowship dinner. I zeroed in on an attractive young lady in the second row. "Miss," I said, looking straight at her, "when you first found out that you were in the world, you already had the makings of blonde hair, blue eyes, a pale face, and good looks. You hadn't done one thing to get them. Now, I don't want to hear you arrogate to yourself any prerogatives based on these features for which you are not responsible. I will give you credit, however, if you take what you were given and embellish on that."

Some blacks like to keep together. They go to black churches. They go to certain nightclubs and joints. Sometimes they say, "Ah, let's just get off to ourselves where we can be niggers." I hate to use that word, but it can express how some black people feel when they want to get away from white influences and let their hair down. I know I'm walking into dangerous water because I'm suggesting the kind of racial stereotyping that racists like Ulrich Bonnell Phillips were guilty of. My uncle told me about the lecture he heard Phillips give at Columbia University on the basic inferiority of black people. "Ladies and gentlemen," my uncle said he said, "I'm not saying there aren't some refined, cultured, highly educated black men. Dr. W.E.B. Du Bois is a good example. He's a keen thinker, and I'd not seek a debate with him on any subject. But even the most educated and refined black people wear the garments of civilization loosely. They may come out in the evening dressed in their black ties and tails and stiff white shirts and have all the elegance of high society. But they're always relieved when they get home and can take off these habiliments of civilization and go back to their savage rites. That is where they belong by nature—even W.E.B. Du Bois with his Ph.D. from Harvard."

Phillips's argument is baloney. I have yet to see a white man dressed in his stiff collar and tuxedo and shiny shoes who wasn't relieved to get home and unbuckle. We're all more comfortable when we're not so formal. That's a human trait, not a Negro trait. Racists have always tried to isolate certain traits and to label them "black" or "white" or "brown" or "yellow," but their stereotyping doesn't stand up to objective scrutiny. A black trait is a human trait. A white trait is a human trait. We all belong to one human family.

Musings of a Militant Pacifist

> I don't want you to have a choice as to whether you treat your fellow
> man right or wrong. I demand that you treat him right!

I'M A PACIFIST. Yet I served in the navy during World War II and was a
member of the Louisville draft board during the Vietnam War. I know that
sounds inconsistent, but I think my experiences show that I've always
tried to be an idealist who operates in a realistic world. I've always believed
that changes are better made from inside rather than from outside the
system.

I was drafted into the navy in 1944. By then the navy had somewhat
relaxed its very snooty attitude toward Negroes. They had always wanted
Negroes to work as stewards in the officers' mess or as servants in the
officers' quarters. Despite the continuing limitations, black sailors made a
significant contribution to the war. Dorie Miller is a good example. He was
working as a black steward on board a navy ship in the Pacific when the
Japanese were giving our ships hell. One day after the Japs had shot up his
ship, killed all the white officers, and were about to sink the ship, Miller
came up from the galley where he worked, took over one of the antiaircraft guns, and shot down a number of the attacking planes. He saved
the ship and brought it in. The president gave him the Medal of Honor.
Here was a man who had officially been denied an opportunity to become
a hero but became one anyway.

I've always felt that blacks should help to defend their country. Back in
1946, I think it was, Philip Randolph called on blacks to refuse to serve in
the army till they received their full rights in civilian society. Randolph
organized the Brotherhood of Pullman Porters and was one of our outstanding Negro leaders. I was teaching a class at Central High School
when a reporter called me to ask what I thought. I said I thought he was all
wet. If two people live in the same house, I said, and the house catches on
fire in 15 degrees-below-zero weather, it doesn't benefit either one to fuss
and scrap about his share of the ashes while the house is burning down.
Likewise, when a war is going on, we both have to protect the house. But
once the war is over, then I can turn the battle on anybody who objects to
my share of the house that I helped to protect. Now if I hadn't helped the
white boy put the fire out, he can legitimately say, "You have no rights in
this house because you didn't help to save it."

That's why Dorie Miller was right in saving his ship, even though he
had been forced to work in the galley. What does it profit me if the ship
we're both on sinks? What good will it do me to say as we're all drowning:

"Boy, didn't I hit that white boy square in the nose? Didn't I blacken both his eyes?"

Don't misunderstand me. I don't think wars have ever been necessary—not even World War II. But people get hotheaded. They begin to argue. Fists begin to fly. Then bullets. So I repeat: Wars are never necessary. But once an arsonist starts the house burning, we all have to help put it out.

I was in the navy from March 1944 till January 1946. I was never sent overseas. I don't know for sure why not. Maybe the navy figured they couldn't trust me completely! One time I said: "There is so much wrong on both sides of this war, I'd like to have a gun that shoots both ways. I would hold it over my head, pull the trigger, and wouldn't give a damn which way the bullet went." I imagine they said, "Good God, we can't send a man like that over there."

I was kept in a segregated camp at Great Lakes Naval Station most of my time in the navy. I was with other so-called educated Negroes the navy raked in from all across the country. No matter how qualified we were, no matter how much education we had, the navy was determined not to make officers out of us. They had given the ensign rank—the lowest officer grade—to twelve blacks and then slammed the door. They scattered the twelve black ensigns out to make them more visible to Negro groups but gave them no authority. I remember an ensign named Nelson up there at Great Lakes. He was a graduate of Fisk and was very handsome with his little clipped mustache. When he was dressed up in his uniform, he really stood tall! He was a delight to see. But he was pitiful too. He had nothing to do. He had no authority whatsoever—not even in the Negro camps. We had white officers over us. One white officer said to us: "You Negroes have more education and other qualifications than most of us who are in charge of you. It isn't our fault that you'll never be officers. When you leave here, you'll only be seamen first class. We have too much respect for you to give you permanent duty in the galley or in the officers' mess. In civilian life we know you were not menial servants, and we'll try not to treat you that way here. We will treat you with as much respect as the Navy Code will let us. So find something you can do on this base in the Negro camp. Then let us know what it is, and we'll say we assigned it to you."

Most of us adopted the project of training the droves of black illiterates who came from states like Alabama and Mississippi by the middle of the war. White boys from Alabama and Mississippi were being drafted and sent to the South Seas—right into a hornet's nest of fanatical Japanese. By then the Japs knew they couldn't win the war but they wouldn't give up. Those suicide dive-bombers began to aim their planes directly at our big aircraft carriers. The American antiaircraft guns could shoot the hell out of the pilot, but that wouldn't turn the plane around. Once the Japanese set their planes so as to hit right in the center of an aircraft carrier, it didn't matter whether the pilot was dead or alive. The planes and the bombs hit their targets.

And who was getting killed? Those little white boys from Alabama and Mississippi! The little black boys were so illiterate they couldn't pass the navy's entrance tests. At last, the chickens had come home to roost! The white children had been sent to school, while the poor blacks had been sent to the cotton fields as cheap labor for goddamn plantation owners like Senator Eastland and his bunch. Cotton pickers didn't need to know how to read and write.

So, lo and behold, it was the white boy who was being killed. That was not the way it was supposed to be! Those white mamas let the U.S. government—from the president on down—know what was happening. "We've got a lot of Nigras down here," they reported, "walking around on the plantation, able-bodied, just as slick and fat and greasy as anything—and they are strong. How dare you turn down these great big able-bodied bucks and take our poor little white boys—the cream of the South—for cannon fodder? Why, these black boys can pick up a pig with one hand and a bale of cotton with the other! Something has got to be done. We don't want our white boys going over there and getting killed by some mad Jap dive-bomber while these niggers are walking around free and eating buttered biscuits. If you can't find anything for them to do in the war, at least put them on a train and carry them away from here." Soon the draft boards began to yield to the pressure, and thousands of black boys were brought out who couldn't read or write their own names. They were brought up north by train, hundreds at a time. They unloaded at Chicago, where buses would pick them up and bring them to Great Lakes. There they were dumped on the ground. And about fifty highly educated Negroes were there doing nothing constructive. So we said: "That's something we can do. Let's see if we can help these men to read and write."

So we built a remedial school for them. We devised most of the techniques and procedures ourselves. Because the students were illiterate, we developed a verbal test to determine whether a man had the brains to learn elementary subjects. After they passed the test, they were turned over to us for twelve weeks. When we finished with them, almost everyone could pass a third-grade test. We thought we were doing marvelous things. And I suppose we were. Perhaps we did more for those illiterate blacks, for the United States Navy, and for the war effort as remedial teachers than we could have done had they sent us into combat.

It was a satisfying but aggravating experience. Here were grown men who couldn't read or write. I'd say: "All right, Townsend, take this pencil, hold it like this, and make this mark. This is what we call the letter 'A.' Now this is the letter 'B.' " And so on. Finally, I'd say, "Now you can put some of these letters together like this, and they make your name: T-O-W-N-S-E-N-D." It was satisfying to see a grown man write his name for the first time. But it was aggravating because I was seeing what a racist society had done to him. Maybe, I decided, the war was a good thing for them. When I'd have a chance to talk to these men, I'd say: "If you go into battle, don't buckle. Don't waiver. If you get your hands on Mr. Hitler, choke him. If you get your hands on Mr. Tojo, tear his guts out and stomp him. But don't forget to thank Mr. Hitler and Mr. Tojo before you kill them. If it weren't for them, you might still be picking cotton down on the old plantation."

My white superior officer called me in time after time and told me to stop talking like that. He said he'd throw me in the brig till the war was over. But I didn't stop, and he didn't throw me in the brig. My friends wondered how I ever got an honorable discharge from the navy! All I was trying to do was to show black people that they must use every opportunity they get. If it hadn't been for that war, black people would still be behind a rock. Maybe we're still behind a rock, but at least it's smaller than it was.

President Truman officially ordered the end of segregation in the military services in 1948, but I remember that some changes were beginning to take place in the summer of 1945. They started taking black sailors from the two camps set aside for Negroes—Camp Moffett and Camp Robert Small—and spreading them all over Great Lakes, mixing them in with white sailors. One day there were seven black barbers cutting black sailors' hair. The next day there were six white barbers and one black barber cutting black and white sailors' hair.

I think World War II changed a lot of thinking in this country. It opened white eyes and black eyes. Whites came to the rude awakening that three-fourths of the world is not white. They were forced to see that being white is not enough to keep up in a scientific, techological society. And they were amazed at how well "colored" countries could operate without white assistance. They were shocked to find out that they could no longer go into Africa or Asia or anywhere showing off their white skins and expect special privileges. A black or brown policeman in India or Nigeria just might crack them over their white heads! So whites have had their conceit cooled off a bit.

At the same time, blacks gained a daring they never had before. I think it was World War II that started many of these changes. When young black soldiers came back from the war, they were a rough bunch of cats. They had faced Hitler and Mussolini and Tojo, and now they were ready to face Mr. Charley down home. "Don't tell me to get back in my place," they said. "Move on over. I'm here to stay." It's an attitude that's been reinforced by Korea and Vietnam. "I've fought for this country—right or wrong—and now I want my piece of it."

I was astounded at the new boldness of black veterans on both sides of the Mason-Dixon Line. After World War II, it even woke up sleepy little Columbia, Tennessee. In late January and early February 1946, a big race riot broke out. The Negroes squared off, barricaded themseves in the little Negro business district, and said to the white police: "Don't come down here. We've shot out the street lights and turned off the lights in our stores. If you come on, you'll get shot." One white policeman went beyond the barricade and got himself shot in the leg. Another one came, and he was also shot and fell on top of the first one. It was a shocking display of anger and determination, but it had been a long time coming.

Columbia was a powder keg, and it took a small match to ignite it. This is how it started. An old black woman took her radio to a repair shop to get it fixed. She was poor and uneducated—a humble sort of woman— and her life was centered on that pitiful little radio. After two weeks she went back to ask about it. "No, it's not ready. I ain't had time to get around to yours yet," the white repairman said. "Go on home. I'll fix it when I get time." The old woman begged the man to fix her radio soon because it was all she had at home to keep her company. A week later she went back, but the man hadn't touched her radio. A few days later she went again. Still nothing had been done. Finally, she pleaded, "Please, sir, when are you going to fix my radio?"

He said: "Woman, that radio didn't cost you more than eight dollars when you bought it. You can buy another one cheaper than I can fix this one. Now take this old box home, throw it in the trash, and get a new one!" But the old woman liked her old radio and followed him to the workshop at the back of the store. She begged: "Please, I want my old radio fixed. Can't you do it?" The white man began to get angry, raised his voice, and started cursing: "Nigger, if you don't get out of my store and take that thing with you, I'll bust it over your head."

Of course, the man was right in wanting to make what money he could, and he knew he couldn't make much on a radio that had only cost maybe eight dollars to begin with. But he was wrong in not understanding how attached the old woman was to her little radio. She probably thought he could put in a twenty-five cent tube and it would be all right again. Maybe that's all it would have taken. He didn't know. He hadn't checked. But his big mistake was in cursing that old lady and using vulgar language. Unknown to him, a young black man had come in the front and was listening to his threats. Suddenly, the black man erupted. "I heard what you've been saying to this woman here. And I've heard enough. Listen, goddammit, she's my mother! And I won't let *any* man talk to her that way! I've been over in Okinawa and just got home. This is the way you people used to treat Negroes down here, but you're not going to get away with it anymore." Then he grabbed the white man by the shoulders and threw him through the plate glass winow in front of the store. The man fell into the street all cut up and bleeding. The soldier looked around and said to his mother: "Mama, you go on home. I don't know where I'm going, but I'd better leave now. This is where they lynch people." When the police came and saw the man all chopped up by the glass, they picked him up and rushed him to the hospital. He told them what had happened, and the police said "Well, we got to get that nigger!" And the search started.

The soldier had run down to the Negro business block. The people down there said: "Oh, boy, if you've done what you say, all hell is going to break loose. We got to get you out of town real quick." It was almost like the underground railroad in operation all over again. Some calls were made to Nashville and secret signals given. Within half an hour, he was on his way north. In Nashville some people hid him till they could get him to Louisville. The people in Louisville got him to Cincinnati, and another bunch got him on up to Detroit.

In Columbia two or three days passed, and the police still hadn't found the fellow. They had searched the town upside down. They'd walk in, with or without search warrants, and look everywhere—in stores and homes and churches. Finally, they said: "Well, dammit, he must be gone. But we've got to put these niggers in their place. And the best way to do that is to lynch one of 'em."

About the third night a howling mob of whites lined up on the two streets surrounding the block of Negro businesses. They paraded up and down, cursing, shouting, and threatening. But they were afraid to go into that Negro block because they had heard that armed Negroes had come in from all the nearby counties. A lot of them had just gotten out of the service and were mad. They said: "We are ready to die on this battlefield if we have to. We were shoved into a war we didn't like and made to fight for something we don't even have right here at home. Freedom! Whose freedom? Well, now we're back home. We've got guns and ammunition. We're here in our own business district. So don't come down here. Don't any of you white people come on our street."

The blacks knew they were trapped. But they also knew the whites were afraid to come in. For a while it was a standoff. Finally, the state militia was called, and the town was put under martial law. The militia did a good job of shooting up the place. They rounded up over 100 Negroes, filled the county jail in Coumbia, and took the rest to Nashville. They wanted to send as many as they could to the electric chair and give the rest of them life sentences to make examples out of them. The charges were murder and insurrection. Some whites had been killed, but blacks had been killed first.

The police took the Negroes they had arrested one by one from the jail and brought them to the main police office for questioning. The walls of the interrogation room were lined with guns. The police claimed that all of a sudden a Negro prisoner reached out for one of the guns. The police cut him down right there, killed him on the spot. Another man was killed the same way. It was a legal lynching! No Negro in his right mind would have tried to reach for a gun when he was in the police station surrounded by five or six armed guards. The police story was thin, but no arrests were ever made for the two killings. The police said: "Those niggers were trying to escape. They were going to shoot their way out. We had to shoot to keep them from escaping and to keep from getting shot."

Of the 105 arrested, only those two men were hurt. The rest were eventually all cleared when the trials were moved to another county. Thurgood Marshall was one of the lawyers who defended them. Not a single white man was ever arrested.

When that tragedy happened, my father and my uncle were old men in their eighties. It started on a Monday and by Friday had reached a high pitch. I was in Louisville teaching. After school on Friday, I went by my home, packed my bag, picked up some sandwiches my wife had made me, and caught the bus down there. I got to Columbia about two o'clock in the morning. Every intersection was guarded in the downtown area. The bus station was two blocks west of the courthouse, and my father lived about eight blocks east of the courthouse. I got off the bus and started walking. At every intersection I was stopped by militiamen. "Fellow," they asked, "where you going? Don't you know this town was torn up and is under martial law?" I explained that I had come to visit my father and uncle who lived out on Ninth Street. At that time my family were the only blacks living on that street. It was cold and pitch dark, and I was dressed in my navy peacoat buckled all the way up to my neck. They never suspected that I was black. "I've just been out of the navy for a few weeks," I said, "And I just wanted to spend a little time with my father and uncle and make sure they are all right. I live in Louisville, and I've been hearing about the trouble down here."

At each intersection they said: "Well, move on. But be careful. There are some mighty bad niggers around here." I made it to the last guarded intersection, just a couple of blocks from my father's place. Then my luck almost ran out. There the guards said: "You better wait here till sunrise. It's not far over there to the nigger quarters, and they are some of the meanest damn niggers on God's earth. If you go any farther, you may get shot. We have orders not to let anything happen that might start the shooting again. The niggers have said that for every one of them who dies, two whites will die. So we don't intend to kill any more niggers because we don't want to lose any more white people."

They went on and on. And there I was shaking from cold and fear too, listening to them tell me their orders and secrets. Hell, I thought, they may make an exception and kill one more "nigger," and I'll be the one! If they find out they've mistaken a Negro for a white man after they've told me all their secrets, then I may be done for! So I knew I could not let those guards keep me there till the sun rose in my face. So I said: "Hell, I'm not afraid of anybody out there. The navy trained me to handle those Japs and Germans, and I certainly can take care of myself around here." I went on bragging about how tough the navy had made me, but I never told them that during my time in service I was never out of the United States! Finally, they said: "Well, all right. We've warned you, but go on if you want to. With your training and war record, you ought to be able to slip through."

That's exactly what I did, and in a few minutes, I tapped at my father's door. It was after three o'clock in the morning, but I could see a little light coming from under the door. Then I heard my father's voice say, "Yes, who is it?" I said: "Open up, Papa. It's Lyman." That convinced him, and he opened the door. Inside, my father and uncle were sitting in the log cabin part of the house by the fireplace. They were sitting in two great big armchairs wrapped in coats and blankets and rugs to keep warm. The fire had almost gone out, but they were awake worrying about the turmoil outside. Each one had a Winchester rifle lying across his knees. My father said: "Son, why did you come down here? It's dangerous. We could be attacked any time. We're not worried about the white people around us, but there may be some outsiders who hear there's a Negro family living next to white people. Son, why did you come?" I said, "Papa, I just came down to see about you."

I was down there all day Saturday and Sunday and came back to Louisville on Sunday night. On Saturday the town looked like a Sunday. Some of the stores were open, but there was no business going on. Nobody went anywhere. The whites stayed in, and the blacks stayed in. One of the best tales connected with the riot had to do with the Negro janitor at the white undertaking establishment. The white undertaker called him in and said: "You go on and stay with your people on your side of town. It won't look right if you keep on working here. We'll clean up and do all your work and pay you anyway." He got a two-week paid vacation! He'd been working at the funeral home for close to twenty years, and during that time he'd learned how to embalm. I expect he did about two-thirds of the work. It was unofficial, of course, because he didn't have an embalmer's license. I believe his boss gave him the extra time off not because he was in danger but because the white man didn't want him to find out how many white people were killed. Officially, no white people were killed. Anybody who died during that time died of "natural causes." But I remember what the white guard told me when I arrived. "We don't want any *more* white folks killed." I know there was a lot of sniping and shooting on both sides. To this day a lot of blacks down there believe a sizable number of whites were killed.

When I got home, I found out that the *Louisville Defender* had sent five people down to cover the story—a reporter, a photographer, a lawyer, a preacher, and a fifth person to drive the station wagon. But they couldn't get any information. They were given militia protection but couldn't find any Negro with nerve enough to talk to them. And the white people were too mad and mean to talk to a bunch of Negroes from "up North" in Louisville. When they found out I had been down, they came to see me, and I gave them all the dope. I was afraid my father and uncle would get into trouble if I was named as the story's source, so I asked the reporter not to identify me. He wrote up a powerful story.

In 1958 after my father and uncle had died and I was handling the business property they left, I went around to the insurance office and pointed out some cracks in a big plate glass window in one of our stores. I said, "I'm afraid those cracks might widen and cause the glass to fall out on somebody and you might get sued." The insurance man said: "Professor, if you'll sign a statement that a boy leaned his bicycle against the glass and cracked it, we'll put in a new one. We both know it was shot by the state troopers in 1946 during the riot. But you can't sue the state. The state will claim that it is not responsible for any damages done when it was trying to subdue a rebellion." My uncle had been trying for several years to get the insurance company to replace the glass, and they had refused. But twelve years after the damage had been done, the insurance man changed his mind. Why? I think after a while most people recognize the wrongs of the past and do their best to correct them. This white man wasn't willing to say, "Mama and Papa were wrong." But he would go so far as to say, "I don't think I would have done it that way." In this manner the southern white can pay proper respect to his elders and not, at the same time, continue their evils.

World War II helped to bring about a better world for the Negro. But as a pacifist I maintain that the good fruits of that war—and all wars—could have been harvested at a lower price. Even the benefits of the Civil War could have been accomplished without war—if only the people in disagreement had sat around a table and talked out a solution. A lot of slaveowners would have welcomed these words. "Now you've got 100 slaves, which you paid good money for, and if you put a reasonable price on each one of them, we'll pay you to turn them loose." What happened was infinitely more expensive—in lives, in money, in everything. Now as glad as I am that the war brought emancipation, I say it was wrong for the northern people not to pay for the slaves. In 1850, say, a law could have been passed that would have allowed the federal government to buy the slaves their freedom. I can imagine slaveowners lining up for a scene like this. "Mr. Smith, you have how many slaves?" And Mr. Smith says, "I got two, and on the going market they're worth $1,000 apiece." And the government man says: "All right, Mr. Smith. That sounds reasonable. Turn them loose and go over to the cashier and pick up your check for $2,000. From now on we're going to have free labor in all this country." It would have worked! Free labor was profitable in the North, and it would have been profitable in the South. But after the North found out that slave labor was unprofitable in their region and unloaded their slaves on the South, they got pious and decided that slavery was wrong. The rascals were hypocritical, and they didn't want to pay for the slaves they had sold the South earlier.

The stakes are higher in our time than ever before. Now it's not just a matter of freeing slaves. It's a matter of human survival. I see the wars of this century as a ball game with four quarters. The first quarter was World War I. The second quarter was World War II. Korea and Vietnam I group as the third quarter. I hope to God we never get around to the fourth quarter. That will be the holocaust. All of us will go up in smoke. Now everybody has bombs—atomic, nitrogen, hydrogen—and guided missiles. When the button is pushed, we'll all go up in one big conflagration. Let's not play that final quarter.

I know that most people are excited by violence and that war is the greatest violence and therefore the greatest excitement. But I do not believe that any sane person wants to die prematurely. In fact, I think that most people would be pacifists if they weren't gamblers. A fellow gambles this way. He says to himself: "I don't want to be killed, but here at the start I have two chances. One chance is that I'll be found able-bodied and will have to become a soldier. On the other hand, if I'm lucky, I'll have some physical defect that will keep me out; and I can enjoy the war from a safe distance. If I have to go, I still have two chances. I may be sent to a battlefield, or I may be kept safe behind the lines. . . ." And the poor fellow rationalizes his chances all the way to the end. "If they shoot at me, one chance is that the bullet will miss. The other chance is that it will only wound me. But even if I die, I still have two chances. I have a chance to go to heaven!" Poor slob. All down the line he's gambling on the better of two chances. Like a habitual gambler, he plays the odds—till his number comes up and it's too late.

I'm more optimistic than I sound. Atomic and hydrogen bombs may force us to be more humane. It's too dangerous not to be. If Russia sends a guided missile toward Detroit, all our president has to do is to push a button and one will go to Moscow. There's absolutely no defense for either side! And I'm glad of it! If we won't be civilized human beings without the pressure of hydrogen bombs, then thank you, Mr. Einstein, thank you for making these bombs possible. It seems we will not behave ourselves— even with all the preaching and all the popes, bishops, and priests.

The one big fault I have with Jesus Christ is that he leaves you with the opportunity to be bad if you want to be. He says: "If you believe in me, behave yourself and live a decent life. Oh, it would be so nice if you did. But if you choose to be a devil, then go ahead and be one. It's your choice." But thank God, with all those horrible weapons we have now, we don't have a choice. We have *got* to be good! Nations, like individuals, have to behave themselves.

I certainly don't think individuals should have a choice. If you are stronger than I am, I don't want you to have a choice whether to choke me or to pat me on the back. I don't want you to have a choice as to whether you can send my child to a little rinky-dink school down there on the corner and yours to a classy one across town. I don't want you to have a choice whether to make me play basketball out in the dirt while your kids get to play on a beautiful hardwood floor. I don't want to have choices like these! I want hardwood floors in all the schools or in none. I don't want you to have a choice as to whether you will be moral or not. I have a grapefruit and an apple in my kitchen. You can choose which you want, and I won't care, because the impact of your choice won't be detrimental to anyone. But I don't want you to have a choice as to whether you treat your fellow man right or wrong. I *demand* that you treat him right!

If this belief goes against free will and attacks God, then God is unjust; and I don't want anything to do with his morality or his heaven. If God is going to be unjust and let one bunch of people have nice, pretty things while I have to peep through a fence to see these things, then I won't believe in him; I won't go to his heaven. I'd just as soon go to hell and burn.

On the other hand, I don't believe God *expects* you to choose as you please. If I saw a mad dog running toward a child who was playing in the yard and I had a pistol in my hand, should I just sit back and give the dog a choice? Of course not! I'm not going to give God any credit at all if he would let the rabid dog bite that child. I don't think, however, we can blame that kind of evil on God. All my days people have told me that God is responsible. We have used him as a kind of divine scapegoat. But God is not responsible. Hell, we're responsible. When we let evil triumph, we have no one to blame but ourselves. When we let disagreements between nations become wars, we are to blame. If we let wars destroy this world, we'll have no one left to hold responsible. We'll all be dead.

The Religion of a Doubting Thomas

I don't believe, and I don't disbelieve.

I'M A Congregationalist now, but like most southern Negroes, I was baptized a Baptist. There's not a lot of difference. Although I have reservations about some aspects of religion—even the Christian religion—I have benefited from its emphasis on education. For two years I went to Knoxville Academy, a Presbyterian school. Those people were too austere and too good for me. It seemed that we had prayer and sermons all the time. Then I went to a Baptist college in Richmond, Virginia.

When I came to Louisville, I stayed first with my sister and brother-in-law, who were staunch Baptists. They lived on Eighteenth Street and went to church at Fifth Street Baptist. They had no car and had to take a taxi every time they went. I'd go with them occasionally on Sunday, but usually I'd sit on their front porch and read the paper while they were riding to church. Then about eleven o'clock I'd put the paper aside, jump up, and walk across to Seventeenth Street, where there was a little Congregational church. I could get back and finish my paper before they got home from their church. I said: "That church down the street is just as good as your church. The minister is intelligent and well educated. His sermons are good. Why spend all the money and time to go to another church?"

Plymouth Congregational Church has always had a reputation as an elitist church for blacks. The reason is that a lot of Louisville's black teachers, doctors, and lawyers were educated at Fisk or Atlanta University, both founded by northern Congregationalists after the Civil War. I'm sure many blacks felt that after their education they didn't want to drop back down to the Baptist or the Methodist culture they came from. The national church subsidized a young man, the Reverend E.G. Harris, to come to Louisville and pastor Plymouth Church. He served about forty-five years.

Harris took over a small group of dissident Methodists who wanted a little more class to their services, and they began to attract other Negro college graduates. Today the church still has a high percentage of educated people, though we welcome people of all races and education levels. To my knowledge, however, we've never had a white member. It is ironic that nationally the Congregational church is a predominantly white church and that in Louisville the only Congregational church is all black. It has sometimes led to embarrassing situations. When executives of big corporations like Ford or General Electric move here from other parts of the country where they were Congregationalists, they look into the phone book, see that our church is the only one in town, and come for a one-time visit. Imagine their surprise when they enter our doors and come into the presence of a sea of black faces! They never call back. They go and join an Episcopal or a Presbyterian church.

There are very few white or black Congregational churches in the South. The church never took root there because it was associated with the antislavery movement before the Civil War and with the black education movement after the war. People in the South used to say: "They're just damn Yankess. Keep them out. They think they're better than we are. They think they're more moral, but they're hypocrites." I have to admit there is some truth to that accusation. Before slavery was abolished in the northern states, members of Congregational churches made huge profits buying and selling slaves. Of course, they shared their profits with the Lord. When they could no longer sell slaves up North, they continued to sell them to the South. When the slave trade was finally stopped, a lot of former slave traders got very moral and became abolitionists and began to support people like William Lloyd Garrison and John Brown. "Turn those slaves loose," they ordered. "It's against the law of God." I certainly wanted the slaves turned loose, but I can also understand the plantation owner who pointed out the New Englanders' tardy conversion to abolition.

But I can live with irony and inconsistency because I like the more formal service at Plymouth Church. I don't like a preacher who gives out all that "wang-doodle stuff." I like a dignified service with an intelligently composed sermon. But the tastes of educated blacks sometimes put us in conflict with the general run of people. It is difficult for us to go out and get a little education and then live on a level of culture and refinement that a university training tends to develop. Other blacks don't always understand that although we are educated and speak a little different brand of English we can still sympathize with them on social and economic levels. They think our desire to live on a more cultured level implies an insult to them. It's hard to communicate with such people.

When educated people select a minister, they ask, "What schools did he go to?" The general run of blacks say: "What in the hell are you talking about? What *schools* did he go to? What we want to know is can he preach? He doesn't have to go to college. If he is a child of God, the Lord will tell him what to say. Moses never went to college, and he was a great leader. Jesus never went to college." One day a friend said to me, "Lyman, I'd come to your church, but you won't let me say 'Amen.' " I said: "Oh, well, you can say it once or twice a service if it'll make you feel any better. We used to have a deacon who said it often, but he's dead now. But come on. Once in a while somebody will still say 'Amen.' "

I see a change in emphasis, however, even in the main black denominations. More and more black churches are demanding educated ministers. "We will not compromise," they say. "We are educated, and we will not tolerate an uneducated minister in our pulpit. Education is important to us, or we wouldn't have spent so much time and money getting educated. What we have demanded of ourselves we now demand of our minister."

More blacks are attending predominantly white churches. Now that Negroes are moving out of the West End, they don't see the point of coming all the way back here on Sunday to go to church. They are being accepted in churches near where they live. There is no fuss made over it. Nobody says: "Hey, folks. Look here. We have a black family on our row now."

Very few blacks belong to such "high" churches as Episcopal or Lutheran. There is one Negro Episcopal Church, the Church of Our Merciful Saviour, but it's not thriving. Once there was even a black Lutheran church, but blacks found their services too cold. They were so cold they didn't need air conditioning even when the temperature hit 103 degrees. When the black Lutheran church had ten people, they thought they had a crowd. There are several black Presbyterian churches, but it's hard for them to finance a decent church. There are also a number of black Catholics in Louisville. St. Augustine is a long-standing Negro church.

Although many of the slaveholders were members of these high churches, the vast majority of blacks today are either Baptists or Methodists. The high churches were just too elegant for the general run of people of either race. Most people back then couldn't read of write. So what good did it do to give them a hymn book or a Bible or a prayer book and ask them to read the service? Those things were out of place. The average person wanted to go to a church where he felt at home, where he could let his emotions out, and where he wouldn't have to read what was in the prayer book. You'd just get up and sing. You'd just get up and pray. You'd just get up and preach. You wouldn't read anything. So the Baptist and Methodist churches, which didn't insist on education for their preachers or their members, were a relief to uneducated people in those days. After the slaves were freed and no longer had to go to their masters' churches, they joined churches where they felt more comfortable. The Baptists said: "Just come right in, brother and sister. Make yourselves at home and have a good time in the spirit of the Lord. Let your hair down and enjoy yourself."

The two main Methodist churches are the African Methodist Episcopal Church and the African Methodist Episcopal Zion Church. When they were started as black churches in the 1770s, they attracted large numbers of blacks in the North who objected to sitting in a segregated balcony and listening to a white preacher. In the South blacks began withdrawing from the white churches after the Civil War and starting their own. Quinn Chapel is the hub church for the AME group in Louisville, and the main AME Zion church is Broadway Temple. Both are large and active.

The majority of Negroes in Louisville belong to one of the several dozen Baptist churches. Each Baptist church runs its own business. There are no bishops to oversee them. I think this kind of home rule appealed to black people and especially to the newly freed slaves. Even after freedom came, there weren't many places where the Negro could make his own decisions. In his Baptist church, he could vote and govern himself. He could make his church be anything he wanted it to be. That's why Baptist churches in Louisville differ so much from each other. The church with the highest flavor of literacy is Fifth Street Baptist. It has a tradition of il-lustrious, well-educated pastors. When I came to Louisville, the pastor was a man who could speak three foreign languages and could translate out of Latin and Greek. He was a philosopher and a scholar.

One of the largest churches is West Chestnut Baptist, whose pastor at one time was a well-educated man named G.K. Offutt. He was one of the first Negroes to graduate from the Southern Baptist Theological Seminary in Louisville. That was in the 1940s, and he had to take courses in the evening that white students took during the day because he wasn't allowed to sit in classes with whites. He'd go to the professors' offices at night, and they would tutor him.

Two churches claim to be the oldest black Baptist church in Louisville, Fifth Street and Calvary. Both churches came out of white churches, and both say that they came out about 1828. I get along very well with both of them. When I go to Fifth Street, I say, "Yes, I understand you all are the first Negro Baptist Church." Then I go over to Calvary and say, "Yes, I understand you all are the first Negro Baptist Church." I don't get into the argument; I let them both be first.

A church that includes the whole spectrum of Negro social and educational life is Mt. Lebanon. It runs from the high to the low, from laborers to doctors and lawyers. One of their pastors, the Reverend Frederick G. Sampson, I knew very well. He knew how to handle both ends of the spectrum. He would preach the congregation into a frenzy, shouting and carrying on. Then all of a sudden, he would wave his hands and say: "All right, folks, settle down. Here's the point. Now don't get so emotional you forget what I'm saying." He'd then go back and pinpoint the main parts of his sermon. His sermons were masterpieces of emotion and reason.

Most blacks, regardless of their educational level, will not tolerate a dull preacher. They think they haven't had a good church experience on

Sunday if the preacher hasn't said enough to make them feel good. History explains why. What have black people had for most of their life in this country? Almost nothing! In their own churches, at least, they could tell Jesus about their troubles in their sermons and shoutings and spirituals. Somehow I think the slaveowners sympathized with them and said: "I'm going to work hell out of them from tomorrow morning to Saturday night. So if they can have a little fun on Sunday, let 'em go ahead."

Even today religion gives blacks a lot of relief from their troubles. Maybe the Communists are right when they say it's just the opiate of the people—just something to console us and to help us bear our worries through this world. It also offers the hope that when Jesus comes to take us to the next world, we'll have everything we missed in this one. Religion has helped to deaden a lot of pain, though I find it handy to have aspirins around to help me bear the pain of my arthritis! But religion seems mighty fine for people faced with problems they can't solve—when they can't get a decent place to live, when they can't get a good job, when they can't afford luxuries other people have. It's a relief to go to church and hear that by and by all the troubles of this world will be over and there will be no more moaning, no more groaning. But what about the next morning? I look out and see that conditions are just as bad as they were before I went to church yesterday. At least the Communists offer answers for the here and now.

At least once or twice a week, however, the church helps cover up the pain of desperately poor and hopeless Negroes. White people have always been tolerantly amused at such Negro church services. I've heard them say: "Let's go slumming. Let's go see the niggers let their hair down. Let's go see them shout and pray and carry on." I've been to services like that, and as far as I could, I've tried to fit in. My etiquette in attending religious services is that I try to catch on to the way the church people are doing things, and I do my best to accommodate it and to go along. If I go to a high service in the Episcopal or Catholic church, I adjust to the situation. On the other hand, if I go to a service where the people are playing leapfrog with the pulpit and hanging on the chandeliers and calling out to Isaiah, Esau, and Moses for two hours, I'll get through that too. I may not go back to a service like that, but at least I'll be polite while I'm there.

I don't mean to knock religion too much. We know we're not ever going to solve all our problems, and religion does give us the guts to go on. At least it keeps us from committing suicide. Sometimes you get so despondent you want to go up to the top of the First National Bank, bust out the glass, jump off, and call it quits! I've felt that way practically all my life. All I know is that I have an instinct to live.

One time I got so depressed over my girlfriend that I walked into the

Atlantic Ocean. I wanted to marry her, and I didn't want to marry her. She was skewed up with her religion, and I was skewed up over my non-religion. I loved her but was afraid married life would be a torment for both of us with our different views. Then I thought about how sincere, kind, and sweet she was and wondered how I could turn my back on her. Rather than face the situation and try to solve it, I said, "Oh, hell," and walked out and out into the ocean. An undertow caught me, and if I hadn't been such a strong swimmer, I expect I'd have drowned. The instinct to stay alive— an instinct we share with other animals—made me keep fighting the waves till I got back to shore. I think a lot of people like me who have tried to commit suicide are living today because instinct took over.

Yet I've always wondered what in the hell I am here for. I solved ten problems today, but I'll awake tomorrow and see twenty-five new ones. Where did they come from? I suppose the ones I killed had babies just before they died. So what's the use in living? I've been working over fifty years trying my best to make conditions better for black people, and now I read in the paper that unemployment for young blacks is 45 percent! What have I done? Have I—or has anyone—accomplished anything? The problems of the Depression that I lived through haven't been solved and probably never will be. So what's the use of trying anymore?

I'm bothered by those questions. Yet I take satisfaction in having done what I could do. That's the reason I haven't jumped out. I won't give up. If I did, I'd be breaking faith with all those people I've encouraged and tried to help all these years. And I won't break faith with my children. Their mother and I tried to rear them to prepare for and have confidence in the future. There is no future when you give up.

Religion, at least, gives us hope for something better to come. It keeps us alive. I've never been concerned with theology or doctrine. Too much of that is hocus-pocus. I think most religion is superstition. Unfortunately, it doesn't help us much in dealing with reality. It teaches us to reach out in space for some supernatural force to handle our problems for us. It may sound good to say that we can cast our burdens upon the Lord, but it doesn't eliminate them.

One of my friends used to be a member of the Methodist church. One day he said: "Lyman, I'm so happy. I've changed churches. My wife has been a Catholic since childhood, and I just started thinking about all the fussing and scrapping and carrying on we do at my church. I decided we waste too much time and energy just debating all the points of church life. Then I noticed that my wife was always so contented, so I decided that I'd give up my church fussing and arguing and join her church and become a Catholic. It's such a relief. When I have problems, I go and tell my priest. I'm sorry I didn't become a Catholic when I married." I said: "That sounds wonderful to me. I guess all your problems are solved." He said: "Oh, no, they're not solved. I just don't worry about them anymore." Too often that's what all religion does. It helps people avoid and cover up their problems.

I believe in God if I can use my own definition. God is the sum total of all that is good. If you could put it in a ball and I could look inside, I'd find truth and honesty and justice. Everything that is good is God. It's also heaven. Everything that is bad is hell. I can even accept the devil as the chief executive of hell. Any doctrine beyond that is man-made, and I don't accept it. The Lord only requires of us that we live honestly, do justice, and walk humbly with him. Anything more is hocus-pocus.

I do not believe in the special divinity of Jesus Christ. To me he was a man like Martin Luther King or Gandhi. I place him at the top of the most outstanding teachers and philosophers of all time, but that's as far as I go. I've always felt sorry for poor Joseph. I suspect that Mary went around the corner, got mixed up with an outside man, and he became the daddy of her baby. Joseph was so wrapped up in religion she pulled the wool over his eyes. He looked at her and said: "Mary, it looks like you're going to have a baby. Where did it come from?" She said, "From God." Joseph may have swallowed that. But I can't. I don't even think Jesus thought he was God. He was too smart to think he could sell that line. The Jews didn't believe it—at least most of them didn't—and they were on the lookout for a messiah.

I think we've ruined the philosophy of Jesus by trying to explain away the fact that he was a bastard. There's nothing wrong with being a bastard. It's not the child's fault. Maybe Jesus got carried away now and then and sometimes let people believe he was God, but I don't think that was his mission. His mission, his philosophy, is the Sermon on the Mount. You can't find better philosophy than the Beatitudes. Nobody has ever taught us a better way to behave toward other people. Once he fed 5,000 hungry people. I'm not sure how he got all that food together. Maybe he started with a little boy's fish and loaves of bread, and everybody started sharing what they had with those who had nothing. He didn't sell tickets. He didn't tell people how much they could eat. He told them to share and not to waste. He didn't say, "If you got twenty-five dollars, follow me down to the Hyatt Regency and eat with me." He said: "Come to my table. I can feed all 5,000 of you. Sit down. Sit down and eat." Anyway he did it, it was a miracle. And when the people finished and started walking away, he said: "Hey, wait a minute. Scrape up those leftovers and put them in the refrigerator. You'll have enough for supper tonight." Preachers should talk about his caring for the poor and hungry and not worry about how he may have suspended natural laws to perform miracles. They shouldn't worry about whether he was divinely conceived. I don't really know what divinely conceived means. I may have been divinely conceived. But I don't worry about it, one way or the other. I had nothing to do with it.

Overall, I like the teachings of Jesus, though I have some reservations about his philosophy of turning the other cheek. I agree more with Thurgood Marshall, who once said: "Ladies and gentlemen, we are told to turn the other cheek. I say the black man in this country got socked on one cheek. So he turned the other one and got socked on it too. Now the Bible doesn't say what you're supposed to do after that. I suppose you're on your own."

I don't know a thing about the Resurrection, so I don't concern myself with it. I plead guilty to having a shallow mind when it comes to religion. When I was baptized all the way under in the Duck River down in Tennessee, people said, "Now, Lyman, all your sins are washed away." I said to myself, "Hogwash."

I've tried to live a good life, but I know I've done things a lot of church members wouldn't approve of. I keep liquor in my house, but I don't usually drink. I keep cigarettes handy, but I don't often smoke. Sometimes if a lot of people are visiting me and they are smoking and drinking, I might light up a cigarette and take a little diluted bourbon. But I'm doing it just to be sociable. That's why I go to church. The difference between me and most people is that I'm just honest about it.

I see value in being a church member. Like every group it has its set of principles and an organization to carry them out. Most of the church's intentions are beautiful. I would rather have my children go to Sunday School and hear a teacher talk about good moral principles than to have them waste time on a street corner. Any good organization teaches its members self-discipline. If I always ate alone, I imagine I'd let myself get sloppy. I wouldn't use a clean napkin. I wouldn't worry about a few spots on my glass. I might get to the point of not using my fork and knife. Like a caveman I might grab a piece of meat, bite it off, chew it, and spit out the gristle on the floor. The discipline of being a member of a group makes me behave like a civilized person.

I don't have to believe everything a group teaches to be a member. When the preacher on Easter Sunday announces, "He is risen," I say, "Go ahead and preach, but what you're saying just hits the top of my head and bounces off." But I have enough discipline to sit there till he finishes. If other people feel the need to believe these things, that's all right with me. Most people seem to need to believe in a hereafter, from Old King Tut to the man next door. King Tut even had a lot of servants and food and household goods buried with him, but in the 3,000 or 4,000 years he's been gone, he doesn't seem to have needed them.

I've been a deacon in my church since 1939. During my first year as deacon—about five weeks before Christmas—the board of deacons was calculating how much money they should take from the deacons' fund to buy grocery baskets for Christmas. They were planning to give ten baskets to poor people in our neighborhood. When it came to a vote, I voted no. They said, "Lyman, how can you vote against giving baskets to the poor at Christmas?" I said: "Well, I did. I warned you ahead of time that I wasn't particularly anxious to be a deacon, but you elected me anyway. Now you've got me!" They said, "But why did you vote against those baskets?" I said: "I'll tell you. I think it's ridiculous to plan five weeks ahead to give ten baskets of food to poor, hungry people at Christmas. If the people are hungry right now, why should we wait till Christmas to fill their bellies? What do we expect them to do for five weeks? Starve? Do you plan to give them more baskets in January?" They said: "Oh, no. No. We can't afford to do that." I said: "It doesn't make sense to me to starve them till Christmas Day—then gorge them—and then starve them again. I say we should starve them on Christmas Day too." They said: "Lyman, you're awful. What you say is unforgivable." I said: "Well, that's the way I feel. Take it or leave it. You can kick me off the board whenever you're ready. You can even kick me out of the church. I don't give a damn whether I'm deacon or not. I don't care whether I am in this church or not. I'm here because most people expect teachers to go to church. It's part of being respectable, and I like respectability. But I think you ought to know my philosophy. My philosophy on helping the poor is that we should help them get a job so they can work and earn their own basket of groceries. That way they'll have fifty-two baskets for the whole year."

I'm afraid the Christian religion has been used to lull people to sleep while they're starving. People are told: "Get down on your knees. Pray. Maybe the Lord will put some meal in your bin." I say: "Get up off your knees. Get to work. Plant you some wheat or corn and grow your own bread. The Lord has given you a rich country. Now make something of it."

Religion has often been used to disguise human greed and self-ishness. Think of the wars and other atrocities that have been justified by religion. For example, during the two world wars, both the French and the Germans fought in the name of God. I'd have said—and perhaps God did—"To hell with both of you."

I don't know what the purpose of life is. Nobody does. Sometimes I think of life as a pendulum constantly swinging, moving just as far to the left as it moves to the right. Let's say the right side is the good side, the positive side, and the left side is the negative or facilitating side. To pay my light and gas bills, to take a little trip, to have a little recreation—to have all the things I enjoy—I've got to work. I've got to swing to the left. When the pendulum stops swinging and comes to dead center, that's the end of life. When you choose not to go into the laboring field on the left, you won't have any gas to get over to the right. When you're tired of working, when you're no longer willing to pay the price that life requires, the pendulum stops. From the cradle to the grave, it's the pendulum swinging. That's life for me.

I'm not interested in what happens to me when my pendulum stops swinging. What happens—or doesn't happen—doesn't interest me. I used to go with a Catholic girl who told me if we got married and I didn't join her church she'd still pray for my salvation. I said: "Darling, don't you worry about it. I'm not." She said: "But that's my training and my desire. I'll pray for you as long as I live." I didn't marry the girl. I haven't joined her church. I hope she hasn't been praying for me all these years. If my pendulum stops right now, I've had over eighty years to swing. If I can't make a good account of my life in that time, I don't deserve another chance, here or anywhere else.

I've always believed in doing good. I've not been concerned about a god who rewards or punishes me in an afterlife. If a label is necessary, call me a humanist, not a Christian. I don't think the word *Christian* means very much—not when "Christian" bankers charge poor people 20 percent interest, not when "Christian" businessmen pay their workers as little as they can get away with, not when "Christian" ministers take the widow's mite and live lives of luxury. To be a good man, you have to *act* good. You can't just *say* it. You make yourself good by doing good. It is the essence of the teaching of Jesus. But he wasn't the only one to teach this morality. Socrates may even have taught a higher form. Jesus said to his people: "I'll soon be leaving to prepare a good place for you to come. In the meantime you continue to do good things and stack up all the credits you can, and you will be rewarded in my father's house after you die." Socrates said: "Do what is right. Do what is honest, just, and truthful. Then you already have your reward. Don't look for any other." I agree with Socrates. You do what's right because it's right—not because of some calculated reward that will come your way later. If you see somebody on the road with a flat tire, help him change it, not because on down the highway you may have a flat and need somebody to help you, but because it's the right thing to do. The good feeling that you've done the right thing is your reward.

Throughout my life I've tried to do what's right. Now in my old age, I feel pretty good. I believe that by helping others you're storing up treasure for yourself in this life, not for some far off hereafter. My father in Tennessee got so much pleasure from seeing former students who came by to visit and to thank him. One of his students became a successful pharmacist in Chicago. He was illegitimate. His mother cooked in the kitchen of the white man who was his father. The boy was brilliant, and my father took a liking to him. Papa advised him: "Son, you can't make it in this town. You've got too many strikes against you. Finish high school, make good grades, and somehow I'll help you go on to college." That's what happened. Thirty years later this man came back to thank my father.

Like my father or any teacher worth his name, I got a kick out of seeing human beings come from hulls. One of my students was a boy who lived on the second floor of an old shack at Eighth and Broadway. It was one of those hovels that blacks used to live in just west of downtown. It was so ramshackle that it looked like a strong wind would topple it over. His mother had finished the eighth grade and his father the seventh. His father was a common laborer and didn't make much pay. Of their five children, only this one seemed interested in going to school and getting his lessons. He didn't get any encouragement from his parents. As a matter of fact, they would whip him when they saw him studying because they thought he was dodging his chores and wasting his time. About five of us teachers at Central took an interest in him. We bought him clothes, shoes, and books. We would give him lunch money and sometimes a little extra change. With our encouragement and help, the boy finished close to the top of his class.

He enrolled at the old Louisville Municipal College, but because he had to work full time and because he had no encouragement from his professors, he couldn't keep his grades up. He had to drop out. He continued working, hoping to save enough money to go back to college. Then World War II came along, and he spent four years in the army. When he came home, he went back to college on the G.I. Bill and made such good marks he received a scholarship to the University of Cincinnati, got his law degree, and set up practice in California. When he comes home to Louisville, he always looks up those five teachers who helped him get started. That kind of appreciation has been my main pay as a teacher. It has made me happy. I couldn't buy a new car with that kind of pay, but I didn't need a new car. I couldn't buy a suit of clothes whenever I wanted to, but I liked the ones I had. Seeing young people develop into successful human beings has been my joy and my earthly reward.

It does pay off when you do good things for other people. It always pays off. It's in the nature of things. Of course, if you do good deeds expecting a certain kind of reward, you're going to be robbed. Do good things, as Socrates says, because they make you feel better and because it's right. I don't think about a reward in another world.

If people want to base their life's meaning on magic and on super-naturalism, that's all right with me. There was a man in my hometown who could hear a ghost when the wind blew in a certain tree. It was merely branches of the tree rubbing against each other. He would tell us children ghost stories that frightened us. "Boys," he'd say, "I can take you to an old, empty house and show you dead people spinning plates. I can take you to a window you can look through and see them dead people spinning plates. I can show you a back window with the glass broke out, and a big black dog will jump through and gallop into that room where them dead people are spinning plates." He said he had seen those dead people in that house many times. He believed what he said. And he almost made us believe it. I was too scared to walk by that house at night. My mother said: "Son, don't pay that old man any mind. He's crazy. I don't want you growing up afraid of ghosts. If there are people in that house, they're alive. If a dog jumps through that broken-out window, it's a live dog."

Some people handle snakes as a part of their religion. That's all right with me. Just leave me out of it. Some people drink wine they say is the blood of Jesus. That's all right. Just don't force me to believe it. Some people insist that a three-headed God governs the universe. I don't waste my time speculating on such matters. I don't believe, and I don't disbelieve. After both sides have presented their cases, all I see on these matters is darkness.

Life is a mystery to me. That's where I leave it. I don't know when we started. I don't know where we started. I don't know how we started. All I know is here I am. That's enough for me.

The Rest of the Dream

I have been a black man for eighty-one years. My race has been a dominant factor in my life. It was not my choice. I have wanted simply to live as a human being. I have not wanted to remember my life as a series of "black experiences," but at birth I was tagged as a black man. My dark skin has been a black man's burden. When I discovered doors labeled "White Only," I knew my race was a tag I couldn't escape. Now, please, I would like to be free.

WHEN I WAS ACTIVE in the teachers' union, I would sometimes meet with other members of the executive committee in downtown Louisville. There would be maybe three blacks and ten whites. We'd work till noon and then decide to go out and get a sandwich. It never occurred to the white teachers to ask, "*Can* we go here or there to eat?" They could go anywhere they wanted to. I remember as if it were yesterday a meeting in 1948. All the committee members, black and white, walked out together. When we got outside, we blacks pulled off to ourselves and stood there at the corner of Fourth and Market. We just stood there while the white people went off down the street. I see the scene as distinctly as a newsreel. We blacks lingered at the corner for thirty-five or forty minutes, killing time and shooting the breeze. Finally, the white teachers drifted back, laughing and talking. Their stomachs were full, and they were gay and happy. We joined in their lighthearted mood, although we were hungry and thirsty because there was no place nearby that served blacks. We had not even had a coke or a drink of water, but we said nothing about it. What had happened was normal for us. What had happened was normal for them.

The white teachers were relaxed and friendly toward us. They had gotten beyond the point of being patronizing. They didn't expect extra credit for treating us as equals. As we walked in to resume our work, the white teachers started comparing the food at several nearby cafés. Then one of them asked, "Lyman where did you all go to eat?" I tried to avoid an answer. "Oh, I don't know," I said. "We're all right." Like a chorus they joined in: "Didn't you all eat anywhere? Weren't you hungry? Didn't you get at least a coke and a hot dog?" Finally, I said: "Please have some common sense. We strolled up and down Fourth Street window-shopping." Then it dawned on one of them, who said, "They didn't have any place to go," and they all began feeling guilty and sympathetic. "We should have known," they said. "We should have done something." But it was too late. Even now it's a painful episode to recall. It's painful for us blacks and for our white friends. It's a burden we still carry. It says a lot about America.

My burdens have not been lifted. Even if the law is on my side now, the burden of memory is still with me. And the rotting roots of prejudice have not all been extracted. Blacks are still denied service and embarrassed in public places. I'm not completely free, and I'm not completely comfortable. I'm allowed to eat at a MacDonald's and sleep in a Holiday Inn, but is it because the law requires it? When I come in the door, do white people see me as a man or as a *black* man? No one will be free till race is irrelevant.

The day of the colorless society has not come, but my day is about over. I'm ready to turn the work over to a new generation of blacks and whites. I've done what I could to fight the battle, hold the line, and advance the cause of human freedom in my own backyard. It's time for new leaders to take over. I've tried to prepare for the new day by coaching young people to fill my shoes. When people have said, "Mr. Johnson, you should head this project because you've had experience," I've said, "No, it's time for you to get some experience because soon I'll be checking out." I try to prepare young people for the jabs they'll receive from their own race. There will always be people who will not do a damn thing, but when you do it and get complimented for it, they'll step up and say, "Old Lyman thinks nobody could have done that but him." To young leaders I say, "Don't worry about critics like that." And then I tell them my own parable. "Working for human rights is like a man who goes out and toils in the cornfield with the hot sun making sweat roll down his body. Another man who is just as strong and capable is sitting over in the shade drinking a cool glass of iced tea and watching the farmer work his crop. When the day is over and the crop is harvested, the lazy man will say: 'That fool thought he was the only one who could work that corn. He killed himself doing it.' Don't worry. There will be honor for the fool who kills himself working a good crop."

I don't kid myself by thinking that because the mountain was moved, Lyman Johnson moved it. If I hadn't done the things I've done, I know someone else would have. No one is indispensable. All in all, I think I've taken advantage of my opportunities. If I had been as fit of pen as of tongue, maybe I could have cut a broader swath through the world. But I'm not crying. I could have done better, but I think I've done pretty well with my resources. I'm not ashamed of my stewardship. I could have done a lot worse! As Lou Rawls sings it in his song, "You Have One Life to Live." I've tried to give my one life all I had.

My paternal grandparents died before I was born and were buried in the little Columbia cemetery. When I was a boy, it was considered a white folks' cemetery, and Negroes weren't supposed to be poking around in there. Not long ago, however, I wandered all over that cemetery and found their graves over to one side. When the cemetery was opened about 1800, it served both whites and blacks. They started burying blacks at one end and whites at the other. During the next 100 years, the races began to meet in the middle. The markers on my grandparents' graves don't identify their color. They say simply "Dyer Johnson" and "Betty Johnson." In that cemetery my dead ancestors are like everybody else's dead ancestors. But there is another, newer cemetery in Columbia. About 1900 the old cemetery was beginning to fill up, and the city bought land in another section of town for a new cemetery. They put up a high brick and stone wall with a wire on top to separate the dead white from the dead black. The white section is called Rose Hill and the black section, Rose Mound. I suppose the city fathers wanted to make sure that the spirits of the dead didn't crawl over the wall and have interracial intercourse with each other. The last time I was there the wall was still up, but it seemed to be decaying. There is a break where the stone and brick have spilled out, and the gap is overgrown with all kinds of honeysuckle and wild jasmine and clinging vines.

I don't care to be buried on either side of the wall. In fact, I don't care to be buried anywhere. I've signed a contract with the University of Louisville Medical School providing that if they can find out where my machine runs out of gas they can come and get the old jalopy and use it for spare parts or tinkering or whatever they need. It will be of no more use to me.

There is something sentimental and consoling about having a grave site. Most of my relatives are buried like that. For years I used to go down to Columbia and cut the grass and trim the hedges around the graves of my mother and father and later my brothers as they were added. It's a melancholy chore. I'd have to wade in weeds almost up to my waist to get to my family's graves. The weeds made the cemetery look like a forgotten territory. Maybe that's the way it should have been. When somebody died, the grave diggers would dig another hole in the weeds. The weeds seemed like a fitting memorial to the dead.

My wife and I agreed that death is just as much a part of existence as life. There's no sense in getting all sentimental about it. She didn't want her body or ashes placed in a particular spot where people would dutifully visit for a few years and then forget. She didn't want any record made of what happened to her remains. I respected her wishes.

After the medical school finishes with my remains, I want them returned to the elements as quickly as possible. Nobody can keep his body separate forever. Even if it takes a million years, a steel vault will eventually corrode and crumble, and its contents will spill and finally merge with the mother elements.

One night when I was a boy, I had a strange dream. I dreamed I was dead and lying there in the bed. Yet somehow I was also outside alive, delivering papers with a mad dog chasing me. I ran home but the front door was locked. From the bed I heard somebody knocking, so I got up and unlocked the door. I opened the door and let myself in, and then I woke up. I woke up and lost the rest of the dream. It never came back. It's worried me all my life. Where is the rest of the dream?

Index